PERFORMING NEW ORLEANS

PERFORMING NEW ORLEANS

Rethinking Resilience in Art and Everyday Life

STUART ANDREWS AND PATRICK DUGGAN
Foreword by Joycelyn Reynolds

Louisiana State University Press ▐▐ Baton Rouge

Published by Louisiana State University Press
lsupress.org

DESIGNER: Michelle A. Neustrom
TYPEFACES: Minion Pro, text; Bicyclette, display

COVER IMAGE: Photograph of the situated artwork *Rising Tables* (2017), by Jennifer Odem,
on the Crescent Park riverbank in New Orleans, 2018. Photo by the authors.

Unless otherwise credited, all photographs are by the authors.

Portions of chapter 3 are based on, and were first published as, "Situation Rooms: Performing
City Resilience in New Orleans," *Liminalities: A Journal of Performance Studies* 15, no. 1 (2019).

Chapter 5 draws on the research report *Performance as City Pandemic Response: Invitations
to Innovate* (Newcastle, UK: Performing City Resilience, 2021), first published open access as
part of the AHRC-funded project "Social Distancing and Reimagining City Life: Performative
Strategies and Practices for Response and Recovery in and beyond Lockdown."

Library of Congress Cataloging-in-Publication Data

Names: Andrews, Stuart, 1975– author | Duggan, Patrick, 1981– author |
   Reynolds, Joycelyn writer of foreword
Title: Performing New Orleans : rethinking resilience in art and everyday life /
   Stuart Andrews and Patrick Duggan ; foreword by Joycelyn Reynolds.
Description: Baton Rouge : Louisiana State University Press, [2025] |
   Includes bibliographical references and index.
Identifiers: LCCN 2025018359 (print) | LCCN 2025018360 (ebook) | ISBN
   978-0-8071-8454-7 (cloth) | ISBN 978-0-8071-8531-5 (epub) | ISBN 978-0-8071-8532-2 (pdf)
Subjects: LCSH: Arts and society—Louisiana—New Orleans | Social adjustment—
   Louisiana—New Orleans
Classification: LCC NX180.S6 A54 2025 (print) | LCC NX180.S6 (ebook) |
   DDC 306.4/70976335—dc23/eng/20250613
LC record available at https://lccn.loc.gov/2025018359
LC ebook record available at https://lccn.loc.gov/2025018360

To our partners, Ellen and Naomi, and to our children, Arthur and Elinora, Elka and Cassian: thank you for enabling this work, without your patience, support, and guidance it would never have been possible. Here's to letting the good times roll!

CONTENTS

FOREWORD

As a native daughter of New Orleans and president/CEO of the Arts Council of New Orleans (dba Arts New Orleans), I am deeply privileged to introduce this seminal work, *Performing New Orleans: Rethinking Resilience in Art and Everyday Life.* Through the lens of performance studies, this book embarks on a profound exploration of our beloved city and its resilience amid adversity.

Art and architecture have been enduring legacies for centuries, transcending generations and preserving our collective memories. This is a city in which our diverse cultural practices, spanning dance, music, theater, opera, visual, and media arts, are the essence of our individual and communal identities. This book recognizes that these practices are vital to the life of the city. It explores their importance to new understandings of questions of community, place, and resilience (often a challenging term for New Orleans). This is achieved by looking across diverse and often under-explored "performances of New Orleans" from theater to tourism, Indigenous arts practice engaged with climate change to creative engagements with civic infrastructure, and even the importance of a warm welcome.

Having borne witness to the indomitable spirit of our artists and arts community, I have seen firsthand how individual artists and organizations such as Ashé Cultural Arts Center, the Ogden Museum of Southern Art, Junebug Productions, and countless others have been instrumental in the city's rebuilding efforts post–Hurricane Katrina and during the COVID-19 pandemic. More recently, the work of organizations such as No Dream Deferred and the André Cailloux Center for Performing Arts and Cultural Justice (ACC) have been continuing and building on these legacies, as Patrick and Stuart explore in this volume. These artists' and organizations' unwavering commitment to preserving our cultural heritage has been pivotal in shaping New Orleans's identity and attracting more than seventeen million visitors annually.

As a Black woman at the helm of Arts New Orleans, I am deeply committed to ensuring that our cultural heritage is accessible to all New Orleanians, especially our Black youth, whom I consider sons and daughters. I have witnessed the transformative power of the arts in the lives of my three daughters, whose paths were illuminated by their exposure to artistic expression. With that in mind, I hope this book illuminates the continuing importance of arts and culture to individuals and communities in the city and beyond.

Performing New Orleans: Rethinking Resilience in Art and Everyday Life is not merely a scholarly endeavor; it is a testament to the resilience and creativity that define our city and points to new ways of engaging creatively with the challenges we will face in the future. It celebrates our rich cultural tapestry and calls on future generations to embrace, nurture, and develop our artistic legacy.

Thank you, Patrick and Stuart, for your commitment to New Orleans.

—Joycelyn Reynolds
President/CEO of Arts New Orleans

ACKNOWLEDGMENTS

As we have begun to understand the city through this book, and in preceding publications, we have always been keen to share our emerging thinking with people in the city, to check our approach. This has been a slow, gradual process of understanding, and it only worked because people in the city spent time with us to help us on what is proving to be a fascinating journey.

We are extraordinarily grateful to everyone who has supported the development of this book and the thinking from which it emerges. It would be impossible to name-check everyone in New Orleans (and beyond) who has been important to this work, though we feel it is essential here to share that the book would not have been possible without the generous and gently critical engagement and feedback of colleagues and friends from across the Crescent City. Many of those who have helped our work are discussed in the main chapters of the book, but we need to say an enormous thank you to those who attended events with us, who helped us make these events possible both practically and in terms of more properly understanding the cultural norms of the city (like making sure there was always a warm welcome and a good bite to eat); individuals and organizations who have given so generously of their time and expertise in interviews, conversations, and workshops; strangers who chatted to us in theaters, bars, music venues, and on streets or in parks; and friends and colleagues who listened and gently guided or corrected our thinking or approaches to the city. Without you all, this book would not have happened. Thank you.

We're very grateful to Jenny Keegan at Louisiana State University Press for her energy and enthusiasm for the book, from meeting to discussing our first sketch of ideas one sunny February day to developing the emerging manuscript. Our thanks also to all colleagues at the press who have supported the finalizing of the book.

Last, the underpinning research took place while we both worked at the University of Surrey and continued as we moved, respectively, to Brunel and Northumbria. We are grateful for the support provided by these institutions and for the intellectual engagement of colleagues in and beyond these universities who provided generous critical feedback and continue to do so.

PERFORMING
NEW ORLEANS

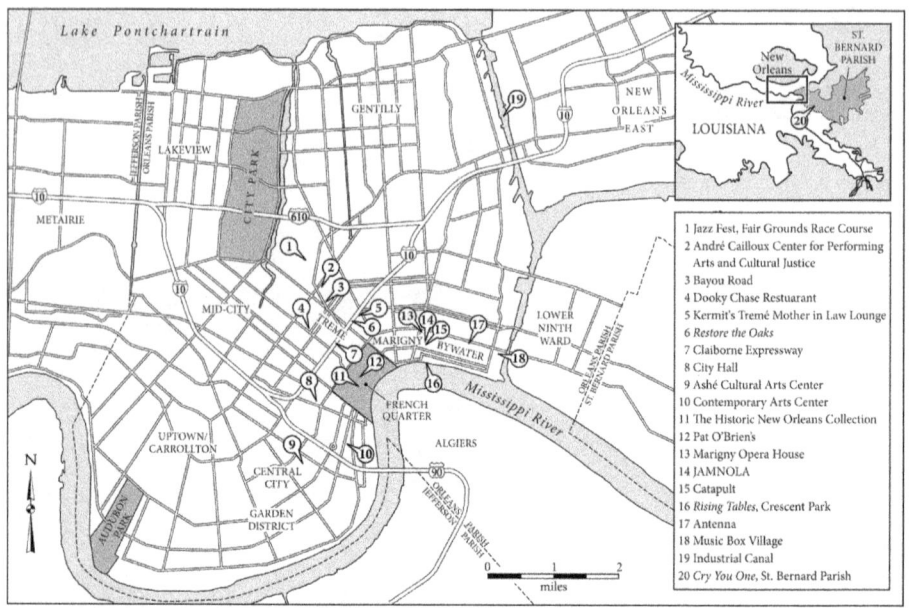

Map of New Orleans, showing the locations of main case studies and key areas of the city discussed in this book. Map by Mary Lee Eggart.

"COME BACK OFTEN"

By Way of Introduction

Beginnings

In mid-2017 we worked at the same university in the United Kingdom and had been thinking about collaborating on research that brought our expertise on "place" and contexts of "crisis" together. With that in mind, we met in Duggan's office to catch up about a conference he had attended in New Orleans in late 2016. From the first moments of that conversation, it was evident that while the conference had not been as engaging as it might have been, the city had offered a captivating professional environment for a performance studies scholar. Not least because the city is one that, as we will explore throughout this book, defines itself through multiple forms of performance and cultural practice: parading, music, the costumed performances of Black Masking Indians, street performances, the "culinary arts." More specifically, we remember discussing the Marigny Opera House, an old church damaged during Hurricane Katrina but subsequently repurposed as a performance venue, multi-arts and cultural hub, and "community meeting place."[1] In deliberately and explicitly seeking to speak at once to the needs of local communities, to developing New Orleans's cultural talent, and to programming professional dance and performance in the Marigny, this "Church for the Arts" seemed emblematic of the importance of the arts to understandings of place and, in having been revitalized post-Katrina, in contexts of recovery from crisis.

While it is a status that needs critiquing and problematizing, New Orleans is, of course, often identified as a "poster city" for thinking through disaster recovery, resilience planning, and emergency management. As resilience scholar Samantha Montano has recently put it, "If you can figure out how to do emergency [resilience] management in New Orleans, you can do emergency management anywhere."[2] In that context, our initial conversation on the

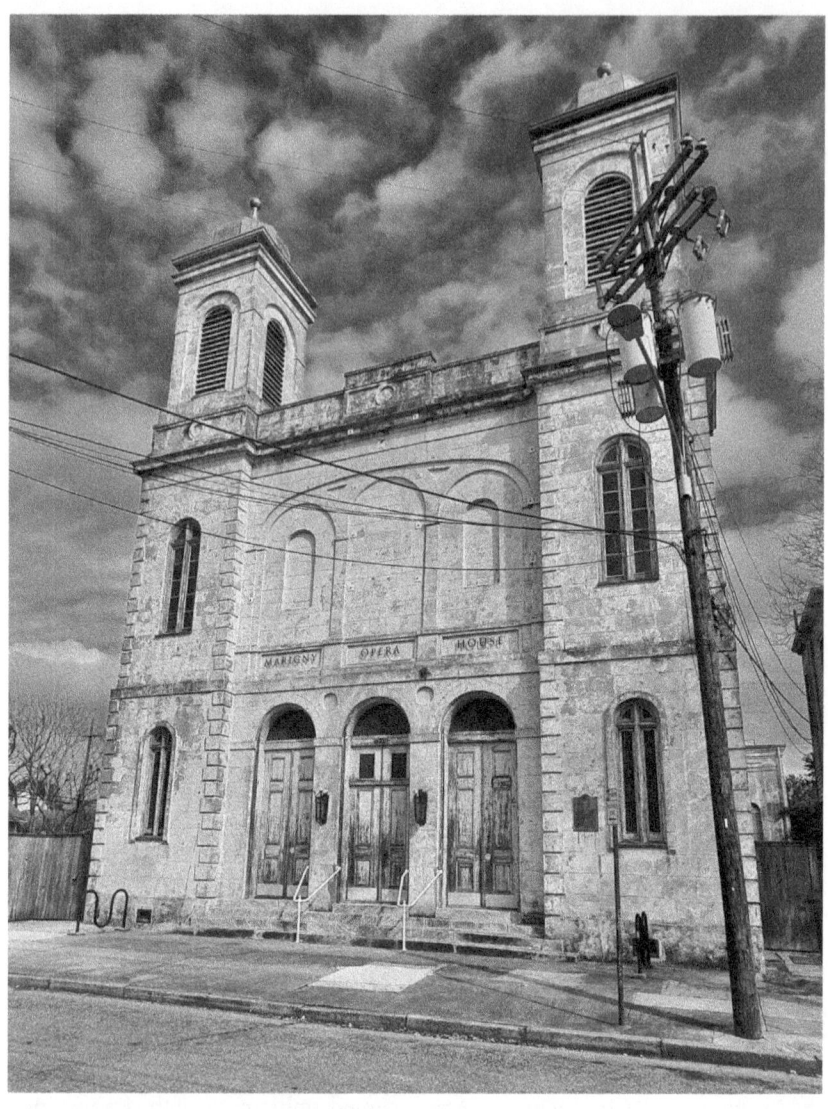

Exterior of Marigny Opera House, 2023.

importance of New Orleans as a performance culture that needed to be taken as seriously as other major cities of culture was compounded by an emerging sense that there was a significant gap in international understandings and theories of resilience. This was because, as we will discuss, the arts were not being valued beyond their capacity to be deployed as communication strategies for resilience professionals, indicatively in the design of public-facing policy-related messaging. This book emerges from our sense that the performance story of contemporary New Orleans is one worthy of scholarly attention and that the catastrophizing narratives of the city that frame much of its "post-Katrina" history need critiquing and reconsidering. Our research "hunch" (after performance theorist Baz Kershaw) at this point was that performance theory and practice could be invaluable in that reconsideration and that from there we might come to understand how performance should be considered as vital in theorizing resilience and practicing emergency preparedness internationally.[3] *Performing New Orleans* analyzes contemporary artistic and everyday performance practices in New Orleans to understand how those practices rethink and recalibrate understandings of resilience challenges in the city. In so doing, we seek to stage productive conversations between arts and resilience professionals in ways that can be internationally useful for rethinking local resilience challenges.

We need to be clear here: we do not advocate that arts and culture should be deployed to implement a preexisting resilience agenda. Nor do we offer a set of specific recommendations for resilience management in New Orleans or elsewhere. Instead, we argue in the chapters that follow that many artistic and everyday performances in New Orleans *already* address critical resilience challenges in the city. Not to recognize this fact is to miss an extraordinary and established body of work by which a city attends to its resilience challenges. Through this book, we seek to reveal and demonstrate the value of arts and culture in terms of resilience. This is not to put arts and cultural practice in the service of resilience agendas but, rather, to identify ways in which arts and culture practitioners may engage in new, productive, and mutually beneficial conversations with resilience professionals to rethink readings of, and responses to, pressing local challenges. Our intention is not to appear to co-opt arts and everyday practice into an argument about resilience; instead, we suggest that, internationally, it is all too easy to misunderstand the seriousness with which practitioners of arts and culture attend to the places in which they live and the challenges facing those places.

While this is a book on performance in New Orleans, we are aware that the arts-resilience approach may appear unfamiliar. As such, it is important we state at the outset that this not a book of quintessential performances of the city, and in particular, it is not a book of quintessential street performances of the city (in part because there have been many excellent studies of these practices previously).[4] We do address some performance forms that might be regarded as familiar practices in the city, but we approach them from angles that may be unfamiliar. For example, while we write of Mardi Gras, we do so from the perspective of performances between spectators (rather than with attention to the parades themselves). Elsewhere, we reflect on Jazz Fest during COVID-19 as part of our wider discussion of pandemic performances in the city (rather than directly addressing either the music of the festival or its place in the city's calendar). We discuss these among a range of performances that rethink resilience. There are, of course, many others that offer compelling and distinctive rethinking, and so we regard this book as part of an ongoing conversation with the city. Indeed, conversation has been vital to our own research approach in the city. The book might be seen, then, to operate as something of a textual conversation between case studies and theories within each chapter and between the arguments we make across the whole. Each chapter holds its own internal logic, argument, and power; however, overlaps between individual chapters (or better yet, between them all) offer increasingly complex yet useful arguments on how cultural production of multiple forms can perform city resilience.

To understand how the arts can address city challenges, we need to resist conventional, often simplistic definitions of arts practice. We need clear understandings of what arts practices are now, what they do (in cities in crises), and how this relates to understandings of place, community, and "resilience" in positive and innovative ways. This book seeks new understandings of the relationship between the arts and resilience. This is not a book only about performance(s); rather, we use a performance studies approach as a means of understanding and analyzing this city. Through this, we attend to both artistic and everyday acts to help make sense of the city. While the book focuses on New Orleans, the arguments and conclusions we make are applicable internationally.

Understanding performance as object of analysis and mode of reflection, the research draws on case studies from social and civic performances such as protests or local practices of place; aesthetic performances such as theater works, public art practice, and music; and performances that occupy a blurry intersection of the two (for instance, decorating potholes or impromptu second lines). Through this approach, the book reflects on the authors' research in the city between 2017 and 2025, to think through what performances in and of a city reveal about that place (socially, politically, culturally, practically). While some case studies occur in the most "famous" areas of New Orleans, others take place in areas that may be less well-known. As a result, while the book offers some degree of geographical representation across the city, and at times beyond the city limits, in being case study focused, it will consciously and inevitably not offer a representative survey of the city.

In "rethinking resilience," we review, critique, and retheorize resilience and the often problematic (political) idea of "being resilient." The book identifies cultural practice as a critical, established, but undervalued means by which the city speaks to and of itself and the necessity for key stakeholders in the city to contribute to and advance this understanding.

Performing Resilience

There is already a degree of intersection between practices of hazard mitigation, theater, and performance: tabletop and live city enactments provide training opportunities and allow for strategies, methods, and practices to be refined or revised. Indeed, as Scott Magelssen has argued, simulation-based performances in the form of "emergency preparedness drills" happen in the "thousands" all across the United States of America (and internationally). Such performances are "rehearsing for future threats and working to prevent them."[5] While our work in this volume explores less directly connected forms of cultural production, Magelssen's argument helps to make clear that the distance to travel between resilience and performance, intellectually and at the level of emergency preparedness practice, is perhaps not as far as might be assumed. For instance, while a scenario-based exercise might quite easily be read as both a performance and a resilience training event, understanding the ways in which something like a performance in a music venue might also constitute both is perhaps less explicitly apparent. This book seeks to join the dots between these practices.

Such synergies are but one aspect of what we argue are profoundly important revelations that performance theory can make to the performance of resilience in a given context. For example, in 2013–14, the academic and artist Stephen Hodge created *Where to Build the Walls That Protect Us* to explicitly question the impact of environmental shocks and stresses on Exeter, in the United Kingdom. The work presented participants with an "opportunity . . . to imagine and model a future city" by walking in the city with Hodge as well as gathering sometime later to reflect on that process and model in clay versions of a future city that understands its resilience challenges.[6] And while Hodge did not frame it in these terms, certainly that is what the performance was capable of doing as a locally situated performance concerned with the challenge of ecological change.[7]

While Hodge's site-specific, participatory project attended to a chronic stress—frequent city flooding—Tony Walsh's live, and then remediated, performance of his poem "This Is the Place" sought to address the acute shock of the Manchester (UK) bombing on 22 May 2017. Written in 2013 for local charity Forever Manchester, the poem was intended both as a way to build support for that charity and as a means to articulate the achievements and plural activities of Manchester historically and in the contemporary moment. It was, then, always already about building resilience: of the charity, of the city and its communities. But in its re-articulation after the bombing, the poem became a rallying cry to unify people in the face of terrorism and, as the writer Jeanette Winterson put it, a means of helping to "face up to the tragedy . . . giving us back the words we need" when "[we] don't know what to say." The "poem becomes part of what has happened, as well as a way of talking about it."[8] In its performance at the vigil in Manchester on 23 May 2017, the poem became a performance of city resilience.[9]

Where these aesthetic moments reveal particular ways of *performing* resilience, our broader argument in this book is concerned with the centrality of arts and culture in a city to wider understandings and practices of resilience in that city. In using performance theory, we reflect both on everyday and artistic performances of New Orleans and on aspects of the city that contribute to the performance of the city, whether these be lived practices or material structures that inform understandings, experiences, and practices of place. In taking this approach, we recognize and reimagine Tommy DeFrantz's reading of performance. For DeFrantz: "People make performances happen, whether they be in the nightclub, in church, in the classroom, on the job, or on a stage. Importantly, performers need to recognize their own performance in order for it to be valuable. It needs to be conscious action, conceived or created as performance."[10]

As DeFrantz identifies the importance of performers recognizing their own performance, so we approach research in similar ways, recognizing our performance as researchers, experiencing and observing the performances that happen in nightclubs, churches, classrooms, or onstage. As DeFrantz suggests that performance needs to be a conscious action, so we begin from the perspective that the act of attending to and researching a performance involves similarly conscious attention to what is present, what is happening, and then beginning to ask questions about what this means and in what ways it is valuable. Writing on the active nature of theoretical analysis, DeFrantz notes: "Theory, in this formation, is the mobilization of practice toward analysis. The taking stock, or noticing, of action to recognize its component parts and its implications, and the extension of that noticing to construct a way to understand, or interpret, what is happening there."[11] The analysis in the book emerges from our investigations of performances in and of the city since 2017.[12] As such, this is not an exhaustive survey of arts and culture in New Orleans. Rather, it is a study in which we seek to understand, in DeFrantz's terms, "what is happening" through a series of case studies. In so doing, we seek to understand how we might read these case studies as resilience performances, how these performances open up new thinking about resilience in New Orleans, and how these case studies speak to contexts beyond the Crescent City.

To illustrate this, the book's structure is to filter or frame these analyses through resilience challenges facing New Orleans. We argue that arts and culture offer new strategic models for emergency response and planning that can be valued intellectually and in practical terms. The task of this book, then, is not to simply survey or document interesting performances but to think through the significance of such works in context. Thus, we take seriously the importance of the place in which they occurred and their relation to other practices in that place. While not a resolvable tension, we recognize the complexity of place-based research in which precision and specificity in addressing a local context must be balanced with the potential applicability of findings beyond a given place.

We (and we are not alone here) are critical of those who have praised the resilience of New Orleanians and not supported that resilience with appropriate resources. We recognize that we may appear to be making a similar argument by finding that arts and culture workers in the city have worked their way to being well placed to address crises. Yet here we are framing the arts and culture as labor. We are not suggesting that New Orleanians are intrinsically resilient; indeed, this neoliberal deployment of resilience is a claim that has been endlessly, uncritically aimed at the city. Rather, we are recognizing the labor of individuals and organizations and identifying it as a vital part of the labor of a city in dealing with its challenges.

With that in mind, our intention is that this book reveals that a truly resilient city is one that supports arts and culture professionals as critical innovators, in good times and in crises. While recognizing the challenges that artists face, particularly freelancers, a resilient city is made up of artists and culture bearers as partners, as people in the room, as critical practitioners of the city. Building from this framing, *Performing New Orleans* seeks to draw attention to the ongoing work of arts ecosystems as critical aspects of resilience in New Orleans, offering models for practice elsewhere. We do not recommend that models from this book are lifted wholesale from New Orleans to be applied elsewhere. However, the works analyzed in this volume demonstrate the critical resilience work undertaken through this city's arts ecosystem, inviting new means of understanding the importance of local arts ecosystems in cities internationally.

Being "Outsiders"

We are performance studies scholars from the United Kingdom; our work addresses the form and practice of place and the ways that people and places respond to challenges and to crises. For the past eight years, we have been exploring intersections between arts and culture and city resilience strategy in New Orleans and in the United Kingdom. We are outsiders to New Orleans, white outsiders. There are risks of this position, particularly from our whiteness. But as others have demonstrated, if carefully considered and the positionality acknowledged, there is also value to being an outsider because it can help to avoid pre-formed biases and conclusions, ensure attention to the data presented, and afford a critical position that is not inculcated in preexisting dynamics and politics.[13] Importantly, our work to date has never been funded by any organization in the city.[14] People in the city have told us, repeatedly, that this matters—perhaps most evocatively artistic director of the Southern Rep Theatre, Aimée Hayes, who contested that it meant we "don't have a dog in the fight."[15]

That positioning has made the work of researching the city practically challenging but has nonetheless been deeply productive, allowing us to return to the place over time, observing changes and differences that may not be wholly visible to those who live "in" those changes. While we have built a solid understanding of the city, that will always be an ongoing process, and our position as outsiders will remain no matter the number of times we visit. What has become very clear through the course of our field research is the importance of returning, of coming back again and again. Indeed, in early 2022, the chief equity officer of the extraordinary Ashé Cultural Arts Center, Asali DeVan

Ecclesiastes, told us to "come back often."[16] Although informal in the context of their delivery (at a live music event outside Ashé), the words hold weight as both an invitation and instruction: it is vital to come back, often. This is because in a city dominated by narratives of temporary engagement by outsiders (especially tourists and conference delegates), to return repeatedly affords opportunities for engagement and relationship building that have been vital to our understandings of performance in and of New Orleans.

In these opening pages, we want explicitly to acknowledge that we recognize the very great dangers of knowing only a little about a place. We write about New Orleans because of its artistic and cultural practices, both aesthetic (music, theater, visual arts) and everyday (beads hanging from trees, signs, and decorations). We recognize the challenges facing the city and the ways in which the city is performed in particular ways to serve particular ends—and, thereby, particular people. We are concerned about the tourist framing of the city and the sometimes catastrophic framing of the city in terms of crime and flooding, particularly in journalism from beyond the city. Representation of New Orleans often seems at odds with the rich variety of the city and with the vast inequity of the city. At root, our concern is with equity: this is an unequal city that is too often represented as a happy-go-lucky place of joy and delight. There is joy and delight here, but there is also acute poverty and systemic and structural racism. In that context, it is important to acknowledge that legacies of race and racism continue to have a significant role in contemporary New Orleans. As such, although not *explicitly* addressed in every chapter, this book is deeply concerned with ensuring proper and meaningful representation of the artistic and scholarly work of Black and Indigenous communities—not least because this work is well-placed to engage with questions of resilience now and in the future. In part, this is because of their situated awareness of and positions in the city, or as theater scholar Harvey Young might have it, their capacity to engage in situated "thoughtful, critical consideration of the experiences of racial interpellation, socialization, and habitus." For Young, while the "concept of race is so ingrained in the operations of societies-at-large that its erasure can be difficult to imagine," cultural production, especially performance, can function as "invitations to reflect upon and evaluate the legacy and enduring relevance of race."[17] Our work in this book, then, is to begin to reveal how performances of the city can unpick neat readings of it and to reveal the ways in which individuals and organizations are engaging in compelling work to critique problematic pasts and imagine possible futures.

The Trouble with Resilience

News media representations of the city often tend to catastrophize the place. From impending environmental doom to headlines about the city being the "nation's murder capital," New Orleans is a city that is often placed into a contradictory tension between cultural and touristic narratives of place and readings of the city as failing to address the multiple challenges it faces.[18] Neither of these narratives do justice to the complexity of this city, but neither are they entirely inaccurate. New Orleans *is* an extraordinary city, rich in culture, art, and performance. It *is* a place facing profound resilience challenges, not least the tension between the city's economy being significantly dependent on tourism and conferencing industries and at the same time being irreparably damaged by both. People flock to New Orleans because of its cultural richness and its sense of abstracted otherness, of hedonism and frivolity, but that puts profound pressure on the infrastructures of the place and its people.

Meanwhile, definitions of *resilience* abound, and while it is something of a contested (or at least debated) concept, most definitions tend toward some variation of Judith Rodin's proposition that it is the ability to "develop greater capacity to bounce back from a crisis, learn from it, and achieve revitalization."[19] This is perhaps a reasonable proposition given that the word's etymological roots are from the Latin *resi-lire,* meaning "to spring back."[20] Nevertheless, the wide-scale adoption of this definition within contemporary academic and professional discourse is perhaps a little too narrowly and (historically at least) uncritically focused on the idea of returning to a previous steady state. Common also is some iteration of Brian Walker's sense that resilience "is the capacity of a system to absorb disturbance and still retain its basic function and structure."[21] These definitions share a predominant focus on hard infrastructure and/or systems that support it, with only occasional (and often passing) attention to human factors being considered. This is, perhaps, to be expected: in the face of an unfolding crisis, the capacity to get the water and electricity running again, for example, is of fundamental importance to human survival. Yet to ignore, or at least to implicitly devalue, human factors is to miss the importance of social interactions as a capacity-building activity and minimizes the importance of places of social interaction as key sites for human survival. This gap in thinking has not gone entirely unnoticed, however. Siambabala Bernard Manyena has proposed that if resilience is to be properly understood socially, politically, and in terms of infrastructure, we "need to address the philosophical questions that continue to blur the concept."[22] Beyond the philosophical, in this book we argue that the arts, and performance in particular, are fundamental to the development of more nuanced understandings of resilience.

Of course, such theory runs the risk of divorcing resilience from the lived reality of the deployment of what we might call "resilience logics" within a given context. For sociologist Kathleen Tierney, extending the work of David Chandler, there is a pervasive problem with resilience discourses in a neoliberal context insofar as they "shift the burden of providing security from the state to the individual." As such, responding to work by Julian Reid, Tierney finds the choices one makes reveal one's capacity to accept and adapt in order to tolerate "suffering" in the face of external challenges.[23]

More worrying still, this leads to a framework in which vulnerable subjects become positioned as the cause of social problems rather than exposing the place of structural inequities in causing those problems.[24] Such an understanding of resilience leads to a deployment of the term and concept in deeply problematic and oppressive ways. In New Orleans, this has played out in very particular forms of environmental racism, notably as the Lower Ninth Ward is essentially cut off from the rest of the city and in political messaging that the city and its people are resilient in the face of environmental and social challenges that are profound in their implications and systemic in their construction.[25] In this context, it is vital that we try to nuance or amend the processes and structures by which resilience is developed at city level to account for individual and community perspectives without apportioning individual responsibility for the delivery of that resilience. In this book, and in our wider Performing City Resilience research, we are particularly concerned with recognizing the contribution of arts practitioners and cultural communities to such city-level thinking. Our argument is that aesthetic and social performances in the arts and cultural arena can be valuable to resilience planning and practice *without* appropriating that work for those ends. That is: established arts and cultural practices of a given city are often already engaged in understanding resilience challenges from new, nuanced, and embedded perspectives. In arguing this, we also argue that it is possible to envision a performance of city resilience that moves past the neoliberal apportioning of responsibility onto the individual.

One of the central arguments of *Performing New Orleans*, then, is that locally situated arts and cultural practices can be useful to understandings and practices of city resilience in a specific geopolitical context (and offer useful models for practice to be shared internationally). While in line with Jen Harvie's arguments in *Theatre and the City*, we recognize that in any given city artists are engaged in demonstrating, producing, critiquing, and influencing urban life, there is currently little research that relates this artistic work on urban life to considerations of urban policy in terms of resilience.[26]

Responding to this lack of scholarly attention, this book seeks to engage with the interrelation of local resilience challenges and locally situated arts practices in New Orleans, so as to "speak back" to resilience thinking and practice in that city and internationally. Our hope is that from the specificity of our case studies in New Orleans, more globally applicable understandings will emerge.

For planning scholar David R. Godschalk, the "overriding goal" of hazard mitigation practice "should be to develop resilient cities."[27] For Godschalk, this is a response to research that revealed the considerable social and economic costs of disasters. As such, and perhaps inevitably, much writing on city hazard mitigation and resilience addresses disaster mitigation and recovery. James R. G. Morris and Paul Kadetz reflect that "culture has seldom been portrayed as an integral factor in the recovery and community rebuilding efforts of disasters." They recognize that the "emphasis in the recovery literature has been predominantly on the rebuilding of physical infrastructure." In contrast, they point to the potential of cultural practices to contribute to "individual and community resilience in the aftermath of disaster."[28] Where they consider how culture might make people or a community resilient, we are concerned with understanding the fundamental usefulness of creative work at the level of strategy and systems thinking, which may involve rethinking resilience. In pushing for an integrated approach to strategy development, and in deploying methodologies from performance studies in hazard mitigation contexts, our research seeks to go further than the important work of highlighting the power of cultural production to community and individual resilience. This is to place arts and culture front and center in the development of city-level resilience planning, strategy, and emergency preparedness practice.

Resilience as Conceptual Frame

There is significant and growing interest in resilience planning in the face of challenges that pose a threat to people and/or place. In his editorial in the first issue of the *Resilience* journal, David Chandler observed that "resilience is now a central concept informing policy frameworks dealing with political, developmental, social, economic and environmental problems in ways that clearly transcend traditional disciplinary boundaries."[29] Interest in resilience is particularly evident in urban contexts, both as it is understood and practiced in individual cities and by organizations that connect to and collaborate with specific cities. In part this may be a result of increasing urbanization, with more than half the world's population living in cities. In 2013, for example, the Rockefeller Foundation set up 100 Resilient Cities (100RC). As its name suggests, 100RC worked with one hundred cities to support the development of long-term resilience strategies and networks, principally by funding a chief resilience officer in each city for a period of two years.

Although the project in its original form ended, 100RC offered critical conceptual and practical frameworks for thinking about resilience internationally. Key among these interventions was identifying resilience in terms of "challenges" that could be classified as either "acute shocks" or "chronic stresses." For 100RC: "Shocks are typically considered single event disasters, such as fires, earthquakes, and floods. Stresses are factors that pressure a city on a daily or reoccurring basis, such as chronic food and water shortages, an overtaxed transportation system, endemic violence or high unemployment."[30] On one level, urban resilience is an issue of infrastructure, but this infrastructure is necessarily engaged in supporting and enabling practices of life and work in a city. For us there is a need also to try to understand the ways in which people *live* in the context of resilience challenges and the ways in which they make sense of this experience of living in a place facing shocks and/or stresses.

Alongside this growth in strategic resilience planning, particularly in urban contexts, theorists have sought to define resilience as a means of conceiving of and practicing place. In 2006 Walker and Salt suggest that resilience is "a way of looking at the world" and "seeing systems, linkages, thresholds, and cycles in the things that are important to us and in the things that drive them."[31] For Walker and Salt, where once the challenges of a city might have been seen and attended to as discrete concerns, resilience takes them together as interconnected and in need of critical analysis and unified response. Similarly, David Chandler argues that "resilience—and its ubiquitous rise across the policy spectrum—is an invitation to critically engage with the world around us, to ask new questions of it and to overcome disciplinary and conceptual divides based upon the understandings of the past."[32] Thought through in such terms, resilience shares much with the by now well-worn understandings of performance as a means through which people understand, practice, and, crucially, materialize the world around them.[33] That is, we might argue, that performance and (understandings of) urban space can be co-constitutive: each enacts something on the other that materially impacts upon its "creation" and its subsequent functioning.[34] While there is currently significant global debate on urban resilience—to understand and respond to challenges in specific cities—there is no work that thinks through the contributions that arts and cultural practices make to resilience thinking internationally, and vice versa. Equally, while artists in a city may well be acutely engaged in articulating and reflecting on the resilience challenges of that city, they may not specifically identify that work as a practice of resilience. That is: the arts are missing from resilience thinking. This book seeks to contribute to filling that gap by arguing that performance can be key to understanding city resilience, and resilience might offer much to understanding the "work" performance, and performance spaces, do in a city.

As arts academics, we are concerned to understand, elucidate, and share emerging conceptions of how the arts can be a meaningful part of contemporary discussions on resilience and associated analysis of what Chandler calls "the world around us." To greater or lesser degrees, much, perhaps all, arts practice asks questions or at least invites us to look again at the world in which we live. Faced with pressing resilience challenges, few policymakers turn to artists for solutions. In the reverse, artists may not be entirely comfortable understanding their work solely—even partly—in terms of resilience. The more art is perceived to have a particular use, the less it is free to critically engage with conditions in the world around us: in such a context, there is a tendency to instrumentalize the arts rather than think about the sociopolitical work they might already be doing in a city. That is, we need to think less about how the arts might be used as communication tools, for example, and more about how they are useful in revealing and articulating new and existing understandings of a city. There is, we sense, a need for conversation, for brokering, for thinking with stakeholders across borders of discipline and role. We might then begin to understand the ways in which the arts rethink the world and how doing so might directly reimagine resilience challenges that, in Chandler's terms, may comprise "political, developmental, social, economic and environmental problems."[35] By taking this perspective, we can look again at existing performances as well as at acts in a city, to begin to understand their contribution to a city and to its performance of resilience.

Why New Orleans?

In New Orleans, the predominant narrative around resilience has been precisely that those who are and have been most vulnerable are and need to continue to be resilient. In a workshop we ran with the Music and Culture Coalition of New Orleans (MaCCNO), it became apparent that little policy or structural change had challenged this narrative of seemingly inherent resilience. Our research begins to redress that imbalance by investigating the possibility that locally situated artistic performances in New Orleans reveal how to understand, live, and work in a place that faces particular structural resilience challenges (environmental, political, social). This is to rethink strategy and architecture scholar Melanie Dodd's argument that city-level policy operates "at the level of the meta-narrative" and lacks the precision needed to take account of the "small-scale, disruptive but necessary differences between different spaces, cultures and areas." For while Dodd excitingly points to the need to value the "diversity, complexity and difference . . . [the] barely balanced chaos and flux" of cities, we propose that thinking from performance to resilience, by way of hazard mitigation, enables a reconsideration of the strategic policy decisions and structures that shape people's lived experience of a place.[36] In this we recognize UNESCO and the World Bank's "CURE Framework," which identifies culture and cultural production as essential to city resilience at formal levels in planning for and implementing city strategy concerning hazard mitigation. If, as our work in New Orleans has, we take seriously the intellectual thinking of cultural practice in terms of how to live with and think through a city's resilience challenges, then it is possible to put local cultural practices into productive conversation with the development of city-level strategy and policy.

One reason why we might need to do this work is because there is a possibility that "resilient" and/or catastrophized narratives of New Orleans dismiss the importance of performance practices in the city or suggest that there might not be anything more to be learned through the analysis of performances in and of this city. Indeed, early in our research, we encountered just such a diminishing of the city in terms of its potential importance for performance scholarship. In late 2018 we approached a very well-respected theater and performance journal with an idea for an essay on performance and New Orleans. Our intention was to explore the potential resilience role arts organizations might already be performing in the city. We wanted to understand what might be revealed by understanding arts organizations as city "situations rooms," like those that help manage the city during major events. While that was published elsewhere (and forms the core of chapter 3), the journal's editor explained via email that theater and performance scholarship "has no real interest in an essay on" New Orleans, especially because so much had been written about Paul Chan's *Waiting for Godot*. In a sense, then, this senior academic was suggesting that performance and theater studies was "done" with New Orleans. Such a dismissal would not be written about performance in any other global city, so why suggest that performances of importance in New Orleans stopped when *Godot* arrived in 2007? This book sets that record straight.

Methodology: "In Conversation with the City"

This book is grounded in embedded practices of field research and iterative analysis. Our project methodology involves a series of intersecting, related practices of observation, experience, conversation, interview, and analysis. This works in an action research framework in which discovery and response to discovery spiral, happening in swift iteration, followed by periods of reflection and further analysis between times spent doing fieldwork.

In this research, we are engaging with tried and tested performance studies approaches to the analysis of both "aesthetic" (such as theater shows) and everyday (such as encounters on the street) performances. Considering this, it is not surprising that we reference the ideas of performance and performativity. With the former, we are focusing on particular events or practices in the city that might be analyzed as "cultural objects," bounded and encountered in time and place. With the latter, we are calling upon the sense that acts and utterances have material consequences in the world: a performative act *does something*; ergo, cultural objects *do* things. As performance scholars Simon Shepherd and Mick Wallis have it, drawing on Elin Diamond, as soon as we come to analyze a performance for the performative qualities of the work, the sociopolitical and cultural aspects of that work become open to scrutiny. Shepherd and Wallis go further, arguing that "[performative acts do] something, [they are] efficacious . . . the more general sense of performativity [is] getting something done. There is also a very general metaphoric usage, especially in other disciplines, of 'performative' in the sense of 'like a performance,' or to index the consideration of something in terms of performance—the 'performative aspects of dentistry,' perhaps."[37] In this volume, unless otherwise stated, *performativity* is used in terms of "getting something done" (as constitutive in the world), rather than an act being metaphorically "like a performance."

Grounded in performance studies methods, research activity included fieldwork and later analysis of fieldnotes, semi-structured interviews, performance analyses, and desk-based/archival research. In this, we draw on established practice from performance ethnography methods, following Richard Schechner and, more recently, Joseph Roach.[38] Importantly, work on every aspect of the research is conducted entirely collaboratively, iteratively, and dialogically; this has come with practical and financial challenges, but the work is significantly strengthened in being refracted through and between our different expertise. Just as we have been committed to collaborative investigation, so we have ensured stakeholders' and participants' voices are core to the research at all stages, both in impact-focused activities in New Orleans and in the development of this book.

Critical to every aspect of the research has been the use of *conversation* as a vital method of both data gathering and data analysis. In this we draw on the work of Swain and King, who point to the vital importance in field research of conversation in "natural, everyday settings." During fieldwork, our practice has been to speak to people about places, practices, and topics that relate to our research. Some people have been known to us and engaged via semi-structured interviews and then more informal follow-up conversations, other conversations have been happenstance but no less critical. Incidental conversations have been particularly important, especially when they occurred as encountered aesthetic or social practices taking place in "natural, everyday settings," causing some degree of collective observation and reflection.[39] Because of this, we have kept detailed fieldnote diaries during every trip and have drawn on them extensively in the work of this volume.

Where we refer to any conversation in this book, we anonymize the identity of the person we met when discussing their comments unless they have given permission for their voice to be recognized.[40] Given the precarity and informality of arts and culture communities in New Orleans, formal documentation processes like "participant information sheets" and "participant consent forms" have presented research risks throughout the work insofar as they can make conversation dry up and overly formalize a process that is supposed to be open and engaging, discursive. For example, if a planned meeting occurred in an arts bar at a busy moment, formal processes of consent and project information sharing can be a particular issue for our research, as many of the people and communities we are engaging with may have experienced recent and/or long-standing exclusion in the city (primarily focused on issues of race and poverty), including from city processes (notably construction of the I-10). People may distrust official processes and forms, even though these forms are designed to offer protection, and so we have worked hard to embed the ethics of such processes in more informal ways and use verbal consent with follow-up communications to ensure fairness of representation in this work.

Where conversation is at the core of our methodology, both with participants and between one another, we have also made use of workshops and events, processes of walking and being in a place that emerge from walking performance practices and cultural geography. On every trip, we try as much as possible to "live in the city"; that is, we share a "home" during the research, shop in local grocery stores, and try to get to know the area as much as is possible in the time we have. This changes the way one understands a place and offers a very different experience to that of staying in a hotel (as we did on one trip).

Our methodology, then, is multimodal—informed as much by the resilience theory outlined and the performance studies approaches of our training as by the lived experience of being in a place over time. Going back repeatedly and checking in with assumptions and findings, seeing things again and again while expanding horizons and understandings, ensures—we very much hope—that this book offers a new approach to thinking about New Orleans, avoiding pitfalls of extractive research that has had something of a history in the city (we address this more fully in the next chapter).

As a result of this, drawing on field notes, thick descriptive accounts of our experiences often form means of reflection and framing for critical analysis and the development of the argument we are making. We have resisted the urge to mark these reflections out typographically because they are integral to the analysis, though they are perhaps tonally distinct. In all our visits to the city, we limited our engagement in conventional "tourist" experiences; that is, fieldwork is for the purpose of research, and while *some* engagement with "normal" tourism is necessary, part of this work is to be in the place for longer durations than most visit and therefore to reflect on different aspects of the city.

Of fundamental importance in our approach has been our desire to avoid extractive research, to be "in conversation" with the city, and people in it, over a sustained period of time, and to do this in the city and as we reflect on that field research from afar. To help ensure that, in June 2023 we shared initial versions of the central argument of the book with members of the community, artists and arts organizations, advocacy groups, resilience professionals, interested publics, and those working in environment and placemaking. Those conversations had direct and meaningful impact on the final refractions of our thinking in this volume, and we are forever grateful for that engagement.

"Contemporary" Performances

Given the centrality of field research to the work of this volume, it is perhaps unsurprising that we would focus on the "contemporary" as our temporal frame for this project. That said, quite what the contemporary moment means is perhaps more complex than it might first appear. It would be easy, for example, to take our moment as "post-Katrina," but as we will argue in the next chapter, this runs the risk of perpetuating problematic academic discourses that always already frame the city as defined by that event and its aftermath. Although undoubtedly critical to all aspects of understanding the city, the extraordinary exhibition *Postmodernism to Post-Katrina* (2019), curated by Jan Gilbert, fundamentally breaks the myth of Katrina as *the* defining feature of the city, illuminating the multivalent contexts, histories, and politics of the place that contextualize and are contextualized by Katrina. The city is infinitely more complex than a single event, no matter how catastrophic.

Not only that, but recent scholarship has shown a deft touch in illuminating the importance of performance and wider cultural practices to what Weston Twardowski refers to as "navigat[ing] the legacy of Katrina." Very much focused on the importance of revealing the ways that performance was powerful in offering post-disaster models of adaptation at speed, Twardowski shows how, in the aftermath of Katrina, performance might "help communities process the 2005 disaster through individual and collective acts of mourning."[41] His work reveals the civic-political and social-personal work performance can do in post-disaster recovery.

Like Katrina, COVID-19 had a profound impact in New Orleans, so much so that it could have acted as the central focus of the book in and of itself. But again, we contend that COVID-19 needs to be considered in the round, not in isolation. Thus, the book is not a survey of the city's cultural practices, though we do try to offer a range of case studies. Nor is our work, then, a history of the city. Rather, structured to focus on particular aspects of the city's "resilience challenges," each chapter focuses on performances since 2017, when this project began, referencing past actions and events to help us make sense of practices "now." Where we analyze works older than this, it is because they occupy critical importance in the cultural memory of the place now. For instance, Mondo Bizarro's and ArtSpot's *Cry You One* was referenced and discussed by both arts practitioners and resilience professionals on every trip we made to New Orleans. Thus, the central case studies of the book are drawn from 2017 onward, though we stretch this to take account of works that are very closely related to the concerns of the volume or that have importance in the city on an ongoing basis. In making these analyses, we draw on personal experience as much as we do documentation and archive. Sometimes we have experienced things several times, sometimes just once, and sometimes, as we reflect in the chapters, that "once" is important.

Even in the eight years we have spent working on the city and on this book, we have become acutely aware that ideas, practices, and strategies of a city can change astonishingly quickly. In a book that seeks to think in new ways about city resilience, we are particularly aware that shocks and underlying stresses can easily and rapidly become particular critical issues. We are, then, interested in this time period as a moment in which to think about the city and to work through the innovations it may be able to offer to New Orleans and to cities elsewhere in facing ever more complex social, political, and environmental realities.

Mapping

The complexities the city of New Orleans faces provide the conceptual mapping for this volume. In each chapter, we will introduce and analyze specific case study performances, identifying ways in which they respond to key resilience challenges in New Orleans and, crucially, afford new thinking about how those challenges might be addressed conceptually and practically. Each chapter is grounded in specific conceptual frameworks that are relevant to the resilience challenges under scrutiny. Consistent in each chapter is our methodological commitment to conversation, performance analysis, and reflection on embodied experience in the city. As will become apparent, while each challenge can be seen as a specific focus of the chapter, they inevitably overlap in the lived reality of the city. So, where (over)tourism might seem a discrete issue (chapter 1), it affects all aspects of the city's emergency and resilience planning (chapter 3), and the economic shock of the pandemic was exacerbated by the "removal" of tourism (chapter 5). Where "living with water" is, on the one hand, a very particular resilience challenge (chapter 4), it directly relates to the lived experience of multiple infrastructural challenges of the city and the ways city residents address the lived reality of their situation, on the other (chapter 2). The book can be broken into sections by chapter if desired but is best read as a coherent argument on the importance of performance to city resilience with New Orleans as the case study.

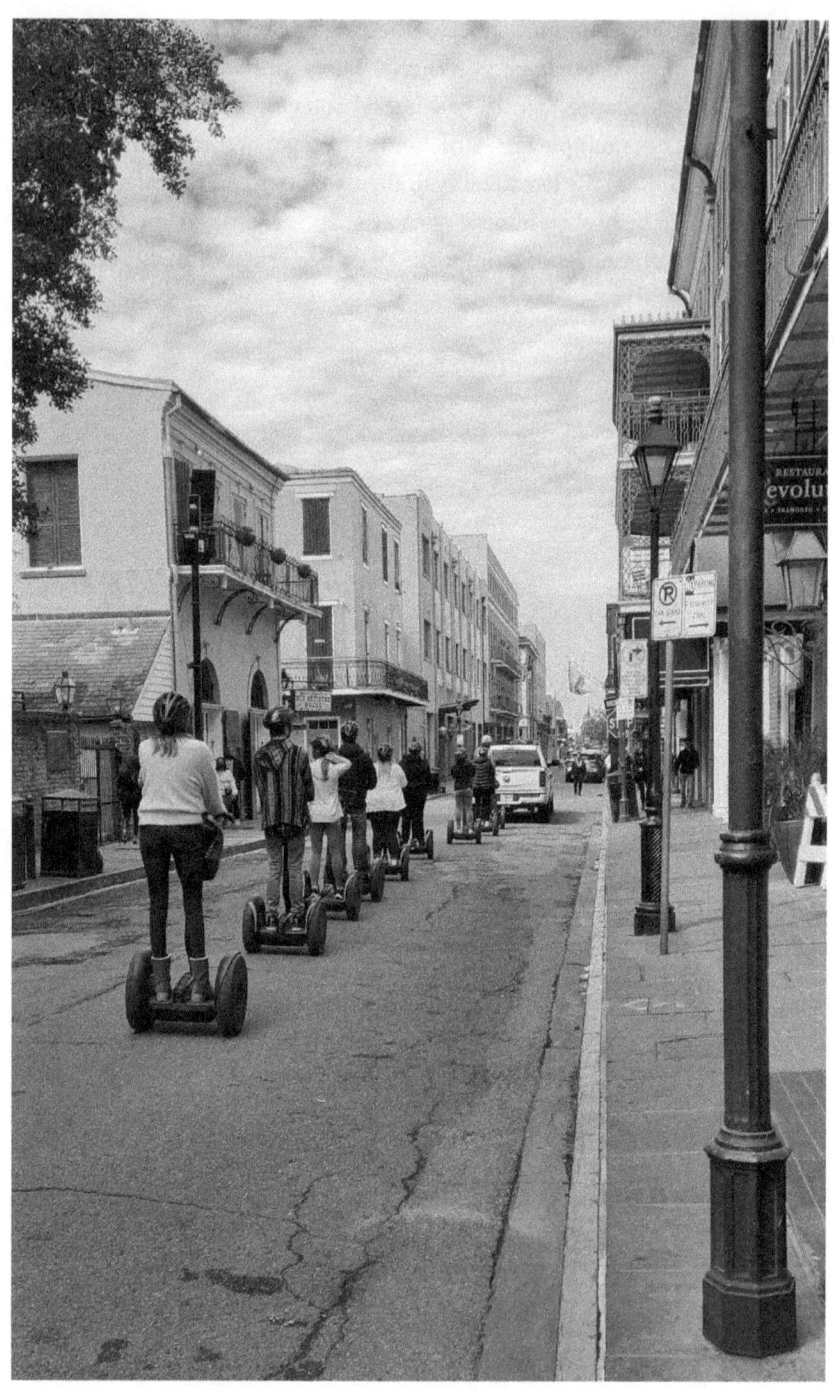

Tourists on Segways in the French Quarter, 2018.

1

AFTER OVERTOURISM

Introduction

In April 2019, just a year before the city would shut its doors to tourists because of the COVID-19 pandemic, the New Orleans Sustainable Tourism Task Force (NOSTTF) released a report exploring "overtourism" and the city's position in relation to this "emerging global crisis." In the report's introduction, it states that "the current course of tourism is clearly unsustainable in many destinations around the world, and specifically in New Orleans."[1] In this chapter we seek to understand how arts and cultural performances can be deployed to help manage tourist conceptions and practices of place that might mitigate overtourism. We ask two interrelated questions: first, how can a performance studies approach to analyzing tourism practices and itineraries be useful to rethinking the dominance of touristic understandings of New Orleans? Second, how might this exploration potentially reveal new practices of, and "management" approaches to, tourist experience in that place? In addressing these questions, we will argue for richer, more nuanced readings of New Orleans that destabilize a current restrictive focus on a limited set of places and practices in and of the city. We call for more recognition of the local in New Orleans, of museums, exhibitions, neighborhoods, and communities that recognize and value New Orleans as a lived city, rather than a tourist city. As our case studies show, there are existing processes and practices in the city that can be drawn on to find new ways to invite visitors to explore the city beyond the predominant tourist "hot spots." We do this by revealing the ways that performance thinking offers means of attending to social and aesthetic encounters in a place that can suggest alternative representations of a place, which can then be enacted as tourist management strategy.

Recent scholarship, and much popular and tourist writing on New Orleans, demonstrates that this is a city that occupies cultural imaginaries in very particular ways. The city exists in films, media, theater, and literature so prominently that understandings of this place have been particularly driven by representation in and from cultural production. More invidiously, perhaps, is the way that these cultural narratives have been inculcated into touristic representations of the city and that the tourist version of New Orleans is now the dominant image of the place. As American studies scholar and native New Orleanian Lynnell L. Thomas puts it: "The historical reality [is] that most outsiders'—and a good deal of insiders'—perceptions of the city have been filtered through travel accounts, literature, film, and other popular depictions . . . even in the midst of unprecedented crisis the portrayal of New Orleans during Hurricane Katrina continued to be dominated by troubling images and ideas of the city's tourist iconography."[2]

Theater scholar Margaret Werry has recently argued that we need to "understand tourism as an inherently performative practice" and that, therefore, "it follows that tourism is the largest, most profitable institution of performance culture of the last century."[3] In line with this proposition, our interest here is in what we term the "performance of tourism": the ways in which particular practices, places, behaviors, and/or areas of the city come performatively to "be" New Orleans. That is, recalling Shepherd and Wallis, such representations of the city are active agents in the world that come to constitute the "reality" of the city as it is perceived in tourist narratives and indeed how it may be experienced. Even at a basic semiotic level, certain performances of tourism in and about the city can be seen to have become codified to such an extent that they operate as the dominant indexical points of reference for understanding the city. So prominent in this indexical relationship are aspects of the city's representation that they have become iconic of it. That is: touristic representations of and performances in New Orleans have come powerfully to be understood as *being* the city.

Given the predominance of such representations and the potency with which they have become embedded in the cultural imaginary of understandings of New Orleans, it is very hard to move beyond them. That is, the power of these representations within understandings of place raises the possibility that folk who do not engage with these areas or itineraries may feel they have not experienced the "real" New Orleans. Rhetorically, these representations operate to raise the prospect that for one to be able to say one went to the Big Easy, one *needs* to have been to the French Quarter, taken photos of beautiful balustrades, and partied until the early morning on Bourbon Street. In so doing, there is a great risk that the details and particularities of a place, this place, get overlooked—that the wrought ironwork so iconic of understandings of the city's architectural vernacular often contains Adinkra symbols. As Karel Sloane-Boekbinder of the Ashé Cultural Arts Center argues, these symbols carry "messages forged into iron shapes [that] have crossed centuries, cultures and continents. As a person's expertise with metal and fire can travel with that person, so can cultural patterns particular to the places they come from."[4] Or that to perambulate through the Quarter is to walk through complex histories of slavery, racism, and segregation that still reverberate through the city in profoundly problematic ways. Stopping to notice, to remember, to question, is not part of dominant perspectives on how to be a tourist in the city, perpetuating practices that might be seen to offer very thin experiences of place that "whitewash" more complex histories and perspectives.

At one level, this is problematic in the ways it reductively narrows understandings of the place to (normally quite trite) misrepresentations or essentializations. At another level, the power of these representations and the city's tourism industrial complex, including its behemoth conferencing economy, has pushed tourism into overtourism, presenting meaningful problems to the city's future and its livability.[5] Crucially, the entanglement of (mis)representations, overtourism, and certain performances of tourism present a complex resilience challenge that requires rethinking in novel ways.

As we will discuss, there is value in approaching this rethinking from outside tourism studies because (some) extant literature on New Orleans has tended to accept dominant (mis)representations and framings of the city without critique or problematization. Our analysis, grounded in performance studies, considers the ways in which tourism actions, representations, events, and attractions might be understood as social performances that have been enabled or curated by the city (for economic ends) and proposes analysis of tourism practices in the city that are not regularly part of the discourse. In order to do this, we discuss a series of case study "performances" that help make sense of tourism in the city and offer strategic means of addressing some aspects of overtourism. By analyzing the prominence of a specific drink in a specific bar in the French Quarter, the Hurricane cocktail at Pat O'Brien's, we explore the impact of tourist itineraries as scripted understandings of the city. Attending to incidental performances of play between spectators and the potential to disperse crowds from tourist hot spots at Mardi Gras, we look at new ways of understanding this mega-event and its impact on New Orleans. Analyzing the ways in which a deliberate tourist attraction, JAMNOLA (from Joy Art Music New Orleans), engages with representations of the place and the work of local artists, we explicate the potential for interventions that encourage tourists to disperse into new areas of the city. By reflecting on our own experience of attending live music at Kermit's Tremé Mother-in-Law Lounge, we offer arguments on the ways that locally situated experiences of welcome and home can resist trite simulacra of the city.

Overtourism

In 2018 the general secretary of the United Nations World Tourism Organization (UNWTO), Zurab Pololikashvili, argued that theories of overtourism have become necessary to reflect the significant "challenges of managing growing tourism flows into urban destinations and the impact of tourism on cities and its residents." He further points out that

> addressing the challenges facing urban tourism today is a much more complex task than is commonly recognized. There is a pressing need to set a sustainable roadmap for urban tourism and position the sector in the wider urban agenda.
> Tourism is one of the few economic sectors relentlessly growing around the world, translating into socio-economic development, employment, infrastructure development and export revenues.

Making these comments in the foreword to the UNWTO's executive summary *"Overtourism"?—Understanding and Managing Urban Tourism Growth beyond Perceptions*—produced in collaboration with the Centre of Expertise Leisure, Tourism & Hospitality (CELTH) of Breda University of Applied Sciences and the European Tourism Futures Institute (ETFI) of NHL Stenden University of Applied Sciences)—Pololikashvili is clear that tourism can only be "sustainable if developed and managed considering both visitors and local communities." The report further argues that this approach takes complex, nuanced engagement from sectors and communities across a given destination.[6] Despite this understanding, as is often the case in addressing complex resilience challenges, the arts are largely absent from debates, theories, and practical projects that seek to address overtourism, even though, recalling Werry, the connections between performance and tourism are profound.

According to the UNWTO, the term *overtourism* was coined by the travel news outlet *Skift* in 2016 as "a simple portmanteau [designed] to appeal to people's baser instincts with an element of alarm and fear in it."[7] Defined variously in tourism scholarship, the term broadly refers to the point at which a destination (regularly) exceeds its "carrying capacity" to the point that excessive and unsustainable pressure is put on that place, negatively impacting quality of life.[8]

As the UNWTO report makes clear, there are multiple contributing and exacerbating factors in overtourism. Its authors outline four key areas: numbers in relation to management capacity (including "seasonality"), localization of tourist activity, infrastructure pressure (including "competition" of visitors and residents/commuters), and the limits of "smart solutions."[9] Of particular interest in this chapter is the relation between localization and seasonality, within which we place perceptions of New Orleans as a "party town" and wider (mis)-representations of place that contribute to driving tourism. This focus emerged out of New Orleans–based discourse on the problem of overtourism in the city.

Overtourism in the Big Easy is related to a complex mix of the city's reputation as a party town, the overfocus on the French Quarter as the locus of attention and activity, the conferencing economy, and a more general analysis of exceeding the city's carrying capacity. Tourism in New Orleans is a yearlong challenge, exacerbated at particular moments associated with festivals, events, and seasonality.[10] As performance theorist Joseph Roach has argued, the city has a complex relationship with tourism:

> The hospitality [tourism] industry is an economic driver—but [New Orleans] could not matter to visitors in the beguiling way that it does unless it mattered to natives like no other place. The cost to the locals shows up on the loss side of the cultural balance sheet as exoticization, dooming them to perform "authenticity" to fit the needs of corporate urban branding (Gotham 2007). The benefit to them registers as the gratification of overdoing what they're doing over. The genius of utilitarian hedonism resides in its capacity to extract novel pleasures from routine necessity, such as at Igor's Bar, Restaurant, Game Room, and Laundromat on St. Charles Avenue, open 24/7, where patrons can do their laundry while enjoying the signature Igor Burger and Bloody Mary as they shoot a game of eight ball with their new friends instead of sitting alone and watching their underwear cycle through spin and tumble dry.[11]

As such, this chapter investigates a series of case study performances of tourism, some that might be seen to operate within dominant paradigms of tourist practices in New Orleans and others, like Roach's example, that disrupt or challenge them.

Narrow Narratives of New Orleans: "Bourbon Street, That's Where It's All At"

Arriving in New Orleans in 2018, we stood in the long queue for passport control and, a little weary from the ten-hour flight, waited in silence as we inched toward entry to the United States. A woman in front of us was visibly excited and chatted happily to folks in the queue. Someone asked her if it was her first time in the city. When she affirmed that it was, the questioner quickly recounted how they had visited once before and that the first-timer "must go to Bourbon Street, that's where it's all at!"[12] Globally infamous as the neon light–festooned party area of the city, Bourbon Street stretches the length of the French Quarter (thirteen blocks, about one mile), at more or less the exact midpoint between its Mississippi River and North Rampart Street boundaries. The sense that this one street might contain "it all" is not only fatuous but is indicative of a wider, pervasive misrepresentation that New Orleans *is* the French Quarter (in part as represented by Bourbon Street). While it is true that the Big Easy is a city that parties easily and that the French Quarter's wrought iron balustrades and Creole architecture are charming, the overfocus on the Quarter in tourism narratives, popular representations, and personal itineraries of the city offers a reductive understanding of the place and its performances.

A quick search of peer-reviewed, academic publications on Google Scholar reveals the extent to which the French Quarter not only operates as the epicenter of tourist activity but is also held up performatively to "be" New Orleans within tourist understandings of the city.[13] For example, the historian and tourism scholar Connie Atkinson describes the French Quarter as the "chief tourist area" of the city; Nina Bălan and Bridget Bordelon, urban and tourism studies scholars from the University of New Orleans, argue that "New Orleans is famous for the French Quarter—the city's oldest and one of the most iconic neighborhoods."[14] Musicologist Christopher Coady writes that the Quarter is "historic," "famous," and "romantic."[15] Meanwhile, geographer Michael Crutcher Jr. has convincingly argued that the French Quarter is perceived to be "the city's showpiece and playground."[16] Although these authors are not uncritical of this (mis)representation of the city, all share something of an acceptance that the French Quarter provides the vernacular iconography of the city within tourism discourses, practices, and marketing. Moreover, each recognizes that it operates as the principal locus of tourist activity because the city has, as Thomas argues, "continued to entrench the boundaries around the French Quarter, abandoning the rest of the city as too dangerous and menacing to rescue or rebuild."[17] Disrupting this ostensibly racist boundary setting is a slow process and one that brings the specter of gentrification with it. As such, the French Quarter continues to have its own gravitational pull, occupying central positions on tourist itineraries and in mythologies of the city.

New Orleans has developed its tourism industry at "the expense of other economic and commercial development."[18] This has been pushed to the point that the city is fundamentally reliant on it. At the same time, tourism and the influx of people throughout the year present fundamental challenges to the city environmentally, politically, and practically: New Orleans's "tourism numbers exceed carrying capacity and potentially pose a risk to local community well-being."[19] As such, in a book seeking to "rethink resilience," it is essential to explore this challenge in relation to tourist performances and to performances that seek to address tourism.

Tourism in New Orleans exists within a complex dichotomy between being economically vital, on the one hand, and being (potentially) profoundly damaging in social, political, ecological, and practical terms, on the other. Although not unproblematic in its valorizing of "bouncing back" and of New Orleans as "thriving" post-Katrina, Judith Rodin's *The Resilience Dividend* offers some pertinent observations concerning the potential impact of tourism and problematically narrow understandings of the city that emerge from it. Rodin, former president of the Rockefeller Foundation, argues that "a sense of identity" is vital to place resilience (in particular, in "revitalization" efforts postcrisis). Rodin contends that in the aftermath of a crisis, people and communities need to fold that crisis (or its threat) into understandings of identity, place, and community: "Resilient entities create narratives that are positive, aspirational, and forward looking without ignoring past difficulties [or future ones] or venturing into the realm of fantasy."[20]

While we might query the dismissal of fantasy, given the power of the fantastical to imagine (im)possible futures, the importance of narrative to understandings of place identity, and the centrality of that to resilience, chimes with our own positioning of performance as central to rethinking resilience. That is, if we understand the stories—the performances—of, from, or about a place, we come to find possible solutions to the challenges facing it.

Rodin goes on to argue that "New Orleans identity" and the impact of Katrina on it has been "endlessly explored" in both documentary and fictional representations across different media. Rightly, she qualifies that none of these representations can "claim to tell the whole or true New Orleans story."[21] In particular, she picks up on the problematic positioning of the city as being defined by "booze, Bourbon Street, Mardi Gras, and parties." This pervasive narrative misses the complexity and diversity of the city in favor of one that "centers on the raucous doings in the French Quarter and excludes the more intimate, culturally vibrant" aspects of Mardi Gras and the city more broadly. This particular narrative of the city's identity is pervasive in global representations of New Orleans, across all media, from novels and plays to films and television series to tourism and investment brochures for the city.

The city's economic reliance on tourism is well documented and discussed, but what is perhaps less well-known is that this "commitment" to tourism and its industries is relatively new.[22] Historian and author of *New Orleans on Parade*, Mark Souther contends that while tourism was certainly understood as an economic force for the city, it was not really until the election of Moon Landrieu as mayor of the city in 1970 that there was explicit political force behind the development of it, with particular focus on the French Quarter.[23]

The adoption of tourism as a key cultural focus of the city accelerated further during the "oil crisis" of the 1980s, when, according to Atkinson (glossed by Laine Kaplan-Levenson), "the city went from overlooking its culture to hawking it." This reliance on the tourist's dollar continued to accelerate from there, with New Orleans journalist and documentary filmmaker Lolis Eric Elie neatly putting it: "One of the problems with being a city that depends so much for its life blood on [the] tourist economy is you are inclined to give the customer more of what they want . . . If they come here on a Monday and enjoy the red beans and rice on Monday, and they start asking for them on Tuesday, the next thing you know, you're selling them on Tuesday. If they find out that the Mardi Gras Indians, or that the second line organizations have their annual parades on Sunday, well, 'Could they do it on Tuesday because our conference ends on Wednesday?' . . . And all of a sudden you got folks doing that stuff."[24]

This is exacerbated by the fact that tourist trips to New Orleans tend to be swift, structured around long weekends or visits to coincide with particular events. John Levendis and Mehmet Dicle suggest an average of 3.3 days, while a 2022 *Tripplo* (UK) report put it at 4.2 nights (using data from New Orleans & Company, which "promote[s] New Orleans as a premier travel destination").[25] While short trips are a familiar feature of tourist practice in many cities internationally—see, for instance, guides for 48 hours in one city or another—the emphasis of such short trips as key to tourism in a place is something very different. Such swift encounters necessarily limit one's capacity for depth of engagement with a place. In that context, it is understandable that framings of the city influence the behaviors of tourists. Online or printed guides to the city become especially valuable, when tourists spend such limited time in the city. Yet tourist reliance on these guides means that certain areas gain prominence. One such context in much literature is the idea of New Orleans as being defined by Hurricane Katrina.

Problematizing "Post-Katrina" Framings in Tourism and Academic Discourse

When one comes to research on contemporary tourism in New Orleans, a great deal of the extant literature frames the scholarship in terms of the city as existing in a post-Katrina context, including work produced since 2015 (ten years after that storm). For us this presents a number of critical challenges. First, the titles of these works (if not always the content) suggest that New Orleans's tourism needs always now to be considered in the context of that meteorological event and the human-caused disasters that followed. Second, it presupposes that the city and its peoples are indeed "post"—beyond, done with, bounced back from—those events. While people do not, as local journalist Doug MacCash put it to us in 2018, "talk about it daily," the city, then and now, is profoundly not done with, or post, Katrina.[26] The legacy of that event lingers in the city. Third, and somewhat at odds with our last point, the post-Katrina framing also yolks the research to Katrina without necessarily acknowledging that the city may in fact have more to say about itself, and its position in the world, than simply its relation to August 2005.

Indeed, the post-Katrina framing runs the risk of essentializing experiences of the city, especially tourist experiences, freezing them and their understandings of the place always already in relation to that now historic event. For instance, in their 2021 article "Personalising Disaster: Community Storytelling and Sharing in New Orleans Post-Katrina Tourism," based on field research in August and October 2014, Churnjeet Mahn, Caroline Scarles, Justin Edwards, and John Tribe contend that Katrina and its memorialization "continues to fuel the tourist industry" in the city.[27] While it is true that the legacy of Katrina continues to be important to questions of place, the environment, and the future of the city, it is not the dominant narrative of the city in tourism literature, policy, or itinerary planning. Indeed, many (if not most) of the event-based Katrina-focused tourism activities, such as the Greyline Hurricane Katrina Tour, no longer operate in the city as dedicated "Katrina tours." Such post-Katrina studies (and tours) were common in the years immediately following the storm; indeed, there is a plethora of academic literature that explores the impact of "Katrina tourism" on the economic regeneration of the city after 2005; tourism-focused studies published as recently as 2022 continue to center post-Katrina as a dominant framing paradigm of the place.[28] It is understandable and practical, of course, to use such a significant event as a historical demarcation, but, we argue, to do so in framing tourism in the city is as problematic as discourses and marketing that predominantly or only center the French Quarter. In both cases, there is an uncritical narrowing of how the city is and can be understood.

However, a great deal of the more recent research seeks to problematize the ethics of those practices rather than valorizing them as vectors of "hope and optimism" that offer "first-hand accounts of how communities rallied together as their homes, families and communities were ripped apart."[29] In the years since Katrina, such narratives of New Orleans's resilience have been widespread and deeply troubling in their assumption of the ways people (in general terms, rather than specific cases) "bounce back" or make do. Indeed, these discourses have now been widely problematized, challenged, and contested both academically and by the city's residents and advocacy groups such as the Music and Culture Coalition of New Orleans. Although not a forensic analysis of tourist itineraries, Tripadvisor's 2023 list of "Top Attractions in New Orleans" does not feature a specific Hurricane Katrina "attraction" aside from, at number 22, a passing reference to "the Katrina exhibit" that is permanently on display at the state-run Presbytère Museum. Far from Katrina "fueling" the tourism industry in the city, if anything tourism might be seen to fuel Katrina narratives; indeed, as we will argue later, we are concerned that rather than New Orleans's place identity driving tourism, the tourist industry is perpetuating and driving myths of that identity.

There is, then, a great risk that post-Katrina framings and analyses of the city, especially in relation to tourism, run the risk of taking a moment in history (particularly anniversaries), and experiences therein, to represent the contemporary city. This is to miss the complexity and nuance of the place. As such, we contest that post-Katrina is at best an anachronistic framing, and while the legacy of Katrina is undoubtedly important in New Orleans, it should not be seen as the dominant force of social, cultural, political, or indeed touristic understandings of place. We hope in this volume, and this chapter in particular, both to acknowledge the ways in which Katrina continues to be a presence in the city and its cultural and resilience infrastructures and to explicate the ways in which New Orleans is about so much more than a post-Katrina narrative.

There are, as Thomas argues, multiple powerfully problematic tourist agendas at play in New Orleans, not least the commodification of Black culture within systems that perpetuate racist understandings of those cultures, whitewash history, and sustain environmental and fiscal racism.[30] The implications of these histories and systems, and analyses of them, help to inform our arguments concerning the two problematic and interrelated narratives of Katrina and the French Quarter. At play in the way that tourism frames understandings of New Orleans are, first, academic tourism discourse, which positions Hurricane Katrina at the epicenter of understandings of place and practices of the city. This refracts understandings of the city through a singular "post-Katrina resilience-recovery" framing. Second, tourism literature and popular cultural representations of the city, especially in travel guides, overwhelmingly center Bourbon Street and the French Quarter, perpetuating a sense of place inscribed with a set of bawdy behaviors seen as fundamental to understanding and being in the city.

Tourist "To-Dos": Hurricanes at Pat O'Brien's

One of the ways in which tourist performances are inculcated is through the proliferation of to-do lists such as Tripadvisor's "The Ten Best Things to Do in New Orleans" and *TimeOut's* "The Best Things to Do in New Orleans Right Now."[31] Such lists and guides are of course ubiquitous in the tourism industry globally. However, the sense that one can "do" New Orleans quickly and easily is a predominant feature of much of the material available for the Crescent City. Indeed, not only do these lists tend to circulate around a relatively small set of activities, venues, and areas, but they very often reduce "the City" to a three- or four-day structure in which one simply works through a set of checkbox experiences, so as to "tick off" New Orleans.[32] Of course, such itinerary setting can provide a sense of security and familiarity, especially in a city that can be frenetic and busy and that has a reputation for violence. These itineraries might also be seen as useful in navigating the city. New Orleans's relation to the Mississippi River means that its geography can be occasionally tricky to understand and navigate: "New Orleans is called the Crescent City because of the way it nestles between the southern shore of Lake Pontchartrain and a horseshoe bend in the Mississippi River. This unique location makes the city's layout confusing, with streets curving to follow the river, and shooting off at odd angles to head inland. Compass points are of little use—locals refer instead to lakeside (toward the lake) and riverside (toward the river), and, using Canal Street as the dividing line, uptown (or upriver) and downtown (downriver)."[33]

Nevertheless, these lists and itineraries also invite practices, ways of being in the city. It is easy to read the city as exceptional, but in the context of unfamiliarity with this particular city, itineraries do pose significant and distinctive challenges to the city because they perpetuate the problematic codification of New Orleans. These structural devices of tourism tell people where to go, funneling thousands of people in any given weekend to a very particular set of areas, not only limiting one's experience of the place but also applying profound pressure to the infrastructure and livability of those places.

Perhaps one of the more (in)famous examples of this is the consumption of the Hurricane cocktail at (or "to go" from) Pat O'Brien's. Situated at the heart of the French Quarter, with entrances on Bourbon Street and on St. Peter Street, O'Brien's is a large bar with multiple indoor and outdoor spaces. Extremely popular and almost always busy, O'Brien's is credited with inventing the Hurricane cocktail. Although named after the hurricane lamp–shaped glass it comes in, given that the annual hurricane "season" presents New Orleanians with a six-month period of heightened awareness of the meteorological threats that the city faces, it is perhaps surprising that the name of the drink persists. Especially as it is no small part of the New Orleans to-do experience, being the "most popular drink with visitors to the French Quarter . . . A perfect place to sip a Hurricane is still in Pat O's legendary courtyard, overlooking the flaming fountain."[34]

We arrive at Pat O'Brien's early and notice we are joining an already formed queue of a dozen or so others at the large double wooden doors. As they open, we file through a dark, enclosed walkway, with rooms leading off to the sides. Ahead is the garden, an L-shaped space with chairs and tables, some open, some covered. There is loud popular and familiar music playing from speakers. A waiter checks if we want to order; it is a convivial space. The hurricane is a sizable drink. We're uneasy about the prospect of drinking it, sensing it will

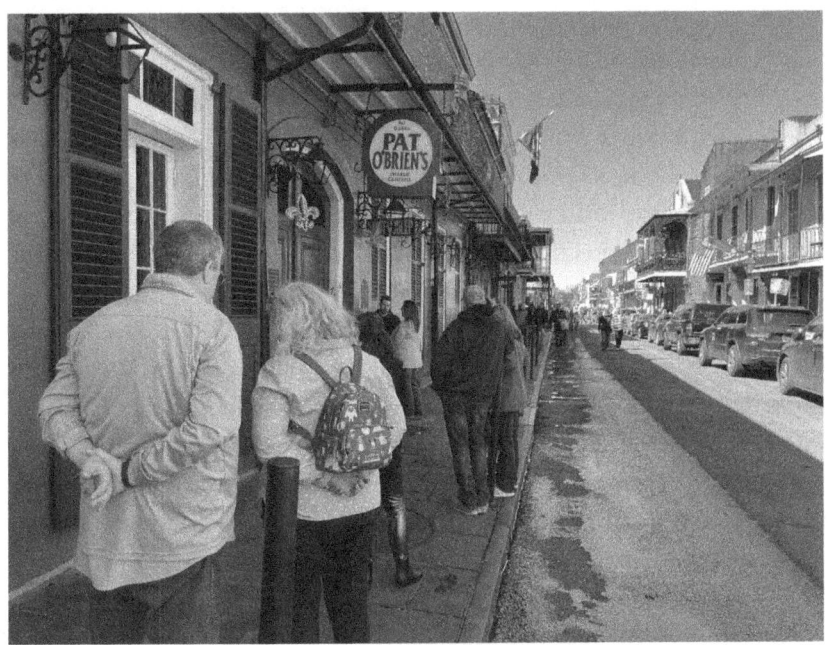

Queue for Pat O'Brien's bar in the French Quarter, 2022.

be sweet and something of a shock to the system. It is sweet, although not as much as we'd imagined, and as the glass is narrower at the top, we make good progress. That said, we reach a point where it feels we may have done enough. We become aware that the dozen or so people who arrived as we did have all ordered Hurricanes.

In their research on overtourism in Yogyakarta, Indonesia, Sarani Pitor Pakan and Intan Purwandani, academics in tourism and geography, found that "tourism-caused overcrowding is often projected as the failure of governance," where "governance consists of myriad aspects and actors." Pakan and Purwandani focus on the influence of travel agents on governing tourist flows through the creation of itineraries. As they find, "local tourism stakeholders should promote not only popular places but (re)distribute the flows and make other places happening as well." Additionally, they argue that beyond travel agents, "tourism actors need to diversify the tourist attraction sites and activities to split the crowds and keep carrying capacities up." More broadly, they find a need to be "aware of tourism" and "not only care about the money" but also consider "the sustainability of tourism."[35] While the performance of tourism may be impacted in New Orleans by governmental support for tourism in the

French Quarter, Pakan and Purwandani recognize there is a body of practitioners in and beyond the city who maintain a particular version of the city by designing strikingly similar tourist itineraries.

By being aware of tourism in New Orleans and its impact on the city, and not only looking to the money, tourist managers might entirely rethink the places and practices of the city and craft more diverse itineraries; critically, they may share with tourists the collective need to be "tourist aware." Ultimately, this will likely involve expanded definitions of the city that involve more diverse experiences of New Orleans. If any city can be ticked off in a few days, the list of what must be seen or done for that city becomes a means by which the city is defined and risks being the only way in which that city is understood, which, as New Orleans and Yogyakarta indicate, is entirely unsustainable.

This is, of course, not to say that one must stay away from the French Quarter, nor is it our intention to bemoan anyone who does want to barhop along Bourbon Street (indeed, in the course of our time researching the city, we may or may not have done this ourselves). These are legitimate experiences of the place, and the Quarter *is* beautiful. It is not our intention to critique the practices and experiences of tourists in the city. Indeed, we are also acutely aware of distinctions between traveler and tourist in travel writing and tourism literature and the risks of critiquing mass tourist practices as opposed to the apparently more sophisticated experience of the traveler.[36]

Our concern is not with tourists in the city but, rather, with the management of tourism: the restricted area of the city that is framed as being safe for tourists and the centrality of Bourbon Street and the Quarter in tourist itineraries. Our argument here is that the itineraries and expected forms of tourist experiences need to be opened up to critique and nuance. This is so that wider, more diverse understandings of place and performances of tourism might be revealed as possible and desirable and that misrepresentations of the city are no longer practiced as familiar, even necessary, tourist acts in the city.

Mardi Gras

One such rethinking is possible in encountering a major driving force of the tourism industry in New Orleans: Mardi Gras. This mega-event is often characterized as "the biggest free party on earth" and annually draws tourists to the city in their tens, if not hundreds, of thousands. In an echo of Judith Rodin's sense of the challenges posed by reputation, performance scholars Leslie Wade, Robin Roberts, and Frank de Caro reflect in *Downtown Mardi Gras* that "on one level, Mardi Gras certainly serves as a potent icon of the city's flair for celebration, performative exuberance, and *laissez-faire* regard for a mainstream American ethos—'New Orleans knows how to party,' a perception that feeds the city's tourism engine and brings millions of visitors to the city each year."[37]

This is, of course, a very narrow reading of a much more complex celebration in the city, one that is as much for local families as it is for out-of-towners, if not more so. As Wade, Roberts, and de Caro go on to explain, "Mardi Gras stands as a key constituent of identity and belonging" for New Orleanians.[38] Nevertheless, the "party town" propaganda persists, creating the dual problems, as noted by the UNWTO, of localizing tourist gatherings and "seasonalizing" activity to (especially) long weekends, festivals, public holidays, and other major events. As the New Orleans Sustainable Tourism Task Force put it: "Decades of '24/7 party town' visitor marketing have resulted in a high volume of party-seeking visitors arriving in New Orleans expecting that to be true—and making it so. The consequent degradation of residential quality of life is placing severe stress on the city's historic neighborhoods and degrading the visitor experience."[39] The Task Force goes further in its short position paper "A Culture Misunderstood" not only to point out that New Orleans is "by any measure . . . a nuanced, richly intriguing, artistically fertile culture" but also to argue that "promoting New Orleans for the past few decades as Party Town USA—one big, raucous, drunken bash—has proved a successful strategy to put heads in (low to moderately-priced) hotel room beds. The problem: New Orleans has never been one big, raucous, drunken bash. Not even on Mardi Gras Day (largely a family affair throughout most of the city)."[40] This sense of Mardi Gras festivities as being family, or at least locally, focused in "most of the city" is worth dwelling on for a moment. Taking one of our own encounters with Mardi Gras celebrations, we argue that more family/locally orientated understandings can be performatively deployed, in the UNWTO's terms, to "stimulate new visitor itineraries and attractions" by recalibrating dominant paradigms of the "24/7 party-town."[41] Simply put: itineraries that could open up the experience of visiting New Orleans to resist simplistic and reductive versions of the city would revolutionize the ways in which tourists make sense of the city. The principal difficulty with tourism in New Orleans is that it is conventionally understood as only requiring three or four days of one's time.

Conversations across St. Charles

In February 2022, after a COVID-19 imposed hiatus, we were back in the city, and, unintentionally, this trip coincided with Carnival season.[42] On 20 February 2022 we walked from our apartment to the intersection of Girod Street and St. Charles Avenue to watch the Krewe of King Arthur roll by. A little daunted by the aggression of some of the throwing of "throws" we witnessed on Canal Street, the "downtown" border of the French Quarter, earlier in the day, we approached with some trepidation (though Patrick was intent on getting a branded throw for his son, Arthur). As we approached, it became clear that the atmosphere here was much different than that on Canal Street: families were gathered, conversation was flowing, and people were helping each other to catch and collect throws.

A few minutes after arriving, we noticed three girls across the street trying to attract the attention of those opposite. Making eye contact, they bounced small rubber balls across the street when the parade came to a halt every now and again. This became an ongoing means of communication across the space; a performance of community, joy, and collaboration evolved over the next ninety minutes or so. Hand signals, reaching to catch, eye contact, pointing, occasional vocal calling, and much laughing came together to create a conversation between strangers: the girls and (what we took to be) their parents on one side, a slowly changing group of parade goers of all ages on the other. There was no hierarchy, no competition. The game was inclusive, spontaneous, and joyful; participants laughed, feigned exasperation if a catch was missed, and actively looked to reengage one another if the "conversation" was interrupted by the passing of floats or marching bands.

An elderly couple danced on a balcony opposite our position. They laughed with one another and with those in the crowd who spotted them and danced "with" them from the pavement. They, and we, sang to familiar lyrics played by passing trucks or brass bands. These performances created and enacted *communitas;* people were brought together through joyful practices that encoded a sense of (temporary) belonging, equality, and understanding. This was an experience of being together in time and space, of being part of something bigger than oneself. This is perhaps an idealized reading of Carnival. There are, for instance, questions to be asked about the performance of sex, sexuality, and race enacted in the costuming of young Black dancers who follow the main floats and the ways in which past traditions of Carnival have been historically racist.

This impromptu community of participants cut a striking difference from the aggression of the earlier parade we had encountered on Canal Street, where throws were thrown with some force while spectators jostled with sharper elbows. The ball game seemed, by design or accident, to enable revelers to participate in the embodied experience of Carnival with a greater degree of connection to one another, rather than clamoring only for the "magnificence" of receiving a particular set of beads, a doubloon or two, or a sought-after handmade gift. We read this performance as a moment in which Carnival became visible as both part of tourist narratives of the city and as an opportunity for connection across race, class, and age lines, between locals and visitors.

This social performance reveals ways of reading and encountering a place through performative interventions that positively disrupt dominant paradigms of "the" tourist experience of a destination. In particular, this reading suggests means of understanding the local, family nature of the Mardi Gras experience that is at once "exceptional" (spectacular, embodied, celebratory) and everyday. Critically, in happening at the edgeland of the main tourist spots—some seven blocks downtown, away from Canal Street and the Quarter—this helps to disperse the dominant geographic locus without necessarily funneling visitors into more residential areas, potentially moving the "problem" from one area to another.

Dispersal

The very first strategy to combat overtourism that the UNWTO recommends is to "promote the dispersal of visitors within the city and beyond."[43] While parade routes stretch through more residential areas—though not generally residential roads, following the city's interventions over time—and are generally open for folk to watch from any point on that route, they tend to follow St. Charles Avenue for long stretches. A major commercial corridor, St. Charles runs more than five miles from Canal Street (on the edge of the French Quarter) to Carrolton Avenue (Uptown). In that span, it affords opportunities to push those visiting the city for Mardi Gras to experience parades and festivities in different areas with very different atmospheres and to spend money in businesses away from the throng of crowds in the French Quarter. Such dispersal has the effect not only of alleviating pressure through geographic dispersal but also of ensuring that "local communities benefit from tourism."[44] City officials and tourism industry professionals (not least as represented by New Orleans

& Company) know this, of course, and there are active moves to engage in systematically enacting such strategies.[45] However, what our work shows is the ways in which performance analysis, and understandings of place that are revealed through the analysis of everyday and more artistic performances, can offer new thinking on the development and implementation of strategies for managing tourist practices.

Our work points to the ways in which tourist management strategy might be informed by close reading of local performances of place that are already stretching geographic and representational understandings of how to be a tourist in the city. This offers ways of visiting (or thinking about being in) that place that diversify understandings of *what* to do, *where*, and *when* as well as contributing to more sustainable *ways* of doing it. By remaking tourist maps and itineraries (as in the work of Pakan and Purwandani), by opening up what appear to be simple activities and events, we can enrich tourist understandings of and engagement in place. In turn, this can potentially distribute tourist resources more widely across the city and to a more diverse set of businesses, enable more sustainable tourism, and draw tourists' attention to their lived performance of tourism in the city.

Different Itineraries, Different Practices

The Music and Culture Coalition of New Orleans points out that "tourism in New Orleans is a $9 billion dollar industry, yet many of our musicians, artists, service industry workers, and traditional culture bearers—the backbone of the tourism industry—are living near the poverty line, and many small cultural businesses are struggling ... We know that this form of 'trickle down tourism,' where massive amounts of money are invested in large developments being pushed by already wealthy developers is both fundamentally inequitable and unsustainable."[46] Rethinking the ways we practice being in a place as tourists may help to alleviate imbalances in the ways that tourism contributes financially to the city. At the 2022 annual American Society of Theatre Research (ASTR) conference, in New Orleans, we hosted a plenary panel discussion with key stakeholders from the city (an event we discuss more fully later).[47] The session sought to explore the idea that performance (cultural practice) might be seen as critical to addressing the resilience challenges of cities internationally, and New Orleans in particular.

In attending to this broad question, one approach to defending against what Souther calls the "Disneyfication" of the city as a result of tourist narratives was offered by both Joycelyn Reynolds (Arts Council New Orleans) and Constance Thompson (Ashé Cultural Arts Center): to visit and spend money in Black-owned businesses. As Thompson put it: "Go eat at Dooky Chase or Willie Mae's, support black owned and local eateries. Do not eat chain restaurant food." Good advice, of course, and we will attend to the cultural and political importance of Dooky Chase at the end of the book. Beyond the general wisdom of encouraging conference delegates to push beyond what are perhaps the easy choices in terms of fiscal contribution to the city, into the locally owned and New Orleans–specific businesses, is the call to diversify engagement with the city geographically and demographically. In calling on conference delegates explicitly to consider where their money, time, and embodied experiences of the city went, both Reynolds and Thompson performatively challenged the predominantly white audience to think beyond the immediate surrounds of the Quarter (where the conference hotel was situated) and into other areas of the city with businesses that have a greater preponderance of Black ownership. This encourages geographic and economic dispersal (as encouraged by the UNWTO) and contributes to nuancing tourist practices in the city.

This is perhaps easier said than done because it requires both a degree of knowledge of the city (how does one identify local, Black-owned businesses?) and a confidence in traversing it, especially after dark, especially given the essential role of the nighttime economy to the city's coffers. But who gets the money, and how, is vitally important in New Orleans, especially given that most musicians and service workers in the city, the people at the very heart of tourism, generally earn minimum wage and rely heavily on tipping. As MaCCNO's *The Good Visitor's Guide to New Orleans (or How You Can Help New Orleans Music and Culture Thrive and Survive)* says:

> Tourism is the lifeblood of our city—we host more than 10 million people a year. But New Orleans and its many distinct neighborhoods are not theme parks; we are a living, breathing city with people from all walks of life. With ever more people enjoying our city's traditions, music, performances, and festivals, it's especially important to share the most sustainable ways to participate in and support our culture . . . Parts of the city that are tourist destinations are also neighborhoods, not theme parks. Enjoy! But please also be respectful of

your neighbors . . . Be respectful of ritual processions, like jazz funerals. Enjoy and observe from the perimeter. It's disrespectful to interfere with the ritual for a photograph . . . Culture and tourism are our livelihoods . . . those of us fueling the [tourism] industry and culture—musicians, artists, performers, and hospitality workers—frequently make a living and support our families on tips alone . . . Please remember to tip when you go out, and make sure to have cash on you. If you like what you hear and see, bring the experience home by purchasing CDs, T-shirts and other merchandise from performers and artists. Follow bands and musicians on social media and introduce their music to your friends.[48]

What MaCCNO's guide makes clear is that how one performs one's tourism in the city (and indeed anywhere) is critical if practices of visitation are to be sustainable and appropriately fiscally rewarding. The guide offers direct means of addressing the UNWTO's finding that sustainable tourism requires engagement with "visitors and local communities."[49]

As such, the call to make a conscious intervention in one's own tourist practice affords opportunities for new cultural experiences that reveal different aspects of the city, many that cut beyond dominant popular understandings of it. This is not to suggest an "authentic" or "essential" New Orleans is accessible in expanding the places one encounters but, rather, to point to the complexity and diversity of experiences that are available across a city—even in the French Quarter. Seeking out such diversity of experience offers, we argue, an internationally applicable model through which it is possible performatively to redraw how one understands a place and how one interacts with it, including, crucially, where the money goes.

Kermit's Tremé Mother-in-Law Lounge

We are both tired by a combination of jet lag, a lot of walking, and having spent a long day working, so decide to eat at our hotel—an easy retreat. We're made welcome by a friendly, chatty server who politely dips in and out of snippets of conversation through the meal. We put laptops away when the food arrives, pleased to have made progress in the day. Despite the fatigue, neither of us can quite determine what time of day our body clocks are registering, and so the prospect of live music is raised. We discuss heading to some of the venues on Frenchmen Street, but neither of us can quite muster the energy needed for that particular strip of New Orleans music establishments. Having missed the opportunity to attend a celebration in memory of Dr. John there in 2019, we have been planning to visit Kermit's Tremé Mother-in-Law Lounge this time round. A local bar and music venue owned and run by the renowned trumpet player Kermit Ruffins, Mother-in-Law Lounge was an important local venue long before it was made famous by HBO's *Tremé* (2010–13). Not quite committing to the idea of venturing out, let alone precisely where, our server seems to sense our indecision and asks if we're thinking of heading out. We mention Mother-in-Law Lounge, and her smile widens. She convinces us we'll have a warm welcome and can be sure there will be live music. Recalling the advice of Constance Thompson, Joycelyn Reynolds, and MaCCNO, we pack up and book a cab.

The bar is on the corner of North Claiborne and Columbus, under the shadow of the infamous I-10 overpass. Music spills out of the open door and greets us as we climb out of the car. A little trepidatious, a little excited, we head into the darkened interior. We expect to find the space crowded but discover it is fairly quiet. We make our way to the bar and are happily welcomed; we order drinks (that arrive much more gin than tonic) and turn to face the musicians playing only a few feet away. A sign made by local artist "Dr. Bob" hangs behind them: BE NICE OR LEAVE!

We had been expecting the place to be bigger, given its importance and presence in the city's music scene, perhaps also because its owner is one of the city's most famous living musicians. However, the space is small, perhaps even cozy, with an almost domestic feel; indeed, while some patrons are watching the music, many, maybe most, seem so at home here that they chat and relax as one might at a friend's party.

At the end of the set, once the applause has died down, three or four notes from a trumpet play out: clear, bright, joyful—a means, it seems, of marking the end of the live set. We turn toward the music and realize that just behind us, maybe three feet away, is Kermit Ruffins, dressed casually in a hoody and lounge wear, sitting with his feet up on a stool. For us this seems extraordinary and exciting, but the rest of the room is apparently nonchalant about Ruffins's presence. Moments later Ruffins asks "Alexa" to start playing various songs and artists through the venue's PA system; there's some debate about what this music should be, both between Ruffins and others in the space and through direct requests to Alexa from patrons enjoying their evening in the Lounge. In these moments, two things become very clearly apparent: that we are the only two people in the bar this evening who are not locals and that this is not exceptional. This is Ruffins's venue, owned *and run* by him; this is a business but one operated with notions of the local, community, home, and welcome at its core.

The sense of welcome extends well beyond being a nice place to listen to music or have a drink. On most days, Ruffins provides free food at the Lounge; often red beans and rice, often BBQ, often cooked by Ruffins himself: "Featuring daily food made by Kermit and other Treme chefs, we're are [sic] always serving up New Orleans Style. Mondays and Thursdays we have Red Beans and rice, and we almost always have the grill going out back."[50] In so doing, the Lounge offers opportunities for nourishment and community, as a practice of good hosting and welcome. In acting as an occasional pop-up vaccine center during the COVID-19 pandemic, the Lounge fulfilled a civic responsibility but acted also as a means to break down barriers to vaccination: this is a trusted space, a place people come to feel at home, and so to be vaccinated here is to be inoculated in a place of safety and familiarity.

Inevitably, there will be times when Kermit's Tremé Mother-in-Law Lounge is much busier, with a crowd more representative of the city's reliance on tourism and the centrality of music to that economy. Paul Oswell, writing for *Condé Nast Traveler*, offers the following reflection on "what are we coming here for?" at the Lounge: "Kermit Ruffins is one of the city's favorite sons, and his civic pride and infectious *joie de vivre* just exude from his bar. Free food, cheap drinks, and music that flows like the lifeblood of this neighborhood."[51] Despite being often mentioned in such tourist narratives, Ruffins being a figure of some fame and acclaim, and the building being flamboyantly and colorfully decorated outside, the Lounge sits at a seemingly inauspicious corner, bordering an underpass that is daunting to traverse (perhaps especially as an outsider) at night, with few other tourist-focused amenities or venues in easy walking distance. As such, in being at a remove from the main thoroughfares of tourism, the Lounge requires of the tourist an encounter with the city that pushes beyond the norm. It offers a view into and from somewhere that both performs being and is very local. Rather than offering a simulacrum of New Orleans such as found often on Bourbon Street and other parts of the main tourist agendas of the city, the Lounge invites tourists into the local, revealing new performances of the place and mixing the local with the outsider in productive, if implicit, ways. The Lounge offers an antithesis to the Hurricane cocktail experience of New Orleans. Although it is a well-known and often recommended venue in the city, it does not occupy space on tourist to-do list experiences of having "done" New Orleans. Kermit's Tremé Mother-in-Law Lounge is a site of and for the city, the Tremé in particular, and it takes this local role seriously.

JAMNOLA

Where Kermit's Tremé Mother-in-Law Lounge is perhaps not geared explicitly toward the tourist market, JAMNOLA absolutely addresses it. Conceived as a "a topsy-turvy stroll through the cultural gems that make the city so special," JAMNOLA is precisely aimed at the tourist economy in its marketing and in content that deploys iconography of and from the city to generate its audience.[52] At the same time, the attraction was developed by local artists and culture leaders, and it continues to support the cultural infrastructure of the city in meaningful ways through efforts such as sponsoring events, advocacy, collaboration with organizations like MaCCNO, and employing local artists, culture practitioners, and residents.

Having booked a timed slot during our fieldwork in February 2022, we decided to walk from our accommodation to the space. We arrived grateful for the blast of air conditioning that greeted us in the foyer of the repurposed warehouse in the Marigny. Although JAMNOLA claims the attraction is "just a 15 minute walk from the French quarter," it had taken us closer to forty minutes from the Canal Street side of the Quarter, as we were staying in the Central Business District (CBD). The fifteen-minute marketing is clearly designed to help alleviate any potential anxiety about venturing out of the Quarter. In so doing, JAMNOLA explicitly situates itself in relation to, if apart from, the dominant space of tourism in the city. Comprised of a series of rooms within which one encounters interactive installations, the experience was designed by a team of more than thirty local artists. Clearly designed to be social media friendly, each room is bright and colorful; patrons are invited to engage with the objects and installations, and there are explicit requests to post pictures of such engagements on Instagram and Facebook (appropriately tagged, of course). One can, for instance, stand within a cartoonish replica of a Black Masking Indian costume or a giant crawfish, pose for pictures on a stoop, or "play dress up like you never have before!"[53] The mise-en-scène of the experience is garish and over the top, designed to draw gasps, giggles, and gigabytes of pictures.

There is a genuine attempt to encourage playful, embodied engagement with the experience, but it is also clearly operating within a self-perpetuating social media marketing feedback loop to increase custom and drive repeat visits. This is not in any way hidden, but the commodification of New Orleans sits a bit uneasily for us when we encounter it: it appears to us to be somewhat exploitative, an explicit over-performance of New Orleansiness (so to speak). But we are perhaps not the intended audience, or perhaps we just have not leaned into letting the good times roll (or maybe we are just a little bit older than the main audience). Certainly, those around us seem to be enjoying the experience hugely. Nevertheless, the theme park quality and aesthetics of the experience leave us unsure what the experience offers to understandings of the city's complexity and depth, wondering what the value of this attraction is to the city.

An initial reading of the experience perhaps points to a problematic politics of capital production and extractive tourism through a Disneyfication effect that is being performed. However, this is too surface level a reading to do justice to JAMNOLA's work in the city. Indeed, as geographers Martin Young and Francis Markham argue, "To theorise the relation between tourist places and the production of value, we need to understand the circumstances under

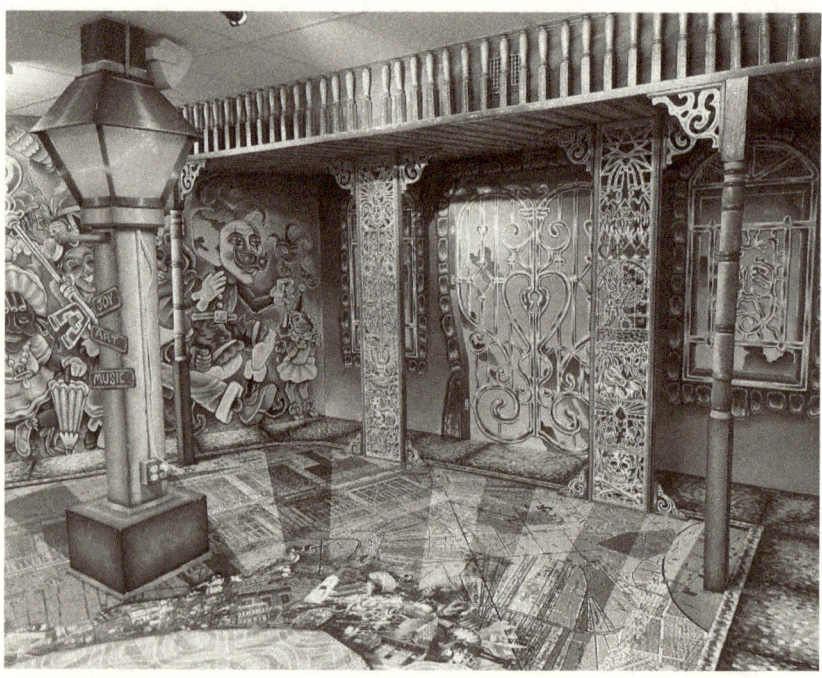

Artistic rendering of the French Quarter inside JAMNOLA, 2022.

which these places take on commodity form." They further contend that "value" can only be understood through greater critical attention to "the transformative power of the tourism industries to reconfigure space and place." While there are undoubtedly, in their terms, "spectacular" examples of this reconfiguration, such as industrial-scale theme parks, "mega casino developments . . . and the conversion of major cities such as Barcelona and Venice into tourist spectacles," we are here interested in the ways that a smaller intervention in New Orleans might be seen to buck the trend of such spectacularizing. Echoing our earlier critiques of New Orleans tourism as both damaging and vitally important to the city, Young and Markham note the broader point that the deliberate construction of tourist attractions and tourist spaces is "highly contested and deeply contradictory." They argue convincingly that this often results in the "subordination of peoples and places as servants of exchange value," which "displaces locals, raises rents, and reduces the quality of life through increased congestion and overcrowding." They further argue that tourist places have a tendency to commodify "the free gifts of nature and culture," without necessarily taking account of how those entities may be impacted by such commodification nor the way it impacts people in those places.[54] This is cognate with critical analyses of tourism in New Orleans and, perhaps more important, with local anecdotal and journalistic accounts of the industry.

Young and Markham argue that "there has been much confusion about what precisely constitutes a tourist commodity, which processes convert spaces into commodities, and what characteristics spaces take on when they assume commodity form."[55] There is no possible confusion about JAMNOLA—it was constructed deliberately and absolutely as a commodity.

For us JAMNOLA attempts to redress imbalances in place "value" by contributing to a redistribution of tourism labor and money while, at the same time, employing local people as hosts in the venue and artists constructing its installations. Moreover, the venue works closely with organizations like MaCCNO to advocate for better conditions for culture workers, hosts events to raise awareness about the underpinning cultures and practices of the place it represents, and disperses tourists to less-trodden parts of the city.

As such, JAMNOLA offers an interesting, complex renegotiation of the "value" of an explicitly designed tourist environment and the ways in which such attractions might be able to perform dual functions that are at once part of the tourism industrial complex of the city and civically focused renegotiations of how tourism might be performed. "Experiential use values such as the consumption of cultural performances, concerts, and tourist spectacles are entirely consistent with the commodity form . . . The production of commodities always involves complex and multiple addition of social meaning throughout the commodity chain."[56] JAMNOLA takes the sign value of New Orleans more broadly (its iconography, history, cultural practices, and popular representations) and deliberately constructs a tourist experience commodity of "pure joy [that] showcases the iconic art, music, food and theatrics of the city through the eyes of over 30 local artists."[57] But in employing local artists, highlighting and supporting their work, and engaging in advocacy, it might be seen to shift its value and social meaning by developing a commodity chain that is variegated and complex, one that uses dominant paradigms of tourism in New Orleans as a way of paying back into the city in positive ways.

Tourism is critical to New Orleans. It brings significant funds to the city, and ongoing tourist interest in the city ensures that New Orleans continues to be known and valued internationally. Yet there are existing and long-standing concerns about tourism, both in terms of how the city can manage overtourism and how tourism impacts those living and working there. We recognize the UNWTO's sense that to address the challenges of tourism, we need to "set a sustainable roadmap for urban tourism and position the sector in the wider urban agenda."[58] To find sustainable solutions to the challenges of contemporary overtourism, we need to look beyond familiar approaches and turn to connected, collaborative, and interdisciplinary perspectives and methods.

As we argue throughout this book, many artists and cultural practitioners in New Orleans are acutely focused on challenges facing the city and are already engaged in means of addressing them, even though this work, as in other cities internationally, is rarely appropriately recognized at the level of strategic change. Many possible answers to city challenges are, then, already alive and present in cities. In terms of tourism, MaCCNO's guide for tourists offers a clear, tangible means of seeking to attend to the challenges of tourism. Further, the guide speaks in the language of tourist itineraries, welcoming tourists but offering *ways* of being in the city, rather than providing a list of the top *places* to be.

There is, however, a disconnect between the lived, embodied excess that is possible in the city and a printed or online guide. The MaCCNO guide offers a moment in which we might look profoundly at changing the practices of tourism in the city, remaking guides, rethinking the places that are the city, recalculating the time it takes to engage with the city. There is critical future work to be done to explore ways in which guides can become embodied, in which tourists extend and enrich their practices of the city. If we acknowledge that issues of overtourism and tourist misreadings of New Orleans are critical, urgent pressures, then not looking to arts and culture for creative thinking is remiss. The challenge, again as in all cases in this book, is to look to the strategic significance of arts and cultural practice for rethinking tourism, rather than requesting or requiring artists to contribute to a strategy that they were not involved in as full stakeholders. JAMNOLA offers one means of attending to this; it is an example of a deliberately constructed tourist destination that will likely become part of future itineraries but in ways that can help to intervene in historically narrow readings of the city. That is, in a city where parading, display, and celebration are so critical, appealing to an Instagram audience is a clear and astute model of diversifying the types of experience available and of welcoming and dispersing crowds to new areas of the city.

In much of our work with arts organizations and local government, we focus on the importance of process, not simply the product. This is not about devaluing the product; Mardi Gras parades are tremendous, extraordinary, at times terrifying, life-affirming practices of being in a city with others, and second lines reveal a comfort in being together with others on a street. Yet there is something of this *communitas*, this togetherness, that might be explored in new ways through tourism management in the city. This kind of thinking, much of it already in play, needs to be developed locally, carefully, thoughtfully. The Mother-in-Law Lounge reveals an existing, established, refined model of generous thinking about people and place. In being described as a "lounge," it confounds easy definitions of a venue; it asks that we think of it as a home in the city, with all the expectations and responsibilities that are bound up in such a term. We write about it here with some reservation, uneasy that we risk driving more tourists to the Lounge in ways that are not locally managed and negotiated. If we seek to develop responsible tourism, and so manage overtourism, then it seems critical that tourists are invited to engage with spaces and practices of responsibility, rather than, as often appears the case in New Orleans, through a predisposition to an irresponsible, party-focused approach to the city. While the lure of the irresponsible may well appeal at times and generate a quick buck for the city, it also fuels the fire of this being read as a "city that care forgot." There are better ways to invite people to a place and to explore different aspects of that place. Such creative and performance-informed "invites" help to understand this city in terms of its established local practices of remembering, valuing, and contributing to New Orleans as a city of care.

Recent work on rethinking Mardi Gras, particularly by relatively new Mardi Gras krewes, offers a further perspective on this idea, illuminating new ways of "parading" and spectating in the city. During COVID-19, in one of many social support projects, the Krewe of Red Beans raised money to fund local restaurateurs to feed local musicians. Where Lolis Eric Elie suggested that tourism might drive restaurants to serve red beans on a Tuesday to meet tourist demand, the Krewe of Red Beans entirely reimagined red beans as a parade, a social enterprise, a way of being and giving in the city. Rather than just providing more of something to meet demand, creative practitioners in the city are demonstrating that there are entirely new ways to address the challenges posed by increased tourism.

In our visits to the city, we have at times been struck by a sense of struggling to balance the needs of the research project's goals (compelling reasons to explore broadly) with the dilemma that we have been visiting a compellingly interesting city with many "essential" things to see and do. Returning from some field research, our experiences in the city have rather confounded friends and colleagues who ask about our experiences only to be disappointed we have been unable to attend to their sense of what one "should" do in the city. Other times, we have walked, occasionally late at night, to and then along Frenchmen Street (a "go-to" area for live music) in order somehow to save ourselves from asking: if we missed Frenchmen Street, if we failed to walk the French Quarter, were we really ever in New Orleans at all?

While facile, this is a question that is so ubiquitous, and thus ingrained, as to be felt in the body. But of course, the Quarter is not the city; no one area of a place can capture the whole. The city we have come to know a little is one of long traditions, extraordinary musical training and practice; it is also a place marked by acute resilience challenges balanced by artistic, civil-city, and community actions that attempt to mitigate those challenges. In that balancing, we might rightly see the educational and community work of the Community Book Center, the civil rights history and activism at the restaurant Dooky Chase, the temporary *communitas* afforded between local families and tourists gathered for Mid-City Mardi Gras, or the importance of putting local spaces into conversation with the touristic at the Mother-in-Law Lounge as offering a completely different order of life to a garish cocktail on Bourbon Street. Crucially, of course, there is a place for both; except that in too many framings and representations of tourism in New Orleans, it is difficult to see a *commitment* to both. As this chapter makes clear, such a commitment can raise the prospect of identifying ways that cities might reveal resilience performances for more sustainable tourism that are already being enacted across locales in a given city.

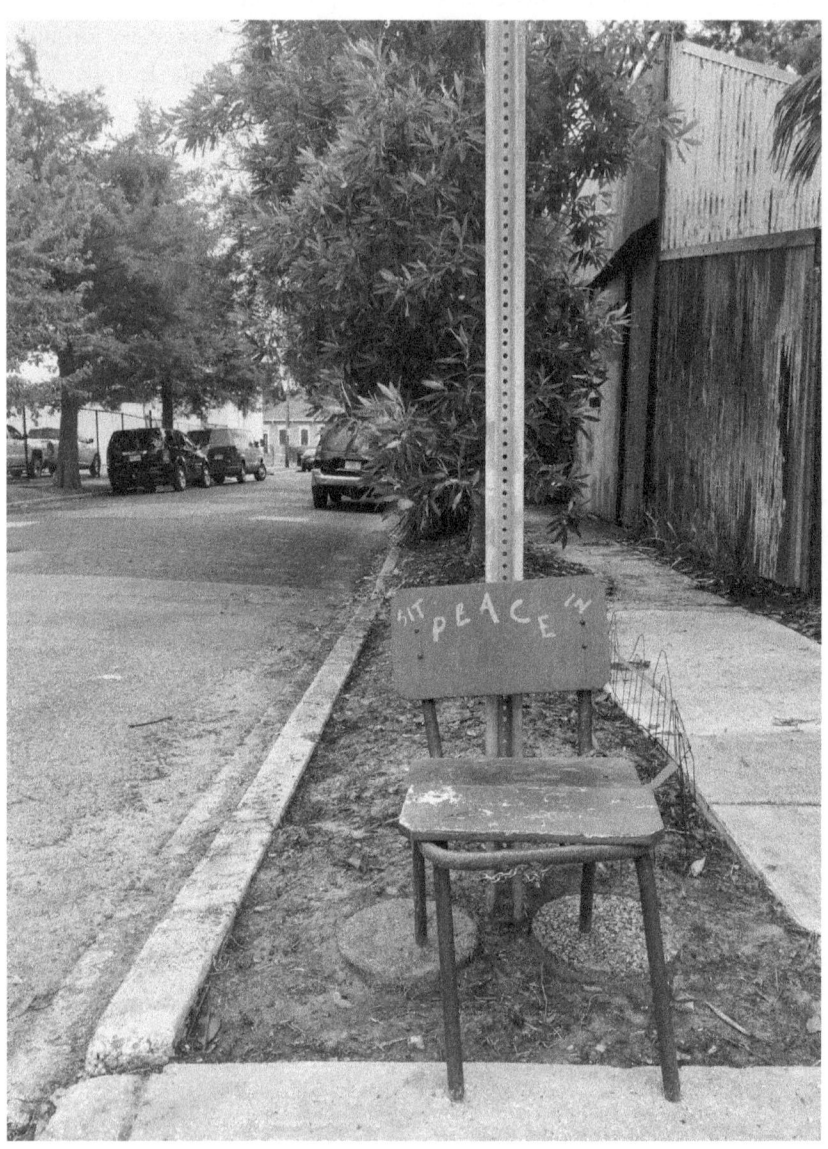

Chair installed on a street corner in the Bywater, 2022.

2

PLAYING IN THE STREETS

On the Importance of Streets in New Orleans

During our visits to New Orleans, people tell us about both the conditions and creative practices of the city's streets. In terms of the challenges, they tell us about driving during Mardi Gras and the time they parked and left their cars until a second line had passed. They describe rain that falls faster than the drains can carry away the water and tell us cautionary tales of streets, and the cars parked there, that can flood with startling speed. They tell us about potholes and recall creative responses that unfolded before holes were fixed. We learn of a second line being held for one pothole, of another pothole being listed on Airbnb, and people lounging in a partially submerged third as if it were a swimming pool, sipping drinks as cars streamed pass. We're aware that the condition of the streets is documented and discussed on social media, and recently, we noticed what may be repair work to the corners of intersections.[1] While we have been familiar with reports of street crime from our early visits, in 2022 people began to tell us about carjackings and appeared reassured that we had not rented a vehicle. That year a cab driver told us about a bump in the road that damaged the underside of his Chevrolet Suburban. When the conversation petered out, we sat awkwardly in the back of the car, listening as it creaked its way over bumps and dips on the route.

Despite what might appear to be considerably negative connotations, streets are incredibly important places politically, socially, and culturally in New Orleans. One simple example of their central role is in the way that people tell us repeatedly, "We dance in the street." Indeed, New Orleans is known internationally for distinctive practices on and of the street, notably in jazz funerals, second lines, Black Masking Indians, marching bands, and parading. Internationally, there is a continuing need to understand how the arts can offer strategic leadership in the management of streets and the lived experience of them, to which this chapter speaks. Drawing attention to diverse practices of street culture in New Orleans, we are interested in how our case study activities remake understandings of what is "performable" and thus what is performatively possible on streets. Each example can be understood as a carefully considered intervention that performatively reimagines spaces in the city and people's relationships with them. In that light, our argument in this chapter models streets as strategic sites of resilience.

Streets in New Orleans are critical sites of political, social, and cultural practice. There is a wealth of practice to be explored in the city that can be useful to modeling internationally applicable approaches to local resilience challenges. As such, we have chosen to analyze three central case studies that engage with and reframe encounters on streets in different ways. First, we investigate *Brass on the Boulevard* (2022), a music performance outside the Ashé Cultural Arts Center, to address the ways in which informal events become critical means of connection in a city. Second, attending to the mural project *Restore the Oaks* (2002), we identify ways in which visual artists brought together stories and perspectives on the historically complex infrastructural development of Claiborne Expressway. Finally, we turn to the performance environment of Mardi Gras, identifying the ways in which street performances intervene productively in everyday practices of place and extra-daily practices of Mardi Gras. In each case, we are interested in the multiple performances that occur in a place and how they contribute to understandings of that place. By employing performance analysis of specific places, we come to understand the significance of artistic and cultural practices and analysis as critical, vital means of experiencing, rethinking, and remaking city streets.

Second Lines

An excellent starting point to highlight the importance of street performance practices in New Orleans is the example of second lines, the practice of dancing in the streets behind a marching band (the first line) at a jazz funeral, an organized social aid and pleasure club event, or a wedding. As Rachel Carrico has argued, second lines are grounded in "the practice [of] black social-ritual spaces," and because they defy easy categorization into "formal systems of knowledge transmission," they help to "maintain ownership of cultural knowledge within the [Black] community, and reinforce the importance of informal settings, from kitchen floors to neighborhood streets, where embodied knowledge is transmitted."[2]

For Joel Dinerstein, a writer on American culture and a member of the Prince of Wales Social Aid and Pleasure Club, second lines are a critical practice of social aid and pleasure clubs, many of which emerged from "post–Civil War freedmen's societies" in New Orleans: "Some forty largely African American social aid and pleasure entities still flourish. They meet year-round, many fund scholarships and charitable causes, and each sponsors an annual second line parade. On the Sunday reserved for a particular club, its members step out in fresh, stylish matching clothes, powered by their favorite brass band. The band and club members constitute the 'first line' and create the space for 'second liners', who dance-walk alongside and all around them as they wind through the city's neighborhoods."[3] For performance theorist Joseph Roach, second lines and jazz funerals are part of an important "year-round cornucopia of Afrocentric forms" that perform in the streets of New Orleans; indeed, the two are tightly linked because while social aid and pleasure clubs may stage their own second lines annually, at a jazz funeral "the deceased is generally accompanied at least part of the way to the cemetery by a brass band and a crowd of mourners who follow an elegant grand marshall (or 'Nelson'). After the body is 'cut loose'—sent on its way in the company of family members—a popular celebration commences, less like a forgetting than a replenishment."[4] A second line dances the deceased on their journey.

As Dinerstein asserts, "In New Orleans, second lining is a noun, a verb, and a cultural institution." Second lines move "lightly like the feathers on our fans yet inexorably like a tank through the streets." Dinerstein cites "Stan," a member of his club, who reflects that "we *own* the streets that day." The effect of being part of a second line can transform one's sense of place in the world while also remaking that place. For Dinerstein: "Sometimes you look up from getting down and don't even know where you're at, even in your own neighborhood. The music shapes the air, the band torques up our internal gyroscopes, the tuba syncs our bodies together. We're getting the street into our system and putting our energy into the street. Like any good ritual, secondlines suspend everyday industrial time."[5] Although they draw on a long history of street performance practices in New Orleans, as Carrico describes, second lines continue to reimagine the practice of the street in the contemporary city, emphasizing the importance of the people in a place.

The flip side of this reimagining of place is the commodification of second lines. In 2022 we met with a member of the arts community at a noisy bar in the French Quarter. While trying to decide whether it was too loud to talk, as if to force our hand, a second line approached along the street. It was, notably, a predominantly white second line. We have seen a few of these events before; they celebrate birthdays, weddings, or even the end of a conference (to recall Elie from chapter 1), and so they recraft the form. Our colleague suggests we head off to avoid the descending crowd. He comments that it is not a "real" second line. There is something in this second line, not least the apparent commercialization of a historically Black cultural practice, that seems to sit awkwardly in the streets, that creates the tanklike sense of imposition but with little of the feathery lightness Dinerstein highlights.

Second lines are only one form of street performance that continue to have political and cultural importance in the contemporary city, alongside, for example, Black Masking Indians and the North Side Skull and Bone Gang.[6] In theatricalizing the streets, second lines attend to the continued importance of playing in, of occupying the streets in New Orleans. As Matt Sakakeeny reflects: "In New Orleans occupying city streets through black cultural traditions articulates a right to the city. Instead of signs, banners, and speeches that enunciate an explicit political agenda, it is music that mobilizes this social movement."[7] In so doing, these traditions illuminate the way in which street performances and wider artistic practices that frame streets as theatrical (or at least as scenographic, such as murals and public art) can adhere to what Harry J. Elam Jr. has argued is the capacity of such theatrical interventions to "transform a seemingly simple act into a powerful moment of theatrical as well as social and cultural significance."[8] Streets, street performances, and interventions in the space of streets matter in New Orleans because they reveal the contested histories of these spaces and the continued importance of Black practices of accessing and politically occupying them.

Beyond New Orleans, there is international and interdisciplinary interest in engaging in practical experimentation to rethink the form and practice of streets, particularly in urban areas. This takes various forms and focuses particularly on the ways in which urban design can focus more clearly on people and their lived experience of a place. This work speaks to broader activity that addresses creative cities. Charles Landry and Franco Bianchini's term "the creative city" has become familiar in thinking on city design.[9] More recently, Rory Shand reflects on "the effects of the creative arts and the creative economy in driving economic development" in the United Kingdom, Germany, and Canada.[10]

Reimagining Streets

Alongside new thinking on creativity and cities, there is research in a range of fields to rethink cities in terms of valuing individuals and local communities and their lived experiences of a place. Source10, a research lab funded by IKEA, explores innovations internationally that explore ideas of "the Ideal City," many of which seek to refocus city thinking on local lines.[11] Juliet Davis, whose work focuses on architecture and urbanism, reflects on cities as sites of care and ways in which urban design can "facilitate, foster, and actually give care."[12] In the context of a city that is often termed "the city that care forgot," it is valuable to understand and take seriously the ways that arts and cultural performances in and of place, space, and infrastructure can enact care.

Writing from the perspective of geography and urban planning, Luca Bertolini reflects that "various street experiments have burgeoned in cities across the world," particularly in terms of managing forms of traffic. For Bertolini such experiments "seek a different balance between motorized and non-motorized traffic in city streets." While Bertolini identifies benefits to these experiments, she also finds that "the current state of research does not allow a full-fledged assessment of the transformative potential of street experiments." Bertolini suggests it is important for policymakers to understand "the elements of city street experiments that can be integrated into long-term plans and policies."[13] This speaks of a broader challenge, of the ways that any experiments might impact a city's strategic development. Our particular concern here is the ways in which existing artistic and cultural practices, especially established and familiar practices, might inform such strategy development. There is a risk that artistic and cultural practices may not be securely or appropriately represented in the thinking and processes of city planning, particularly if they sit outside formal "experiments" to rethink city streets. Our work in this book seeks to address this gap in thinking.

Creative interventions into the practices of streets can result in significant impacts on a city. William Riggs, writing on transport, urban design, and development, argues that streets are "the lifeblood of a city." Where he defines roads as "automobile-oriented," Riggs finds that streets are "cultural" and "facilitate more than how we travel, but how we live, work and play." Riggs's interest lies in "understanding the intangibles that make roads more *livable* and *complete*, and to help define and take action to make these streets more *inclusive*."[14] On a similar theme, Amelia Thorpe, a law professor, reflects on "PARK(ing) Day," an international event each September, in which people pay for city parking spaces and transform them into temporary public parks. Thorpe identifies PARK(ing) Day as an example of "DIY urbanism," which she identifies in "the shipping container bars, pallet seats, pavement chalk, and knitted bike racks that are now familiar in cities around the world."[15]

For Thorpe, and echoing Sakakeeny on Black cultural traditions in New Orleans, advocates of DIY urbanism point to its "potential to enact the right to the city, perhaps even a new urban politics and in turn a new kind of city."[16] As Riggs and Thorpe reveal, streets can become sites of action by local people, at times enacting a new politics of the street. There are issues with implementing learning from creative experiments of practicing streets. From a professional planning perspective, Janette Sadik-Khan, New York City's transportation commissioner from 2007 to 2013, writing with Seth Solomonow, a media strategist, then at the Transportation Department, identifies that "city dwellers around the world are beginning to see the potential of their city streets and want to reclaim them." While Sadik-Khan and Solomonow identify a series of practices that they suggest have reimagined city spaces, they reflect that "few of these strategies have been incorporated into the way that cities operate from the street up."[17] There is, then, a pressing need to find means of connecting innovative street practice with practices of street management, design, and redesign. There are further issues with street experiments. Thorpe cautions that many of those engaged in such practices "invariably emerge from a position of privilege."[18] Turning to arts and cultural practice by communities that have been marginalized, particularly those in the Global Majority, will in some way reset the communities whose innovations inform any emerging strategy. By looking creatively, strategically, and equitably at existing practices of a street, we will discover ways in which people across a city are already engaging in playful, creative practices of the streets in that place and ways in which city authorities might productively embed this existing work within practice and strategy of city management (as we will see with *Brass on the Boulevard* and *Restore the Oaks*).

Writing from the United Kingdom, we are acutely aware that theories of city streets have been significantly influenced by writing on the design and practice of European streets, notably in Walter Benjamin's writing on the arcades and boulevards of Paris, and, subsequently, the work of the Situationists.[19] Alesia Montgomery, an ethnographer focusing on social and environmental justice, who writes particularly on Detroit, reflects that "long before the situationists in France, or the pleasure activists in the [Cass] Corridor, Congo Square in New Orleans served as a gathering place for enslaved Africans, who were allowed to use it on Sundays for drumming, dancing, and socializing and for selling deliciously tempting goods such as pralines."[20] Montgomery's work recognizes the degree to which studies of playful practices of cities internationally are informed by Eurocentric, and primarily white, readings of place. For Marcus Anthony Hunter and his coauthors, it is not simply that Black voices and practices have been obscured in urban theory but, rather, as they suggest, that they have been reported negatively. In response, and in their study of Black placemaking in Chicago, Hunter and his colleagues call directly on the potential for Black placemaking to offer "fun," "witty," "soulful," "smart," "biting" forms of rejuvenation that can lead to "a more just and equitable city and world."[21] In seeking to rethink place through creative performance experimentation, it is critical that we recognize, democratize, and value the ways such performances speak powerfully of past practices, echoing Montgomery's understanding of shared practices in Congo Square.

Playfulness

In the United Kingdom, "playful cities" initiatives have resulted in artists and local officials rethinking place. The Playable Cities project, which began in Bristol, a city in the southwest of England, has developed in cities internationally and invites people in a place "to play in public space, to begin a conversation about the kind of city you want to live in."[22] Also starting in Bristol, Playing Out has become a model of street play that has, similarly, been taken up internationally.[23] In the Playful Streets projects, streets are closed to enable children to play.[24] Playable Cities Open Streets Cape Town (South Africa) closes streets to enable playful pedestrian activity. Such practices inquire into streets and the ways in which we might reimagine them as sites for performance practices or use performance to engage in critical contemporary questions (such as the impact of technological innovation, like Artificial Intelligence [AI]).

Through the Playable Cities project, playful approaches to managing streets have emerged through interdisciplinary practice in which the arts are embedded. Projects focus on technological innovations and individual playful connections and encounters. In many cases, innovations reimagine the city streets and invite new perspectives on them. In *Play Me, I'm Yours* (2008), Luke Jerram installed pianos in the city and invited passersby to play them—a work that has been subsequently introduced in seventy cities internationally. In *How (Not) to Be Hit by a Self-Driving Car* (2023), Tomo Kihara and Playfool (Daniel Coppen and Saki Maruyama) invited participants "to avoid being detected by an AI-powered camera."[25] These projects, and many other Playable Cities events, offer thoughtful interventions in cities, several of them posing questions about the implied limits of creative spaces in cities (as Jerram does in opening up new spaces with each new piano) and systems through which those cities operate (as in Kihara and Playfool's testing of AI capabilities).

Alongside artistic projects, there are significant cultural and everyday practices of streets that bring into question the form, politics, and practice of specific streets. In the late spring and summer of 2020, despite the restrictions of COVID-19, there were significant Black Lives Matter protests (both in the United States and internationally) following the murder of George Floyd. In those moments, the need to speak out about people's lack of safety and the need to protest with others became more important than the need stay apart from others to protect against COVID-19 transmission. In June 2020, in Bristol, a crowd toppled the statue of Edward Colston, a merchant and slave trader, who had been born in the city. The act followed the removal of monuments in New Orleans, including the demounting of the bronze statue of Robert E. Lee, a Confederate general, from the plinth atop a tall pillar at "Lee Circle" in 2017. This removal and the later reversion to the local name of the area as Tivoli Circle (as it had been known until February 1884, before the erection of the monument to Lee) contributed to wider discourses on statue and monument dismantling and street and school renaming in the United States. Such interventions reveal ways in which the material form of streets, and places and objects on or close to those streets, can be understood to perform particular politics.

The Politics of the Streets in New Orleans

To begin to think about practices of the streets of New Orleans, it is critical to understand the local significance of streets in this city, as these may well have an impact, to greater or lesser extents, on practices of those particular streets. We might turn here to the history of New Orleans streets, which is so bound up in the politics of the city. New Orleans geographer Richard Campanella notes that certain streets in New Orleans reveal significant details of the city's past and, specifically, of histories of plantations and of slave ownership. Campanella observes that in the decades after the Good Friday fire in 1788, plantation owners moved from agriculture to housing, building roads within the footprint of their plantation land. For Campanella, this led to "jogs," "angles," and misalignment of streets on neighboring plantations, as "ancient geometrical rationale continues to affect the daily life of citizens today."[26] As we have reflected already, disruption is similarly evident in the state of the city's roads, especially in the uneven recovery of the city after Hurricane Katrina. Lynnell Thomas identifies the city's "irregular recovery process" after Katrina, "with some roads repaved, others still crumbling and impassable, and still others being constructed."[27] The form, aspect, and intersections of streets in the city, their position and condition, all speak of critical politics of the city and issues that powerfully impact the lives of those who live in the Crescent City as well as the lives of those who lived before them.

In the present, Wade, Roberts, and de Caro support Louise McKinney's observation that "the streets are the best places to see the face, or faces of this city."[28] In their discussion of Mardi Gras, and citing Mustafa Dikeç, Wade and their colleagues find that the streets of the city "serve as significant sites of expression and encounter. Streets also serve as a kind of laboratory, giving 'rise to new forms and modes of perceiving the world and relating to it.'"[29]

While this might well be the case, we are struck throughout this book that the performance of practices in the city have not been taken as seriously as they might be. Our concern is that while performances of the streets in New Orleans offer valuable means of perceiving and relating to the world, there has been relatively limited attention paid to these practices in planning initiatives internationally, particularly initiatives focused on playfulness. It has, perhaps, been too easy to dismiss the practices of New Orleans's streets as something exceptional to the city, somehow other to the rest of the country and perhaps the world. Indeed, as we recognize throughout this book, New Orleans is distinctive, as all places are or should be. Yet as has been widely discussed, a frame of exceptionalism limits the degree to which the practices of the city's streets may be taken seriously both in the development of streets in the city and as means of inspiring local transformation in urban neighborhoods and in cities beyond NOLA.

Brass on the Boulevard: Music on the Streets

It is early evening, the sky still light, in the midst of Mardi Gras 2022. We're standing in the car park outside the Ashé Cultural Arts Center on Oretha Castle Haley Boulevard. A band, Kings of Brass, plays, with the end wall of Ashé as the backdrop and the pavement repurposed as raised stage. A couple of high tables have been set out close by, draped with deep-red tablecloths that blow in the light breeze. As the evening passes, people gather, listen, drink, and talk. We buy some beers from staff who are operating a pop-up bar. This is a mixed event, particularly in age and demographic; there are groups of teenagers and older adults, some in couples. It's a warm evening, people gather, move, meet and greet; a woman dances with her young daughter.

Brass on the Boulevard has the feel of a low-key event, planned but informal. There is no fee, apart from making contributions through buying drinks at the bar and tipping the band; there is no boundary cordon or fencing. The apparent lightness of organization carries an air of the spontaneous. We had visited Ashé a day or so earlier, and staff had suggested we come along to this event. Without that invitation, we would most likely never have found our

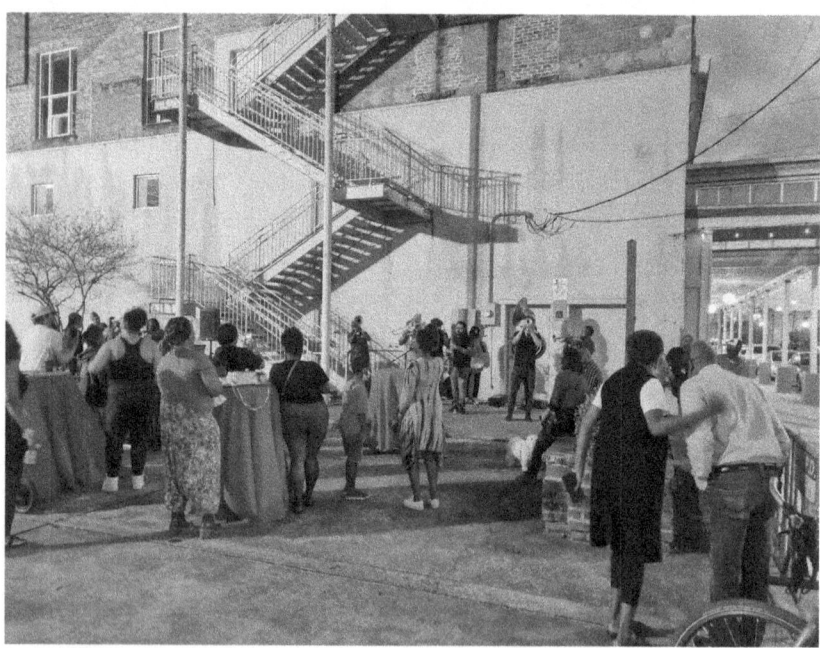

Performance at *Brass on the Boulevard,* 2022.

way here. As the evening winds on, the sun sets. To our left, a mural fills the entire end wall of a neighboring building. There are singers, musicians, and Black Masking Indians smiling in a bustling celebration of people and brightly colored buildings. Above them, the mural depicts a light-blue sky, with few clouds, and two dancers, a man and a woman, each in mid-leap. As the light fades, the mural is illuminated against the blue-black of the sky.

Kurt Iveson, Craig Lyons, Stephanie Clark, and Sara Weir identify established literature on informality in urban culture. They write that in an urban context, the term *informality* is typically used to denote activities in cities that do not conform to existing legal regulations. As Iveson and coauthors note, this work emerged in studies of cities in the Global South but has become increasingly relevant in cities in the Global North. Writing on Sydney, Australia, they observe a "high degree to which the spaces of everyday cultures are typified by informality." They find that this is particularly evident in "the practice of musical performances in urban space, which has increasingly informalized in recent times" as "resident complaints," "security and fire safety requirements," "gentrification," and "licensing reforms" led music venues to close. Similar pressures have become key issues in New Orleans, as has been identified by the Music and Culture Coalition of New Orleans. Iveson and coauthors recognize "a steady growth in the number of informal or DIY music venues generally operating in devalued, or 'rent-gap', land sites in city fringe locations."[30] As the places of performance change, so the character, structure, and politics of this practice shifts.

While Iverson and colleagues recognize that informality has often been understood in terms of legal definitions, we are interested in practices that perform informality on the street, even though they may exist within well managed city codes.[31] It is not the legal issues that interest us here, although we recognize the enormous value in attending to these, particularly in terms of understanding how those who face challenging economic conditions sustain life and work in a city. And further, we are concerned at the creeping conditions that are restricting live culture in cities, although in this instance, that is not the focus of our work. Rather, we are concerned with how that informality on the street productively reimagines the street and resists imposed conventional and appropriate practices of a place. We are less concerned with the legality of such work than with the ways in which practices on the street perform, animate, and activate the street, inviting us to reimagine this space in a city.

Iveson and coauthors identify "the usefulness of informality as a lens through which to understand the ways in which Australian cities are lived, governed and contested."[32] As we discuss later in reflections on practices undertaken during the pandemic, these informal spaces, particularly porches, became vital sites for connection and some conviviality, within the terms of restrictions. If we only refer to informality in terms of legality, we run the risk of missing the potential of performance to create the context to rethink the street, to debate, to discuss, to experience, streets in myriad ways. Such work wears away at formal boundaries of place. Recalling Sakakeeny, this reveals the ways everyday and artistic performances can weave in, out, and through a street, changing tone and form at corners, steps, and stoops. *Brass on the Boulevard* operates as an informal practice of the street, cohering with DIY practices and yet operating, we assume, within clear codes. In terms of rethinking the place and function of streets in resilience contexts, such informal practices need to be valued as performances with the potential to reclaim or remake local spaces as sites in which to think differently about the relationship between human-scale events (a music concert) and industrial-scale infrastructures of vehicles and roads.

Claiborne Expressway

Where we might understand many roads in the city as being materially broken in the present, the I-10 at the Claiborne Expressway was, and continues to be, the cause of significant breakages to the places, patterns, and practices of life for Black communities in the city.[33] We might describe this road as passing through the city, and yet that does little to address the impact of the road on the areas through which it "passes." In the present, this road which has caused such damage, is now itself in need of repair, posing critical questions about what an act of repair might *enact* for the city and for those whose homes and lives have been—and continue to be—so affected by its presence.

The *Advocate* reports that construction began on Interstate 10 in Louisiana in 1957.[34] As the transport journalist Benjamin Schneider writes, it was not until 1966 that the oaks on Claiborne Avenue began to be removed and pilings for the expressway were driven into the ground. Benjamin writes that "the elevated highway and its tangle of off-ramps destroyed some 500 homes and 326 Black-owned businesses."[35] Tremé was, after all, as *Krewe Magazine* reports, "the first neighborhood where African American citizens could freely congregate, play music, sell goods, and create a home."[36] For Richard Campanella, the overpass was then "an intrusion, a barrier, a destroyer of Black businesses, a trigger of community disinvestment and an example of racist urban planning."[37] The impact of interstate highways on cities is not limited to New Orleans, as numerous interstate developments impacted established Black communities in the United States. Adding to the imposition on communities, historian Mia Bay writes, that "American identity has long been defined by mobility and freedom of the open road, but African Americans have never fully shared in that freedom."[38] In Bay's terms, the freedom of the open road came at the cost of communities through which the interstate highways passed. Deborah N. Archer, a law professor, reflects on the history of the highways and the question of what to do with them in the present. She writes that "America's highways are part of the racial architecture of our country, with barriers both visible and invisible. The question before the country is whether and how we will truly confront those barriers."[39] In terms of the physical form of the highways, the question of their future is becoming ever more pressing. For Shawn Wilson, previously secretary to the Louisiana Department of Transportation and Development, the expressway is "at the end of its useful life."[40] There is a live discussion in New Orleans over what to do with the overpass as well as similar conversations in cities across the United States.

In 2021 President Joe Biden signed the Infrastructure Investment and Jobs Act, which recognized the racism and harm done to the place and community, singling out the expressway: "Too often, past transportation investments divided communities—like the Claiborne Expressway in New Orleans or I-81 in Syracuse—or it left out the people most in need of affordable transportation options. In particular, significant portions of the interstate highway system were built through Black neighborhoods."[41] Despite having so significantly impacted the Black community life of Claiborne Avenue, Schneider identifies differing perspectives on the future of the overpass. He suggests that, in part, Tremé has learned to live with the interstate that cleaved it in two. Second line neighborhood parades often end up "under the bridge," and marching bands practice there when it's raining.[42] As a result, Schneider identifies considerable public concern about the kinds of transformation that may follow any removal of the highway. He cites Asali DeVan Ecclesiastes, Ashé Cultural Arts Center's chief equity officer: "In all of those places where the interstate was taken down, that community was aggressively displaced."[43]

The complexity of what to do with the highways is an issue both within the United States and internationally. To understand this, Fahimeh Khalaj,

Dorina Pojani, Neil Sipe, and Jonathan Corcoran surveyed recent literature on the removal of highways in cities. They identify that "a scientific consensus has recently emerged suggesting that the dominant 20th century paradigm of solving transportation congestion problems by building more freeways failed. The legacy of the freeway construction era is clearly visible in polluted and congested cities worldwide. To battle these ills, planning academics have been promoting more sustainable built form aligned with dedicated public/active transport provision." Yet they note that "a paradigm shift has arguably not yet taken place in transportation planning." Instead, they find that innovations to "create human-scale and active transport spaces" are conducted "to coexist alongside freeways."[44] In this context, it becomes vital to understand how practices engage with and reencounter the expressway, particularly if the overpass remains (in the near future at least).

Under the Expressway

It is midmorning on a bright June day. We've been walking through the city and stop for a moment outside a well-maintained wooden house in the Tremé, just off North Claiborne Avenue. There are low steps up to the front doors and an overhanging porch held in place by decorative supports. The steps from the house lead down to the sidewalk and then to a well-planted bed that separates the sidewalk from the street. There is an established tree in this bed, most likely an oak, with a wide trunk and thick branches in full leaf, which shades the street. This is the last house on the street before it meets North Claiborne Avenue and, above it, the expressway.

We are struck by the speed of the cars on North Claiborne Avenue, and it had taken us a while to judge a safe moment to cross the Avenue to reach this point. There is, then, already a contrast between the Avenue and this side street. Yet this traffic exists on the same level as the street. There might be arguments to calm or slow the traffic or to manage vehicles in ways that relieve the juxtaposition between this major road and side streets. At the same time, there is a relation between the Avenue and the adjoining streets.

The overpass offers more of a contrast. In the grass just beyond the house, there is a single concrete pillar, which helps supports one of the expressway ramps. The pillar's gray has been stained with a gray-black substance, although the lower section of the pillar has been painted cream in color to match the house. The six lanes of the I-10 are raised above the wide median (or "neutral ground," in local parlance) between the two-lane carriageways of North Claiborne Avenue.[45] Together with the Avenue, and on-off ramps, there are twelve lanes of traffic between this side of Claiborne Avenue and the other side. Across the other side, we can see the road that leads away opposite, itself planted with established trees, yet it is too far to see much of the life of the street. These major roads intervene in the practice of life on the street, particularly the expressway, a road that in being an interstate highway, interrupts performances of the local.

We are aware the house has small dormer windows on an upper story. The view from these rooms, one or more of which may be bedrooms, will be quite different to the view from below. From these windows, the disjunction between the scale of the street and that of the highway must be even more acute. We turn and walk on along the street, leaving the overpass behind us. Plants spill onto the sidewalk, leading us to walk on the carriageway at times. There is something inconceivable about the expressway being at the end of this and so many other streets.

The scale of the I-10 means that it can be difficult to attend to specific points that draw the eye, that call attention. The length of the road, the many points of impact can be difficult to separate, and it can be difficult to focus on the local. Yet by stopping, by attending to the local and looking to the structure in the context of the local, seeing it in this precise place, it becomes more possible to identify and attend to the particularities of the infrastructure—the pillar close to a house, the black of the stain, the ramp close to windows, the distance of the street across the roads, the quantity of road. By attending to the specifics of place here, by looking to the details of the built environment and the practice of the environment, we can begin to unpick any idea that the road and the cars pass through a place and understand more about the ways the road and the motorized traffic has become part of the place.

Restore the Oaks

It is later in the day, and we find ourselves back at the same stretch of the expressway, our attention caught by paintings on the pillars beneath the carriageways. We stand for a time beneath the expressway, taking these in. On the pillar to our right, a central band of the structure has been painted gold, with top and bottom bands and patterns painted in shades of blue, bronze, and green. On the gold band, a figure has been painted, its head turned to one side,

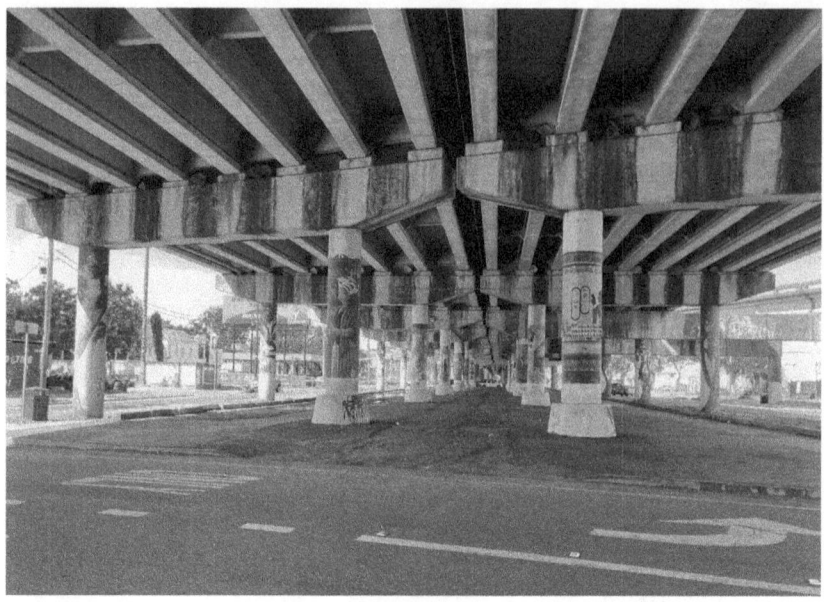

Restore the Oaks art installation on Claiborne Avenue, 2023.

wearing the same gold, blue, and green of the background. The figure's hand is raised upward, and within touching distance, two sets of hieroglyphs have been painted. The style of the painting recalls ancient Egyptian art, perhaps reimagining the pillar as an element of ancient architecture, a long-preserved message from the past. Overlaid on this image are words in English that appear to have been written from the present. PEACE and LOVE have been written close to each set of hieroglyphs. On the lower blue band, a set of words speaks of "our culture." There are other, later additions, in the form of graffiti that may have been added by a separate artist, and at the time of our visit, pictures appear to have been stuck to the pillar.

This is *Restore the Oaks* (2002). Katy Reckdahl, a journalist in the city, explains that the project was led by Richard Thomas, a painter and teacher, and developed with the African American Museum of Art and Culture.[46] For Natalie Dessens, a historian in France, local artists were invited to depict "the people, places, and events that have defined the area's soul."[47] The project was revisited in an exhibition, *Art under the Overpass in Treme* (2010). As we stand in this section of the artwork, the five sets of pillars ahead of us have all been painted with murals. To our left, a woman is depicted carrying a candle and standing in front of a wooden dresser. The image on the next pillar is more stylized: a man, shirtless, reaches up in distress. Above him and emerging from him, a larger man reaches out powerfully against a background of orange and red. The styles are all markedly different. While some images depict a single scene, others comprise montages of faces or images: musical notes, shapes, and colors. As Dessens reflects: "The paintings represent the neighborhood, evoke music, highlight the Civil Rights Movement, but also introduce important figures of the community (like the first black activists of the nineteenth century, the first black surgeon, and Marie Laveau, the great nineteenth-century Voodoo priestess)."[48]

The breadth of styles and subjects in these murals comprise an assemblage of voices, stories, and perspectives, a memory place on the median. Where previously the expressway had been a singular structure imposed on the site, the murals diminish this singularity. The paintings appear as much a part of the neutral ground as of the overpass above. While the artworks do not undo the damage of the expressway, they offer compelling means of breaking up such a structure and valuing the people and stories of the place through which it passes. None of the painted pillars have been marked with the dirt and pollution from above. As such, the murals intervene in the experience of the road, claiming the pillars for the median, the neutral ground of Claiborne Avenue. In that the painting stops at the top of the pillars, there is a separation between the pillars and the I-10 above. We think, then, if the overpass is removed, the pillars should remain, as performative traces of the I-10's historic impact on the area.

This use of murals to rethink place leads us to recall Brandon "BMike" Odums's work on *Project BE,* in the Florida Housing Project, and *Exhibit BE* in Degaulle Manor, an abandoned apartment complex.[49] In both projects, Odums transformed existing infrastructure into a site for people, creative practices, and stories. In a city where infrastructure has been particularly challenged, the use of murals focuses attention on the people of the city, resisting catastrophizing narratives and repurposing space to represent African Americans as key to the city. During our time in the Central Business District, we have long been struck by the optimism of *Survive,* in which Odums and the Young Artist Movement depicted a Black man holding a child above water. In a catastrophized narrative of New Orleans, the father may be lifting his son from flooding, yet both father and child are smiling, and the water is a collage of water-themed images and colors. This, then, is a story of playful engagement with water, perhaps with the sea, a river, or pool. Given the context of narratives of catastrophe from beyond the city, it is unsurprising that mural artists in the city have engaged so richly with sharing the life of the city and with sharing joyful, celebratory images of the importance of Black experience in the city. Odums's work and *Restore the Oaks* demonstrate the ways in which identity can be celebrated in the context of infrastructural challenges. In each case, the work celebrates and so transcends the failure of infrastructure, and narratives that risk destabilizing the city, and Black life and identity in the city. The works are generous, grassroots, emerging from people in a place. This is precisely the energy that reinvigorates streets.

As part of the *Restore the Oaks* project and on several of the outer pillars of the overpass, oak trees have been painted, one on each pillar. Wide trunks grow into branches, some of which have been trimmed. From beneath the overpass, we see both the painted trees and real trees beyond. In 2016 WWNO reported that trees on North Claiborne Avenue once comprised "the longest single strand of oak trees in the country." To install the expressway, "the state cleared over 200 oak trees."[50]

We wonder if the trees painted on the columns depict specific and, perhaps, remembered trees. Perhaps the lines and curve of each trunk, and of the winding branches, re-member individual oaks that grew here until relatively recently. We wonder if the signs of management, the cuts to branches, speak of familiar cuts; we wonder who managed the trees here. The painting of oaks, of trees that would have been familiar, known, loved, on this site is a critical act. Yet of course, these are not the trees that once stood here. This said, these depictions of trees do powerful work. From beneath the expressway, looking out, the combination of trees on the pillars and the trees beyond invites recognition that once there were trees here. These carefully painted trees, the signs of careful management, their apparent established growth, questions the recency of the overpass.

By entering into dialogue with surrounding trees, the artists unsettle the separateness of the overpass with the neutral ground. In the context of this book, the painting of the oaks reveals the ways that artists can trouble distinctions between places and can resist the politics of these separations. The work is an act of remembrance and resistance, a complex curatorial engagement with a challenging site. It points to the ways that creative performances of place can reveal issues that remain live despite the passing of time. And it speaks of the people of a place. For Diana Nawi, cocurator of Prospect.5, the arts triennial in the city, "making and sharing art" allows us to "resist mortality, proclaim our existence, and act as a collective."[51] Collective acts of art, shared beneath the overpass do all of this, albeit in the lightest of ways, in the "simple" act of painting trees.

From close attention to the form and practice of streets and the road above, we turn now to Mardi Gras and look specifically to the varying performances that comprised Mardi Gras. We begin with an early act in the Krewe of Elvi, in which krewe members journeyed along Magazine Street as part of preparations for their parade that night. As second lines are one form of parading in the city and adding murals to streets is a form of remaking the street, so Mardi Gras is another major practice of the street, and similarly this is far from a singular experience. Indeed, in addressing single instances of parades, we seek to draw attention to particular events and the experience of those events. Our desire is to resist generalizations of familiar practices, especially given the tendency of such representations to be marketed internationally, and thereby offer powerful definitions of city practices.

Mardi Gras: Repurposing the Streets

A ROOSTER-HEADED ELVIS

We're sitting outside on benches at a place on Magazine Street. It is early afternoon on 24 February. We watch as, with some poise, a man rides past us on what the Krewe of the Rolling Elvi describe simply as "scooters."[52] He is, ostensibly, dressed as Elvis, in a black all-in-one suit, with trousers that flare out to reveal pink-and-black slashes at the calf. He stands one foot ahead, one behind, a purposeful pose, launching himself at the future. At the same time, he wears what appears to be a mock rooster's head as a form of hat, complete with bright yellow beak, large white eyes with pupils staring upward and slightly backward, bright pinkish-red comb and wattle, and a feathery mane in electric blue. As he rides, a pink cape billows at his back, even at the relatively stately pace of his scooter. The man's eyes are wrapped in sparkling sunglasses or eye mask; his attention is locked on the road ahead.

We had little sense, as we'd set out for Magazine Street that morning, that the Krewe of the Rolling Elvi would pass by. We're aware of the Rolling Elvi around us as we walk along the street, yet in this moment, of watching this solo Elvis pass, we notice the individual in the crowd. The parade is a whole, a collective enterprise. Yet it is comprised of careful individual commitment. After this Elvis, the street is quiet again. This is early in the day, before the krewe processes through the city with Muses that night. It is not primarily an event for spectators but, rather, a gathering phase for the krewe, before the parade that evening.[53] We watch the Rolling Elvi later, their scooters bedecked with lights, their baskets filled with bags of throws to cast to the crowds on either side of the street.

While the parades close and fill city streets, practices of Mardi Gras also weave into familiar practices of the streets. The Rolling Elvi threaded their way through activities on a morning on Magazine Street. While in the city in 2022, Nick Slie introduced us to the notion of "deep gras," coined and articulated by Dominique Lejeune in 2020 in *The Updated List of Mardi Gras Terminology 2020*. For Lejeune, Deep Gras comprises the "period starting on noon Wednesday and ending on noon Ash Wednesday. Your entire life becomes Mardi Gras and nothing else."[54]

The term *deep gras* speaks of the altered sense of time and life that can occur during a festival, particularly in the final phase of a festival that runs for as long as Mardi Gras does and impacts the city so much. As the Rolling Elvi reveal, the streets can become sites for creative practice. Yet this is a city in which parades are a familiar and critical practice.

For philosopher Richard Shusterman, "cities are largely defined by their complex network of busy streets and the diverse multitudes of busy people that populate and animate those streets through their physical presence and bodily actions."[55] As the Krewe of the Rolling Elvi reveal, Mardi Gras creates a context for playful engagement in the streets and, thereby, of the city. Indeed, one of the challenges facing the city is that specific performances, indicative of Mardi Gras in the French Quarter, perform specific versions of an event and the city as a whole. One way of resolving this is to expand the ways in which we understand the performance of Mardi Gras, to recognize the varying and multiple performances by which we understand the scale of Mardi Gras, and to reflect on what these individual events reveal about the city and what understandings they open up. In this vein, in turning to look at Mardi Gras, we attend to different versions of the experience in the CBD and in Mid-City. In each case, we find that the context through which the parade passes becomes fundamental to the experience of the parade.

Neutral Ground

We're on St. Charles Avenue in Central City. People gather on either side of one carriageway. While some stand or sit on the sidewalk, others have brought chairs, tables, and drink coolers, sometimes in a wheeled trolley. There are families, couples, friends. The atmosphere is relaxed; there is space for everyone. Many of those gathered here are Black, although this is a mixed crowd, and of young and old. This makes for a compelling experience, although we recognize that the experience of Mardi Gras is not always so open. As the social anthropologist Martha Radice recognizes, "Reflecting New Orleans society, carnival is socially stratified and relatively racially segregated."[56] In this context, the model(s) of Mardi Gras that exist in popular discourse become important in maintaining or destabilizing segregation in the event.

Children run up and down the streetcar lines that run and cut across the neutral ground; a small boy crouches with a gold striped ball, perhaps a throw from a previous parade. On the street, two children play with toy lightsabers close to the sidewalk. The road is broadly empty, but people drift onto the edge, cross, and cycle slowly. Across the street from us, a man looks up from his phone, perhaps taking in a nearby tree that has been richly festooned with throws, which shine in the light. On the road behind us, people are walking past, perhaps seeking a good spot to watch the parade, perhaps just passing by. There is an air of expectation. The position of the crowds along the street calls for a performance; the slippage of the crowd onto the carriageway marks the relaxation of familiar restrictions. The first cars of the parade appear in the distance.

The parade begins, as many do, with a series of vehicles—police, the NOLA Ready car, a figure walking the route. There are Baby Doll dancers in bright metallic green and purple, red, and silver. There are police along the route; some wear masks, sometimes informally. This is the Krewe of Ancient Druids, an all-male krewe that is comprised of members of other Carnival organizations, all of whom are masked, most in blank gold full-face masks. There are motorcyclists, their bikes decked with LED strips that glow green and then red. The first float is the Archdruid, a masked man in white feather headdress, black-and-gold costume. He sits high on a gold throne on gold steps.

We walk a little, following the route of the parade and a blue-and-orange swirling float. Music pours from the float, as the black-costumed riders cast throws to those along the route. People cheer, whistles blare, a siren passes, people stroll across the neutral ground to the parade, beads arc through the sky. People watch, hold their arms high in the air for throws, lowering them as the float passes. Farther on, we pass under the Pontchartrain Expressway, which encloses the parade. We see fewer families here; there are fewer hands in the air. We might be at a concert or in a nightclub. A bright-white light illu-

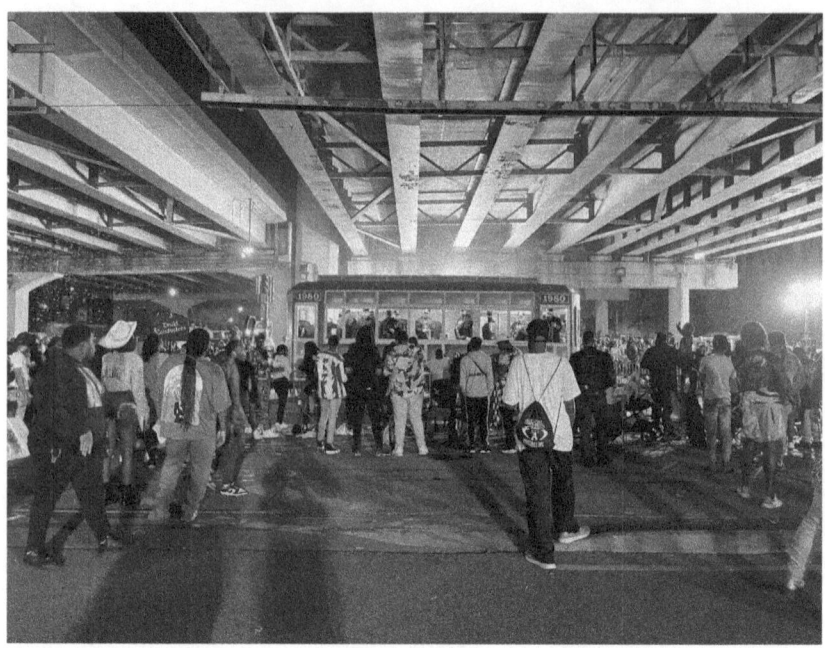

Krewe of Ancient Druids parade passes under the Pontchartrain Expressway during Carnival, 2022.

minates the supporting beams above and ahead of us. Soon after, we're out the other side, close to Harmony Circle, previously Lee Circle; the neutral ground appears busier.

As the floats fill the street, so separate practices occur along the edge of the carriageways and across the wide neutral ground. This phase of the event reveals how the openness of the neutral ground can provide perspective on the passing parade. It allows observers to follow floats and to gather and play where the parade pauses. The shift in practice of spectatorship under the bridge begins to reveal the ways that spectators, as well as the krewe, shape that activity of a Mardi Gras parade.

Throws, Catches, and the Lowering of Goblets

We are in the CBD. It is busy, but the crowds are not extraordinary, perhaps because these are the first Mardi Gras parades after the lifting of COVID-19 restrictions. We are here to catch the Krewe of King Arthur, to try and gather throws for Patrick's son, Arthur. Large floats roll past, their inhabitants high above us, casting throws into the air. Doug MacCash, a journalist in the city, has written on the history and significance of Mardi Gras beads. He cites Bordnick, a behavioral scientist and Mardi Gras fan, "Throwing and catching beads is 'like smiling at someone and having them smile back. Biologically, it feels good.'"[57] We have prepared for the parade by wearing beads from a previous parade, a trick we learned from others and noted by MacCash. MacCash cites Mac Coerce, a Tulane law student, who shared his strategy of wearing beads from previous parades. "The more you wear and show," he said, the more the float riders recognize that you're "invested in Mardi Gras."[58] The wearing of beads speaks of that investment, of one's commitment to "smile back."

MacCash has written compellingly of the appeal and excess of beads and about the unsustainability of plastic novelty shapes and their flashing lights. In this context, there are ongoing initiatives to intervene in the "throwaway" culture of the throw. A nonprofit organization formed to help reduce the waste caused by Mardi Gras throws, Grounds Krewe now supplies homemade, recycled, and sometimes useful throws: coffee, toothbrushes, and bathroom tissues and "throw packages," where items are supplied with a jute bag for krewe members to carry onto their float. This project builds local artist economies while endeavoring to reduce the environmental harm caused by the Mardi Gras throw industry as well as the economic impact on throws being outsourced for production. Although a potentially exciting intervention into Mardi Gras production processes, while the throws are ecologically (and perhaps aesthetically) preferential to the plastic ones, they come at a significant economic cost that may be prohibitive for some float riders.

Nevertheless, for all its challenges, as we stand on the street, and as we call for and catch throws, we delight in the wonder and excess, amassing a fair stash of treasure. Someone throws down a bag from a float, which they had most likely used to bring their throws to the parade, and we use this to store our haul, having learned this trick from others a few days earlier. Among the objects we catch, one or two stand out. As one float passes us by, a woman releases a goblet decorated in rich purple glitter, with an eye mask attached. She passes it down carefully, gingerly, to Stuart. It is a committed act, a highwire maneuver to transfer this object before the enormous float moves on, a wondrous, extraordinary thing, handmade with time and care. In among the excess, such a particular object appears remarkable. A few nights later, we return to the same spot, although now it is busier, and we walk down the street a little. We meet a mother and daughter while watching Muses. The daughter screams out for "A Shoe!" with extraordinary power. Perhaps a planned moment, perhaps lucky, she wins two of these highly prized throws from the Muses. Again, the presence of handmade throws amid the quantity of more mass-produced items stands out as being something extraordinary, all the more extraordinary in that this is such a small, fleeting moment in the scale of the floats on the streets.

Handmade objects are a critical part of Mardi Gras, and specific krewes are known for their DIY throws, particularly the coconuts of Zulu and shoes of Muses. Kezia Setyawan, a journalist writing for WWNO, reflects that the act of crafting throws can often be a collective social practice. She describes Muses riders gathering at the NOLA Craft Culture shop and the shop owner, Lisette Constantin, who explains that, "for the most part, people come over and bring a bottle of wine or some bubbly and some snacks."[59] The throw is not simply important in the act of being "thrown"—or carefully delivered. Rather, this is an object crafted over time, a personal investment of time, skills, and experience and a distinctive and direct individual contribution to the collective practice of the krewe, the parade, Mardi Gras, and the city.

While the act of creating handmade throws may often be social, the work is also focused on recipients of the throw. Jennifer L. Erdely, a communications researcher, reflects on her experiences of making costumes for Mardi Gras, and subsequently masks in response to COVID-19, as acts of care for others. She frames her experience of crafting in terms of the work of Belinda MacGill, an artist and education researcher who locates crafting in terms of an "ethics of care."[60] Reading MacGill, Erdely writes that "the craft is for another person, not the crafter."[61] The act of handing a handmade throw to a recipient is a significant act in a parade. Constantin notes that "when you give it to a total stranger, it's indescribable. I've had people chase me for blocks, because I pointed to them because I like their costume or their sign or whatever. And I'm like, 'yes, you come here', And then they literally run for blocks until I can get the shoe to them [. . .] Then it's like victory—it's so much fun."[62]

These acts of passing and receiving offer particular opportunities for connection between riders and those on the streets. Each Muses rider only carries eleven shoes, which imposes a clear limit on these moments. The extended act of passing these throws focuses on a singular moment, rather than the whirl of activity, and the individuals rather than the crowds. Despite the emphasis on connection, this is also an act performed across a distance with the risk of loss. As throws are gingerly passed, lowered, or thrown, the success of the interaction is both possible and in doubt.

Alongside the handmade throw, Wade, Roberts, and de Caro identify a shift toward the human and the handmade in Mardi Gras. They reflect that "post-Katrina New Orleans has witnessed a new order of celebration, evidenced in the proliferation of do-it-yourself walking krewes that add novel energy and fresh numbers to the Mardi Gras experience."[63] Even in the "super krewe" parades, and even amid the scale of plastic throws, there are compelling opportunities to engage socially—and politically—in powerful ways.[64] Rebecca Sheehan identifies opportunities for "social-spatial interactions in the urban landscape" when discussing the Camel Toe Lady Steppers parade. She writes that "the rhythms of the parade, including the time the parade occurs, the 'wait' at the lineup, the moving and stopping, and the trailing end of the parade provide time and spaces of opportunity for unscripted interactions."[65] For Sheehan, these moments are productive in unsettling conventions and in allowing for meeting and valuing others. Such meetings challenge ongoing politics in Mardi Gras and that of life in the city. In recognizing the playfulness of Mardi Gras and the complex and ongoing politics of the event, the making and gifting of handmade and creative inventions offers tangible opportunities to rethink practices on the street and, thereby, in the world.

In the moments of interaction, in the smiling and smiling back, the casting and the lowering, there are chances for interaction in the crowd, for human connection. The scale of this interaction in parades across the city is a compelling example of multiple playful practices drawn together in and of the city, and of the significance of interaction, connection, and recognition that can be possible, albeit with important caveats about the politics of past and present practices.

The projects here each reveal ways in which artistic and cultural practices of a street constitute critical parts of a street. *Brass on the Boulevard* and the dancing of second lines reveal the ways in which music and dance can resist boundaries; Mardi Gras brings parades and embodied interactions in the street, such as playing, dancing, and marching. The murals on the pillars beneath the Claiborne Expressway repurpose and reimagine each pillar, unsettling their connection to the road above. The streets themselves are performative. The overpass is a continuing performative presence in the city, forever juxtaposed with the streets, the homes, the communities on and off North Claiborne Avenue. In some cases, these projects comprise and call for movement: the dancing of second lines; the parading and the casting, bestowing, and catching of Mardi Gras throws. In others, the work is more settled—the murals call for a slowing of movement, for one to stop under the I-10.

As these practices form part of practice of the streets, they enact particular opportunities to attend to and reflect on the street. The challenge is to look to the ways that these practices, these ways of thinking creatively about urban spaces, can be placed into productive conversation with means and methods of managing and developing streets into the future. From the filling of potholes to debates on the future of the Expressway, decisions on the future form of streets in the city will impact the practices of the street, particularly if fixing the streets leads to gentrification, changes to the form and familiar markers and signs of a place, and the imposition of noise ordinances that restrict live music venues. Indeed, the material form and legal conditions of streets may profoundly limit the potential for creative practice.

In our work beyond this book, we are interested in finding ways of brokering critical conversations between artists, culture bearers, and city officials to find new, collaborative means of rethinking and remaking streets as a form of connected and collective practice. The significance, but also the fragility, of arts and culture on the street in New Orleans constitutes an invitation to the city, and cities internationally, to develop sensitive local strategic practices of managing streets that attend to and enable current and emerging creative and cultural practices. As Montgomery demonstrates, theories of the street are too bound up in Eurocentric models, and there is a need for a new reading of the established practices of streets, particularly by those who, too often, find themselves out of place on city streets.

The more that we can look to the possibilities of existing creative practices, the more we can draw on long-established traditions of experimentation and innovation. This is not to suggest that no new experimentation is required— quite the opposite, there will always be exciting opportunities for playful rethinking of places and practices of a street. There is a vital need, however, to recognize the significance of existing practices, especially when those practices have long histories and speak in critical ways to local communities. Yet recognition of the value of arts and culture is not easily achieved. There has been considerable debate internationally on "cultural value." We need to consider how artistic and cultural practices are understood and valued in city planning processes. Where arts and culture are perceived as being "nice to have" or, less generously, as an engaging but noisy neighbor, they are unlikely to be taken seriously in city management processes. If, instead, and as we have illustrated, they are understood as constituting a rich, considered practice that operates performatively to reimagine the city, then their strategic contribution to the city, their acts of making and remaking of the city, are far more likely to be understood and taken seriously. This book contributes to a growing body of work that argues for arts and culture as sophisticated, vital elements of the life of a street, neighborhood, and city.

There are risks of separation here, of understanding specific artistic and cultural practices in isolation, rather than in terms of the form and broader practices of a street. Such an approach is controlling, limiting. It becomes easy to set aside particular practices of a street, whether arts practices or tents under the I-10, rather than look for the possibilities that emerge from the weaving together of people, practices, and places. To attend to the I-10, the murals beneath, the painting of a telegraph pole, the passing of traffic and the passing of a parade, reveals an established and layered environment. Performance analysis allows us to understand the practices of the street as being in combination and allows us to look for possible points of intersection, of dialogue and collaboration. While this work speaks directly to New Orleans, it also offers a model for mapping, understanding, and valuing street practice internationally.

Taken together, the case studies considered here reveal ways in which practitioners of the city have contributed to practices of the street and the ways in which their work may help us understand and value the practices of streets in the city. They offer innovative means of attending to local practices of streets in cities internationally. It is not that the practices of New Orleans's streets should be exported internationally, although there may be a case for this in some instances. Rather, we suggest that the practice of attending to local arts and cultural practices of streets may offer a productive means of informing collaborative approaches to the care and management of single streets, neighborhoods, and towns and cities.

One of Judith Rodin's key claims in looking to achieve a "resilience dividend" is that it "cannot be achieved without people's intense commitment and engagement." Moreover, she suggests, people will not engage with challenges nor return to a place after a profound crisis like Hurricane Katrina simply because "basic services are restored." By inviting people in the city to join creative practices of the streets, artists and culture bearers in New Orleans offer invitations to look beyond their relationship with basic services. In Rodin's terms, this can be seen to encourage people to "take pride in strengthening" their cities in the face of its resilience challenges.[66] As each of the examples in this chapter illustrates, everyday and aesthetic street performances and performative interventions on streets can be enormously powerful as markers and drivers of pride in place. Such performances function to mobilize communities to (re)consider their environment in new ways, to value informal events of gathering as productive spaces to remake relationships with infrastructures, to performatively claim and assert belonging, and to imagine possible futures while accounting for complex, sometimes violent histories.

3

THE ART AND PERFORMANCE
OF SITUATION ROOMS

Very early in our first research visit to New Orleans, we visited City Hall to meet the chief resilience officer for the city. Following an initial formal meeting, discussion, and interview, the encounter opened up into a more exploratory conversation and a tour of the top floor "situation room" in City Hall. That experience, alongside two other site visits during that trip, became foundational in our thinking about the ways performance might enable a rethinking of resilience. In this chapter, then, we look at how three situation rooms in New Orleans might be seen to be "performing resilience" through practices and processes of everyday and aesthetic performance, architecture, and community. In each instance, the situation rooms enable critical stakeholders to draw on existing and emerging knowledges and intelligences so that they might understand and respond to specific present and/or future "situations." City Hall explicitly uses performance as a mechanism through which the city and city officials can come to know the city and how it functions at times of crisis and/or pressure. For us, the second space, the Music Box Village, can be seen to examine and renegotiate relationships to water and to the edgelands of the city. Last, we turn to think about the André Cailloux Center for Performing Arts and Cultural Justice, a performance venue that seeks to renegotiate social and racial relations in an area of the city, trying to bring people into it by leveraging an understanding of the city to inform the redesign of the building so as to open the building to the city.[1] This final case study is a theater built into a church, where we consider both the development process of the venue by Southern Rep Theatre, before its formal closure in July 2022, and the redevelopment and practice of the space as the André Cailloux Center and home for the No Dream Deferred theater company.

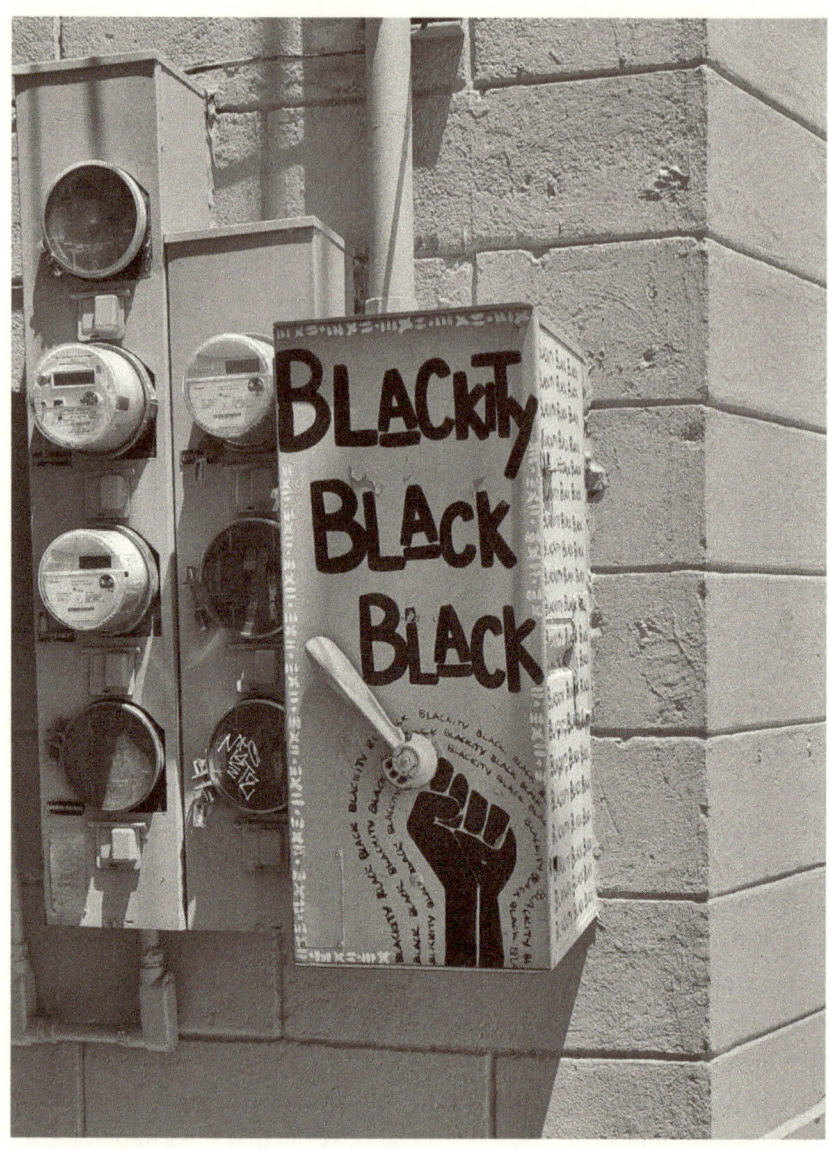

Graffiti on utility box, Bayou Road, 2023.

Situation rooms, also described as control rooms (especially in the United Kingdom), have been discussed in academic literature and in professional contexts, where they are critical sites for emergency planning. The cultural-political geographer Ben Anderson and social researcher Rachel Gordon reflect that "a necessary and constant background to today's interdependent infrastructural life, control rooms are critical to the achievement of continuity." As Anderson and Gordon recognize, control rooms deal with "a series of actualities and potentialities, each of which has an established, recognized sequence of 'next step' actions, whilst also remaining imbued with ambiguity."[2] Control rooms involve carefully managed processes of reading unfolding practices and determining appropriate means of response. Meanwhile, Judith Rodin argues that "gathering and sharing information and, even more important . . . establishing feedback loops (so that information can be gathered, analyzed, and then fed back to inform action) during a crisis are critical to a response effort." This produces key "situational awareness" that is vital to embedding adaptability, efficiency, and clarity of action as a crisis unfolds.[3] Where Rodin is interested in the "technologies" of such action, in this chapter we argue that the spaces that make use of the data gathered, where "actualities and potentialities" are analyzed, and responses are rehearsed, performed, and disseminated, are similarly critical. Importantly, for us, this happens not only in formal situation rooms but also in arts centers and venues throughout a city, albeit in a different form. That is, each of the sites explored in this chapter operate as situation rooms because they *rehearse* the city in different ways: they practice the city, get to know it, analyze it, and, in Rodin's terms, feed back situational awareness on how to be in it. These spaces are also *performing* the city, opening up new understandings of place, inviting people to be in the city differently. Each is about resilience insofar as it is about honing the complex functioning of social, civic, and cultural systems in the city.

City Hall, New Orleans, 2 April 2018

We are standing on the top floor of City Hall in New Orleans, surrounded by a series of meeting room–style tables. Individual working areas are demarcated by chairs, each one with a telephone and laptop in front of it. Small printed cards on stands designate the function of the table. These designations are echoed on large triangular signs that hang from the ceiling so as to be visible from almost any corner of the space: OPS Table 1, Situation/Documentation, Logistics, Planning, Purchasing/Finance. At several of these stations, a high-vis jacket of orange or yellow hangs over an empty chair, signifying the position that the "table lead" will occupy. At one, a dark-blue cardigan hangs incongruously where we would expect high-vis.

The room has windows on two sides. The view from one window, by "OPS

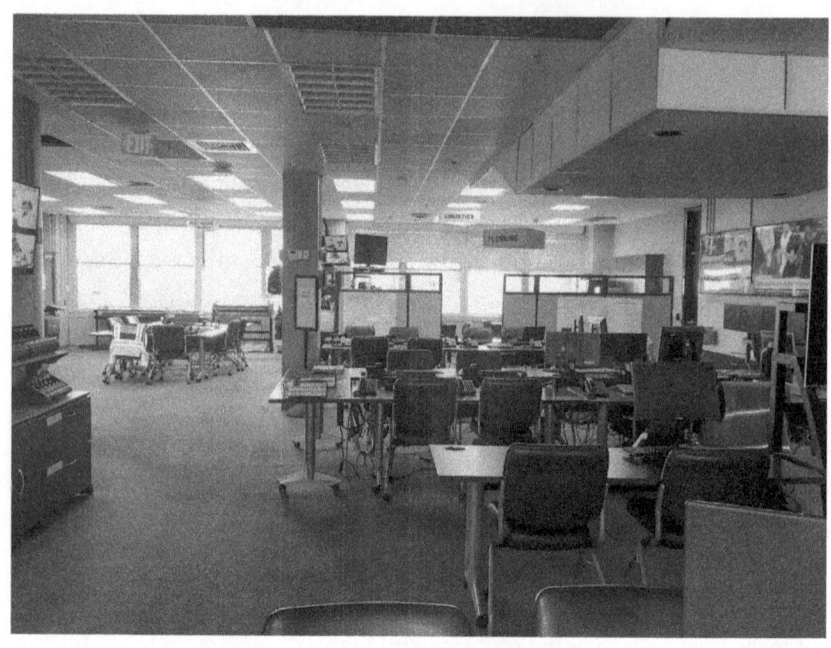

Interior of a "situation room" at City Hall, 2018.

Table 2," where we find ourselves, is obscured by a storm force blind that can withstand the impact of a hurricane at least as strong as Katrina. From the window next to it, we can look out to the northeast of the city—across the French Quarter, the Seventh Ward, and the Marigny. The room behind us is eerily quiet yet busy with the flickering of multiple television screens showing rolling news. This large, multi-sectioned room of prime real estate lies dormant but clearly ready to perform its function as one of the city's three situation rooms.

We are being shown this room by Ryan Mast, who was at the time hazard mitigation administrator and acting chief resilience officer for New Orleans. He describes the room's function as a place from which the city is managed in different contexts, both those of crisis and those of significant "pressure" on the city. In this room, performances of crises are played out in three ways: "table-top" exercises in which key players in crisis management talk through various scenarios; live simulations of real crises that play out across the city with volunteers, emergency services, and city crisis managers role-playing; live events, both planned city-scale events like Mardis Gras or the Super Bowl, and emergencies, such as mass evacuations due to storm warnings or live shooting attacks. Through different simulations, the room *rehearses* events in the city. In the instance of a live crisis, the room also *performs* in the city: intelligence received here is processed, analyzed, and acted upon, and this affects the actions of individuals and teams across the city. We confess to Ryan about being rather surprised at how often the situation room is used, particularly for sporting events. While we are there, the city is preparing for WrestleMania.

In this room, confronted by the everyday and the extraordinary ways it is put to work through performance, we become aware of the multiple places (and spaces) in the city that we might consider to be fulfilling similarly strategic functions. Although perhaps not framed in these terms, this is a city where there is a plurality of places that function *as* situation rooms; places where people from, and information about, the city are brought together to generate, share, analyze, and challenge intelligences *about* the city. That is, there are places that think though (rehearse) and materialize (perform) the city politically, socially, and culturally. These spaces afford "on-the-ground" perspectives on the city and the resilience challenges it faces. To holistically understand how a city is and can be resilient, we need to take seriously the places in which people come together to generate new understandings and formulations of that city—that is, the places, the situation rooms, in which city resilience is *performed*.

Framing Situation Rooms

The term *Situation Room* emerged in response to what Michael K. Bohn identifies as the "Bay of Pigs disaster," the failed attempt by the United States to invade Cuba in 1961. Visually, perhaps the idea of a situation room is most familiar to us in the contemporary moment through the image *Situation Room*, taken by White House photographer Pete Souza in 2011, of Obama's administration during Operation Neptune Spear, which led to the assassination of Osama bin Laden. Bohn writes that either McGeorge Bundy, special assistant to the president for national security, or Walt W. Rostow, deputy special assistant to the president for national security, reflected that "we could have avoided [the Bay of Pigs] fiasco if only we had a crisis centre in the White House."[4] That is, a situation room provides an opportunity for key stakeholders to gather, receive critical and up-to-date information, analyze it, and make swift decisions that impact the operation of people on the ground during whichever situation is being played out. As noted in the Obama White House archives, the "Sit Room" serves as a conference facility, a processing center for secure communications, a hub of intelligence gathering, and a center for emergency operations.[5] Key here, we think, is the idea of intelligence gathering and communication as a mechanism through which crises can be analyzed and responded to as a considered, if responsive, and strategic practice.

Situation rooms have become a familiar trope in some contemporary performance practices. For example, in 2016, Split Britches presented *The Situation Room,* a "performance-conversation . . . with elder audience participants."[6] Staged in the immediate aftermath of the Brexit referendum in the United Kingdom and the 2016 U.S. presidential election, the piece deployed a scenography recognizable as that of a situation room from news media and popular culture. This included well-lit tables arranged in a circular formation, a red telephone, headsets, and information screens above that displayed maps of the world and particular geopolitical contexts. In the same year, Fuel Theatre presented *The Situation Room: Prejudice and Perception,* a series of events intended to "better understand the fractures in our society . . . a place for audiences, artists and researchers to talk about the big issue, to meet other minds and to be entertained."[7] In 2015 Micol Hebron turned her double garage into The Situation Room, a gallery in Los Angeles. For Hebron "the name is general enough to cover any potential situation—nuclear war, terrorist attacks, military coups, spy business, or, who knows, maybe sexual transgressions happen there, too."[8] In each instance, the situation room is considered as an element of the diegesis, a setting in which the action takes place.[9] Moreover, echoing UK theater critic Lyn Gardner's critique of the work by Fuel, such performances are not properly engaging with the complexities and possibilities of rethinking situation rooms and the usefulness of contemporary performance to understanding local, regional, or national "situations."[10]

Alongside work directly engaged with situation rooms, performance practitioners and theorists have addressed ideas and practices that directly speak to the kinds of practices that play out in situation rooms. This relates particularly to the performance theorist Scott Magelssen's work on "simming," which he defines as "a simulated, immersive, performance environment" that uses "theatre and performance practices to stage environments in which participants [play] out a scripted or improvised narrative in order to gain or produce understandings of a situation and its context." For Magelssen, simming stages "emergency response" by "extrapolat[ing] from the past to imaginatively anticipate moments of trauma and crisis in the future." As Magelssen's work demonstrates, there is something significant about being located in a specific place and engaging in a particular situation in that place. As a form of performance practice, Magelssen's observation that simmings have a powerful "ability to witness another's experience through physical embodiment and even discomfort" places this type of resilience exercise and theater practice into direct dialogue.[11]

However, it is also worth noting that simming, especially when conducted by civic authorities, is not neutral and can "present multiple challenges and dilemmas when it comes to issues of power, agency, and representation." This seems particularly important in the context of New Orleans, where community relationships with city authorities, including Homeland Security within which Emergency Preparedness sits, is not always straightforward in terms of processes of power, agency, and representation. While arts spaces are not exempt from these complexities, very often they have meaningful, long-standing relationships with the plural communities they represent and serve.

In this chapter we are concerned to move beyond engagement with the situation room as content/setting/simulated environment to consider how performance spaces are doing the work of situation rooms in a city in relation to its resilience challenges. As is perhaps now so well rehearsed as to be commonplace, for Michel de Certeau a city operates as a signifying system within which architecture operates performatively to constitute a "place" based on how that architecture intervenes in and interacts with its multiple users and local geography.[12] This will, of course, ripple out across the city more broadly, especially where an architectural intervention or recalibration is deliberately attempting to (re)negotiate understandings of place and community by adding something new to an environment, be that people, practices, meeting spaces, and/or things to do, see, eat. In this way, as geographer Amanda Rogers may have it, "cities are a particular type of place where the performing arts are staged, but there are a variety of relationships between performance and urban space" that serve to ensure that "urban space is continually re-created."[13] This happens in a number of ways—for example, through participation in performance practices, from going to the theater to see a play to taking part in a protest to cheering and catching throws along a Mardis Gras parade route. It is also evidenced in the ways that arts organizations and performance venues *perform* in the city, such as in how they interact with the communities that they represent and present and how their spaces might be seen to intervene in urban geographies.

City Hall

The situation room at the top of City Hall operates formally as a site of information processing, observation, and decision-making *about* New Orleans as critical events unfold in real time. New Orleans's City Hall sits at 1300 Perdido Street in the Central Business District, more or less on the edge of the French Quarter. We decide to walk there from a meeting we had in a different part of the city. The two-mile walk feels longer than it is because of the heat of the day. We arrive hot and anxious not to be late. The building is imposing and, well, ugly: an evidently municipal design, it is essentially an enormous cuboid of weather-worn gray-white block work and reflective glass. A large, faded-red CITY HALL adorns the top of the structure. We enter the building into a surprisingly small foyer that is reminiscent of the security area at a small airport: metal detectors, security guards, and X-ray machines. As we are being ushered through the security protocols, a guard asks what room we are going to. We say we are meeting with Ryan Mast, but the guard does not recognize the name. We don't know where we are going and so ensues an awkward (possibly peculiarly British) sort of choreography of apologies, fumbling for mobiles, frantic email searching, and nervous laughter. The guard doesn't seem to mind: perhaps he is amused; perhaps he is used to it.

Once on the top floor of the building, we arrive at the determinedly locked door of the Office of Homeland Security and Emergency Preparedness and are buzzed in after giving our names. At the end of an hour-long interview with Mast, he asks if we'd like a tour to see where his work happens. We weren't expecting to see the situation room; indeed, neither of us knew it was there.

In our conversation with Mast, he noted that his work within the Office of Homeland Security and Emergency Preparedness has "historically . . . focused on the hard emergency management component of disaster recovery."[14] In our discussions with him, Mast reflected on the need to protect cultural infrastructure and artifacts as well as to understand the cultural underpinnings of the city's identity, especially in terms of music and "everyday" performances such as second lines.[15] Moving beyond these "strategic" concerns, one of the things that became clear when Ryan showed us around the situation room was that this was a space that "staged" its thinking. That is: in a space conventionally associated with responding to resilience challenges, rehearsal performances are played out both in round-table and live-action simulations as means of planning for and thinking through "the real thing." But also, in the event of a real crisis or large-scale city event like WrestleMania, this is a "venue" in which *performances* of resilience practice happen. So in the same way that we are making the argument for arts being understood as a means through which a city thinks itself through, so, too, is performance a practice that the city deploys in its processes of city management.

Mast walks us through the space, pointing out the various stations and functions of them. He talks about the strength of the storm blinds and tells us that the space has its own dedicated power generator. It is clear that this is a serious space, one in which important work is done by people who are highly skilled and proficient. An impression backed up by Mast's own relaxed performance in the space: he seems uncannily at ease here, practiced and precise. As we take in the contradiction between the banality of the space, a fairly generic office space on the surface of it, and the complexity of the work carried out here, Mast mentions that they carry out "simulations." They rehearse their work through live performances of crisis scenarios that are enacted across the city, making use of volunteers to help emergency and other services "play out" the event. They also do "tabletop" talk-throughs of situations with key members of the city who would be present in the situation room should a real event unfold. We ask him how the scenarios are put together; he tells us an external company writes them. We comment to Mast that these are performances and that they make use of techniques and practices of the theater. That is, this is a place that is operational only in and through performance.

As Bohn reflects of the White House situation room, staff in City Hall, New Orleans, use this room for a variety of situations. In some instances, only a few people will work here; in others, the room will be busier. Thus, the practice of the room varies in terms of the scale of the event and its implications, the breadth of intelligence gathered, and the types of decision-making and activities undertaken. A single situation room is, necessarily, flexible and open to varying levels of use. The actions within the situation room are connected to systems within and associated with practices of city governance. The scale of events is, therefore, filtered through standardized processes, however much these may be nuanced in particular cases. Nevertheless, in each instance of its use, this room operates to understand the city and make it resilient (in the sense that it prepares the city to attend to crises) in what we might call a "performance-like" mode. If, as Manyena observes, resilience thinking needs to account for more than just "vulnerability reduction," then performance thinking might give us compelling ways of identifying an extended understanding of resilience practices.[16] The practices and techniques of theater and performance underpin operational and skills development processes of the situation room: rehearsals, particular and designed scenographies, use of semiotic conventions, assigned roles that people perform (and perform well), codified practices of procedure and timing. Moreover, it is *performative* insofar as decisions taken in this room directly impact operational performances on the ground and the (immediate) future of the urban environment.

This situation room, like all such civic situation rooms, we imagine, very clearly performs city resilience in relation to understanding a city and how it might prepare for and/or respond to a crisis. It is a venue that performs its thinking, sometimes publicly, sometimes in closed rehearsals, but in each case this is a space that performs resilience. That said, we find this room differs from those we turn to next in this chapter but in ways that are productive to understanding how all of these sites are alive to their situation and their relation to the situations that are active around them.

The Music Box Village

It is early on a spring evening in 2018. Our taxi driver stops, with some uncertainty, just beyond the last of the houses on the street. Beyond these, the road appears to peter out. On either side, the ground is rough, there is some parking to the left, and farther on and to the right, a railroad crosses the street. Ahead of us, we see the grass bank of the Industrial Canal. We're a little tight for time, and the driver's uncertainty makes us uneasy that we might have this all wrong, that we may have mixed up the location. That said, we're reassured by the presence of people moving this way. It is not exactly a crowd, but we join a stream of people, in pairs and small groups, heading toward the end of the street. We cross the ground to the left, passing in between and beneath the canopy of trees, to a building that lies well back from the street. There is a sense of disconnection between the order of the streets, of satellite navigation systems, and the building, which we remember as being only partly visible from the houses on the street. Stopping briefly at the box office and a table where our tickets are checked, we work our way around the structure, through a wide entrance, into an enclosed, open-air interior.[17]

The Music Box Village, which opened in 2016, is a "sonic garden," a "sound art installation/performance venue" just off St. Claude Avenue.[18] It was built and is managed by New Orleans Airlift, a nonprofit arts organization in the

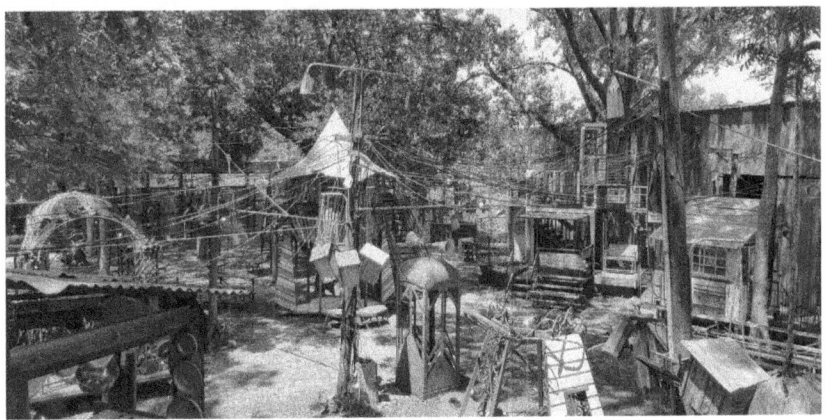

Music Box Village, 2018.

city, which was established following Hurricane Katrina. In contacting the organization about our work in the city, we were offered tickets to a show. We invite—albeit at their expense—two of Patrick's friends who live in the city and who have helped us orientate ourselves. On the evening we visit, we watch *From These Roots,* a performance by musicians and three dancers. The venue comprises a central stage area used by the dancers and a series of buildings or booths on two levels. In building the venue, New Orleans Airlift invited local and international artists to construct these "percussive homes," spaces that can house performances but that might also be "played" musically in some way. The structure has, in part at least, been constructed from reclaimed materials, which may be both practical and pointedly political. This is a case of needing to use that which remains in a city facing considerable resilience challenges, including pronounced poverty and legacy damage from Katrina and more recent storms. Although we are "inside" the venue, its architecture is more like an enclosure, open to the elements with the percussive "houses" in and between the trees. We buy a drink and food at stalls just inside the venue and find a spot to watch the performance. Spectators gather around the stage, on fixed seating or standing at gaps between the ground-floor structures and on a staircase and viewing platform. The use of the buildings as instruments appears distinctive.

Afterward, the performers retire, and spectators roam the site; many of the lights from the performance remain on, and the space takes on an otherworldly, almost magical air. We walk out of the exit, which opens onto the car park, into an evening that is not quite dark. We climb the bank of the canal and become aware of the scale of the water and an industrial structure on the far side. Beyond us is the Lower Ninth Ward, one of the areas most devastated by Katrina. In that storm, the Industrial Canal was a critical site of flooding, as a result of the failure of the levee system to cope with the severity of the water's power as it surged from the Gulf. We descend the embankment, duck under a chain-link fence, and begin walking along the train tracks. After a few minutes, we pass an abandoned military base: the F. Edward Hebert Defense Complex. The friends we had invited explain this is inhabited by people who are homeless. We step off the railroad and become acutely aware of the lack of barriers between the people who live here and the freight trains that pass through the area. As we walk through this place, the darkness of evening has descended, and the absence of street lighting is palpable. Only the occasional external light of a house offers relief from the gloom.

For Delaney Martin, who was cofounder and artistic director of New Orleans Airlift from 2007 to 2023, Music Box Village offers a space for "deep and radical collaboration" in a complex geopolitical environment.[19] Located at what felt then like an edgeland of the city, with ships looming imposingly above the top-line of the tall corrugated iron walls, the venue makes apparent the complex relation of the city to its industrial infrastructures and ecological challenges. The space reveals the enormity of the canal, its power and potential for devastation. And in its proximity to and juxtaposition with abandoned infrastructures now "home" to the homeless, the space articulates other challenges in the city to do with housing, and economic and race inequities. Yet at the same time, the venue *performs* resilience by gathering people together through performance to inhabit a previously disused industrial site, in order to experience, rethink, and then, potentially, celebrate a formerly "abandoned" area.

As Martin explained, when we met her at the Music Box Village a few days after the performance, the venue is the latest in a series of iterations in which local participants have been concerned to maintain and make sense of arts practice in the city. Martin described her sense of devastation that culture might not return to the city in the aftermath of Hurricane Katrina. A friend had suggested bringing art from New Orleans to Berlin, a version of the Berlin Airlift, with airplanes bringing arts practice, rather than food. This work led to a project not far from the current site that involved building a percussive home—a precursor of the homes that inhabit the Music Box Village.

We return to the site in 2023. While we are more certain on how to make our way there, the site has continued to grow. Notably, a house sits just outside the venue, perhaps newly built, perhaps newly included in the "village." The actions and decisions about the site continue to impact the form of the site, resisting any sense that it is completely familiar or completely finished. This process begins to reveal the ways in which decisions in a space can contribute to the form of that space. Through the development of a single home to the construction of a self-contained arts space, comprising multiple performance areas, Music Box Village reveals an iterative process of reflection on the place of arts in the city. The process also illuminates new means of building sites for arts practice in the city that take account of the environmental and economic contexts of its initial construction. The use of reclaimed materials, the relatively low height of the structure, the indistinct nature of the boundaries of the site all speak of an approach to place and to art making in this place that involves the accumulation of materials, practices, and ideas. The iterative process of reclamation, reflection, and reinvention involved in the development of Music Box Village indicates a process not only of venue development but also a profound articulation of the ethos that led to its construction in this place. The venue offers a live space for audiences and performers to reflect on their situated experiences of this place and also stands as a physical articulation of Anderson and Gordon's sense that situation rooms attend to the "actualities and potentialities" of the context and environment within which they operate.[20] Music Box Village, then, is not simply a site that has been constructed for ideas to be explored through live performances. Rather, in developing over time, the venue itself performs an articulation of resilience while leaving open a space for practitioners to investigate ideas by performing in and with the building.

Theater on the Bayou Road, 2018: The Potential of a Theater in Development

In early April 2018, just before nine in the morning, we found ourselves standing on the sidewalk in front of St. Rose de Lima Church on the historic Bayou Road, just before it crosses North Broad Street. In front of the church, the sidewalk widens; the building itself is set back from the street. We noticed what appeared to be an administrative building for Uber opposite, a house, perhaps two, a music store to the left of the church, and shops and housing to the right. The redbrick and stone church is a significant feature on the street. It is tall in comparison to the one- or two-story structures close by. The building is surrounded by metal fencing, weighed down with sandbags: redevelopment works have made the church and its immediate surroundings a building site.

We were there to meet Aimée Hayes, then producing artistic director of what was the Southern Rep Theatre, which was in the process of taking over the church as a new permanent home in time for the 2018 autumn season. We had met with Hayes a few days earlier to discuss her work at Southern Rep Theatre in the context of city resilience, and she had invited us to visit the site.[21] At the time, Southern Rep identified as the only year-round theater company in New Orleans, seeking to "develop and produce new plays that reflect the diversity of the city we call home."[22] In that context, the intention, Hayes told us and their website made clear, was to use the new venue as "a cultural anchor on the Bayou Road corridor."[23] This was a compelling if complicated goal, not least given the company was moving from existing as a city-based but peripatetic company to having its first permanent venue in more than six years. Nevertheless, Hayes was acutely aware that a theater venue offers significant possibilities as a place for people in a city to gather, be, and think together.

At the point of its development, this space was intended to be far more than the site of theater events, something the company was explicitly attending to in its approach to the new space. Indeed, we discussed the potential for a theater venue on this site and tried to identify design, architectural, and policy means for the theater to become a valuable and critical site of local community gathering, cultural expressions, and experiences. Later, financial pressures, the damaging impact of the COVID-19 pandemic on live events, and the challenges of bringing a particular model of theater making to the site led to the closure of this company. Recently, the building has been redeveloped as the André Cailloux Center for Performing Arts and Cultural Justice.

When Hayes led us into the building via a side door, the new spaces of the arts venue were beginning to emerge: renovations to the structure were accompanied by new additions, in particular the newly constructed walls of the auditorium. As we walked through the space, elements of our previous conversations with Hayes took more tangible form as we began to see the lay of the land, both in and outside the church. In particular, we were caught by the relation between interior and exterior, between the theater emerging in the church and its potential for conversation with the streets and the city outside. Hayes had suggested that theater is counterintuitive in New Orleans because everything is normally outside. At the time of our tour, the intention was to blur the sense of inside-outside; the plan was not to have a fence or any kind of barrier between the street and the theater. Instead, glass doors would always be open, hoping to invite regular audiences and newcomers alike. Tables and chairs would, we were told, spill from the café-bar foyer into an inviting court-yard that met the street. Similarly, drawing on the particular context of the city, the Rep would offer a form of "lagniappe," a little something extra, before (or after) the ticketed shows: free performances of music, dance, theater in the foyer of the building and on an outside stage adjoining the sidewalk.[24] Such practices had the potential to become locally situated strategies to mitigate resilience challenges, not least in offering an open space of cultural encounter and/or simple refuge from extreme heat or pouring rain. The hope, in 2018, was that this approach would facilitate a situation in which the established Rep audience, local residents, and business owners (who may or may not be new to the theater) would be able to meet, happenstance, over a drink or free performance.

The new theater was a significant development for Southern Rep Theatre financially, politically, and artistically. From 2012, when a lease expired on a previous property, the Rep had been without a permanent base. Hayes told us of long-drawn-out processes of setting up shows in various venues in the city, often in places with limited facilities. Before each performance, audiences would need to be welcomed and thanked for bearing with the, at times challenging, conditions. Despite the difficulties of these venues, the Rep had been keen to fulfill civic functions and add value to the effort of the "counterintuitive" experience of going to the theater, for instance by setting up voter registration booths in a foyer. In establishing the new venue, the concern was to maintain an established conversation with the company's existing audience and to develop new audiences in its new home, both in the city and, particularly, in the local area.

The Rep was not a venue, nor a company, that identified itself in terms of city resilience or indeed, in broader terms, of maintaining or enhancing the city. Yet the articulation of the underpinning design and artistic strategies in 2018 made explicit a desire to engage with the city and the richness and diversity of the local community it had the potential to serve and represent. That stated goal was important in the context of gentrification, a pronounced citywide phenomenon; in "keeping the doors open" and inviting engagement, the company had hoped to be aware of its potentially gentrifying power and to deliberately counter it.

The development of the theater space afforded the Southern Rep an *opportunity* to think expansively about the potential civic impact of its work and how the new venue might operate as a social-civic cultural space in the area. The *potential* of the site and the goals of the company as articulated to us at the time were ambitious in their focus but were ultimately undone through a combination of financial hardship, exacerbated by the COVID-19 pandemic, and too slowly recognizing a need to address the company's own culpability in systemic racism.

Indeed, it is apparent in statements released by the Southern Rep Theatre in the run-up to and during the process of its closure that while the theater had often staged works that thematically addressed questions of racism and inequity, as an organization it had been systemically guilty of perpetuating some of the harms these works sought to highlight and address. As Hayes stated in announcing her resignation in 2020, "It is essential for Southern Rep to focus on the structural effects of bias and racism in how we work."[25] In June 2021, in response to the murder of George Floyd and the emergence of the Black Lives Matter movement, the company released a public statement via Facebook noting that "white privilege, bias, and structural racism were baked into our democracy and economy from the very start. As racism infects our systems and our institutions, it infects us all as people. Despite our best intentions, we have been party to this corruption. We must and we will do better."[26] It is apparent, then, that the hopes articulated for the theater in 2018 were not fully or properly achieved, ultimately contributing to its closure.

More positively, however, the possibilities of that potential are being explored and now realized by Lauren Turner Hines (with colleagues) through her work as cofounder and artistic director of the André Cailloux Center for Performing Arts and Cultural Justice and as producing artistic director of the theater company No Dream Deferred. What is interesting about more recent developments in this local area is that the businesses are now (again) predominantly Black owned.[27] In taking up residence in the old church, the ACC states that "IN SPITE OF COLONIZATION and its progeny, gentrification, BAYOU ROAD REMAINS a center of transnational and multicultural exchange. We are reclaiming the historic narrative and purpose of this corridor."[28] The transformation of the St. Rose de Lima building into a theater and the opportunities to think through what a theater might do on this site remain profound.

Theater on the Bayou Road, 2023: A Venue Realized

We are sitting at a high table in the foyer of the André Cailloux Center for Performing Arts and Cultural Justice, where a stage has been constructed for the performance of *The Defiance of Dandelions* by local writer Philana Imade

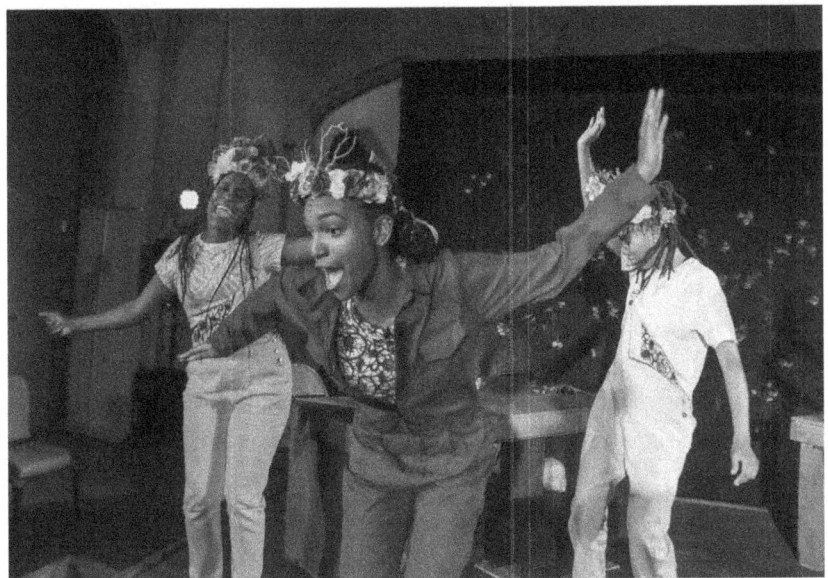

Actors (*left to right*) Constance Thompson, Aria Jackson, and Erin King performing *The Defiance of Dandelions*, by Philana Imade Omorotionmwan, as part of the No Dream Deferred, WE WILL DREAM: New Works Festival at the André Cailloux Center for Performing Arts and Cultural Justice, 2023. Photo by OLM Photography.

Omorotionmwan, to be performed by a cast of Black female performers from New Orleans. Staged as part of the WE WILL DREAM: New Works Festival, a biennial theater festival on the Bayou Road corridor that positions itself as "the 'national meeting place' for Black playwrights originating/working in the American South to engage with compelling artistic, intellectual, and cultural dialogue and community exploration."[29]

Occupying most of the foyer, the performance area asks spectators to face back toward the main entrance, the bar behind them. The repurposing of the foyer as a performance space draws attention to the building's architecture, to its history and longevity. In particular, the configuration encourages time to study an enormous triptych of paintings that celebrate André Cailloux, "an African American army captain, one of the first black officers of any North American military unit," whose funeral was conducted here in July 1863 and after whom the center is named.[30]

Before the performance "proper" begins, we are treated to a lagniappe music performance. This little something extra is provided by a school-age musician; learning their craft in New Orleans must be no mean feat, but the opportunity to perform in public, in a center for performing arts, is seized by the young performer, who sings and plays violin and piano. The audience is modest in size but encouraging and supportive throughout the short performance. Setting a tone of appreciation and concentration, the performance enacts the ACC's commitment to being a "multidisciplinary, community-centered arts [and] cultural" hub that platforms the talent "development [of] Black makers" at all levels.[31]

Shortly after the music ends, we hear a chorus of voices emerging from a hidden space off to our right and behind us. At first muffled and disrupted by the acoustics and the noise of the company members' footsteps as they confidently and happily march into the space down a long wooden ramp, the words they speak in singsong voice become clear as they enter the space: "I am deliberate and afraid of nothing," an affirmation that becomes rallying cry and acclamation throughout the play.

Directed by Nicole Brewer, a Yale University professor known for her anti-racist theater work, the play poetically explores the lived experience of young Black women. Often damagingly controlled and restricted—their behavior, appearance, and activities dictated by systems, structures, and people in "power"—the piece elliptically, through repetition and movement, explores questions of racist control, systems of power, and the possibilities of reclaiming identity and collective agency.

Although not explicitly about New Orleans, in being staged in the city, on the Bayou Road, with a local, all-Black cast, it is hard not to read the work as directly addressing the city, offering a reflection from this center for cultural justice in this historically Black neighborhood back to New Orleans, one that asks searching questions about the contemporary city. In the main, this happens allegorically, but at one point the question is posed: "Why are there tents under the I-10?" The potential of this situation room had been clear when we visited the building site in 2018, but seeing the space animated now showed it had realized that potential, as the work being performed explicitly called attention to questions of inequity, the housing crisis, and poverty in the city and, through form and content, challenged the audience (and so the city) to think through systemic racism and the control of Black women in contemporary America.

Whereas the Southern Rep wanted to create a cultural anchor on the Bayou Road corridor, No Dream Deferred identifies itself as "a community-anchored theatre that prioritizes New Orleans."[32] Similarly prioritizing the importance of place and place identity in their strategic focus, these are very different articulations of the "anchoring" role of the venue and the role theater can play in that. One centers the cultural production, the other those creating and experiencing it. While neither is perhaps better than the other, the distinction speaks to the importance of radically foregrounding minoritized voices in this city, particularly on the Bayou Road corridor. For No Dream Deferred, programming and advocacy afford opportunities to build "a future where art leaders of color are not the exception but the norm."[33]

We meet Lauren Turner Hines in June 2023. She tells us about the importance of creating a home for Black theater in the city, of the significance of there being a building, when so many Black arts organizations in the city have long been unable to access space to develop and share their work. The André Cailloux Center offers space for seven organizations to create and program public work in the building. While this is a single "center," by housing multiple inhabitants, it provides a collaborative context to address and respond to issues and practices faced by people and communities in the city.

There is significant interest in shared use of space in contemporary cities, particularly familiar in coworking spaces that enable people to work together without requiring a dedicated personal space. While this can, in part, be practical and economically efficient, it also offers the potential for more substantial opportunities to remake ways of living and working in a place. Indeed, Laura Wynne and Chris Riedy identify "the transformative potential of communal forms of sharing in our cities."[34] The André Cailloux Center shares space as a political act, creating opportunities and platforms for those whose voices and stories have too often not been heard.

In its home on the Bayou Road, this is a place where stories from the community are welcomed in, developed into performances, and shared with New Orleanians. Read as a situation room, this is a place that invites people from the city to share their stories, whether actual or imagined. The company and venue, then, create a space for those stories to be processed, explored, and understood. Finally, in one of the few majority-minority cities in the United States, the venue uses its established practices of sharing work with the city. In so doing, and in its own terms, the theater is sharing understandings of place that emerge properly from that place, in order to invite public recalibrations that understand the centrality and importance of art made by people of color as the norm.

The theater offers a model of a collective situation room and creates the

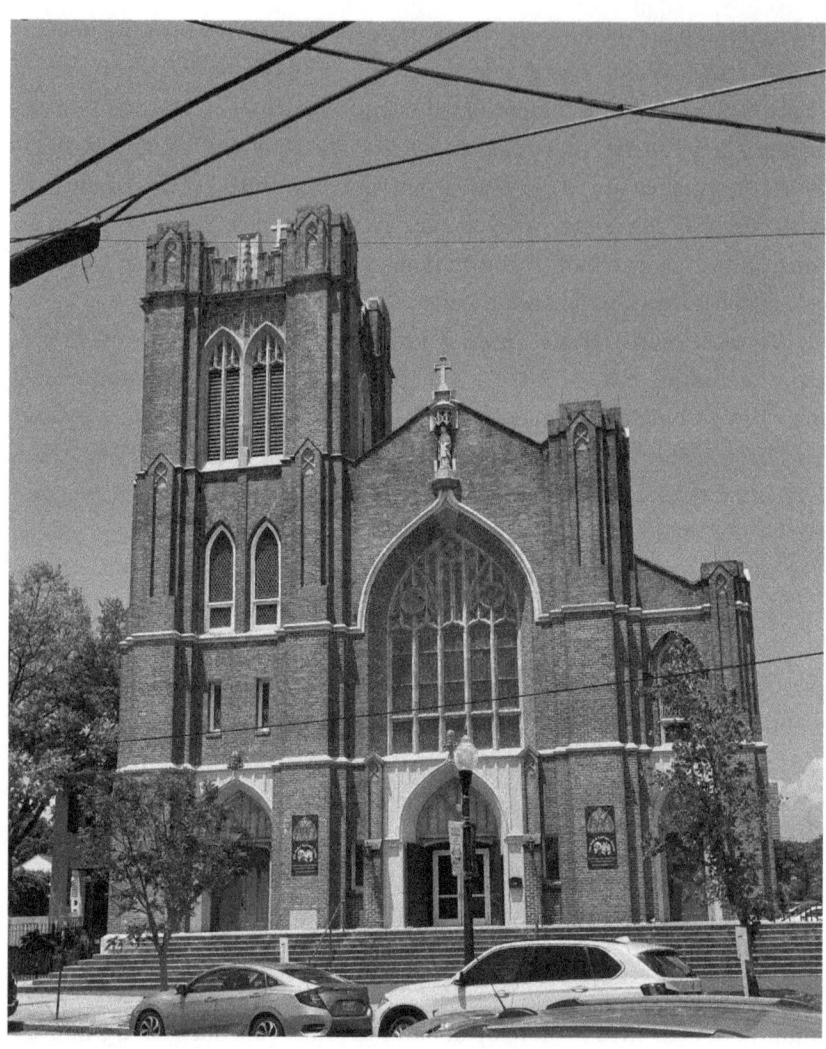

André Cailloux Center for Performing Arts and Cultural Justice, 2023.

potential for multiple, nuanced responses to life in the city and its challenges. Indeed, for Turner Hines, finding responses to challenges is a critical element of her work in theater. Reflecting on her experience of making work through the COVID-19 pandemic, Turner Hines explains that she is concerned with what it is possible to discover through creative practice during a crisis.[35]

The work of the theater is not limited to the building itself; rather, Turner Hines and colleagues are very much focused on the contribution of the venue to Bayou Road. The presence of the ACC on Bayou Road is political; it reclaims space for Black and Indigenous people in the area and centers the work of Black artists on public stages on the street and in the city. Bayou Road is a significant route for people of color in the city. The Bayou Road Business Association identifies that well before the formation of the city, Native Americans had used this "elevated passageway" that led from Bayou St. John to the Mississippi. The association identifies the connection of the road to areas of the city that are historically Black. The association notes that the 2400 and 2500 blocks of the road, along with areas of neighboring streets, "are now home to several Black-owned businesses and cultural centers whose presence and energy help to define the Bayou Road district while serving as a source of pride in the history and culture of the area and as an example of the spirit of cooperative entrepreneurship."[36]

In this context, it becomes valuable to attend to the local situation of the theater on the road. Such an approach recognizes the ways in which acts of sharing can operate within an area of a city or in a city as a whole. As Wynne and Riedy write: "While much can be achieved at the scale of individual buildings and precincts, the real potential of the sharing paradigm can only be realised when we shift our attention to the scale of the whole city."[37]

In opening up performance spaces to the community, the theater operates as a critical site for shared stories on the street. Yet this does not happen in isolation. Next door to the theater is the Community Book Center (CBC), which identifies itself as "a literary, cultural and social hub on historic Bayou Road" and "the oldest Black-owned bookstore in the New Orleans area." We have been aware of the bookshop from our first trip, struck by a mural that covers one side of the building and that depicts a young Black girl being handed a book. This image fills one wall along the plaza outside the ACC. By being connected to both the bookshop and ACC, the plaza places these two institutions into conversation, a conversation about Black and Indigenous people and other minoritized groups in New Orleans. The shop is, as it suggests, "more than a bookstore" and hosts events through the year, which, in 2023, included book signings, a workshop to support children reading at home, music performance, and a monthly meet-up for Black women creatives in the city. The CBC also contributed to HomeFest, a festival for the 2400 and 2500 blocks of Bayou Road.

We are struck by the echoes between the work of the ACC and bookshop and ways in which both are "more than" the terms by which we might usually understand such spaces. To regard one as a theater and the other as a bookshop misunderstands the breadth of practices that each employs to engage with and enable people of color in the city. To understand these as separate spaces, connected only by their geographical proximity, misunderstands the potential of sites operating separately but also in combination. These, then, are both situation rooms in the city, both engaged in gathering and welcoming perspectives, processing, understanding, and sharing these perspectives with the city. They reveal a model of situation rooms as shared spaces that operate in a local network. In the context of established racial inequity in and beyond the city, these networked situation rooms offer powerful means to value stories and find new means of celebrating and lifting up those whose voices have too often not been heard. They demonstrate the ways that situation rooms can operate in close combination, and at times in dialogue, framing a street as a layered, nuanced place to reflect, process, make discoveries, determine future actions, and support future leaders.

This takes on particular significance in the context of the work of Mario Gooden, an architecture theorist. Writing on architecture in the United States, Gooden critiques "the absorption of [Black] spatial and cultural practices into a dominant culture." Instead, he calls for an alternate approach, arguing that "as a cultural practice, architecture must interpret and translate the historical, social, and political contexts of a place and how one comes to terms with that place. Such an architecture should reveal meanings, situations, and conditions (both apparent and subliminal) and allow for individual participatory action, the affirmation of 'presence' in life, and a recognition of existential meaning and knowledge—the confirmation of that life, liberty, and pursuit of happiness."[38]

The ownership and design of businesses and organizations, and the practices that play out in and between many of these buildings and the street, speak directly to the political context of Bayou Road. They open up new ways that current inhabitants of the city might attend to this significant route through the land and city. Further, the performativity of ownership and the cultural practice of performance on Bayou Road constitute means of affirmation and engagement in life. Architecture, design, and performance are vital practices of revealing identity in the present, and they are all the more important in the context of that identity having been resisted and incorporated by an alternate culture—both in the past and as these practices continue in the present. Gooden cites bell hooks: "No matter how poor you were in the shack, no matter if you owned the shack or not, there you could allow your needs and desires to articulate interior design and exterior surroundings."[39] As both Gooden and hooks reveal, design and architecture matter. And, we suggest, so too does performance and the means by which needs and desires are articulated in performative acts—whether onstage, in a workshop, or in daily performances of a city street. The design and practice of buildings on Bayou Road speak of needs and desires, read through both Indigenous knowledge and way finding through this place and the centrality of life on this street in the present. Whether it is young musicians performing onstage, writers sharing their work with city publics, sales and events at the bookshop, the contemporary practices of Bayou Road value and center the life of individual people here, especially the life of Black and Indigenous people, in this neighborhood and in the city as a whole.

When we visited the street in 2018, we were aware that some of the businesses appeared closed, and we noted the presence of an Uber building opposite the church. In 2023 Uber had left; the area seemed bright, exciting, alive. On one level, these are anecdotal observations, affected very much by the time and situation of our visits. Yet as we sat in Addis, an Ethiopian restaurant and bar across from the church, enjoying a cold drink on a terrifyingly warm day, we were struck by the ways in which businesses in the area were each contributing to this area and celebrating Black experience in ways that were less fully marked only a few years earlier. This is not simply about the buildings themselves; it is also present in the artistic and creative interventions on and between buildings. On several of our trips to the Bayou Road, our attention has been caught by words painted onto what may be an electrical box outside the bookshop. Painted in black letters on a pink background, BLACKITY BLACK BLACK makes a playful intervention to the street. Words, murals, the markers of people and place in and between buildings, frame situation rooms in terms of their surroundings. Whether formal shop front or informal graffiti, these interventions into the street tell stories of the people who inhabit a place, who live here, who are from here, and of those who have been here and their importance in shaping these places. On a very practical level, this, for us as white outsiders, is an area of the city in which it is easy to live up to Constance Thompson's and Joycelyn Reynolds's generous instruction that in order to be a constructive visitor to the city, it is important to spend money in and support Black-owned businesses. Yet at the same time, it is far more than this and recognizes both the contemporary, lived community of Bayou Road and the importance of addressing its established history as the oldest road in New Orleans and a route that predates the city.

In thinking through the complexities of how an entity can be resilient, Rodin suggests that it is "important that people engage in activities that celebrate their identity and also that bring the crisis into that identity rather than ignore or negate it."[40] That sense of establishing, renewing, and renegotiating identity is part of the operation of the arts venues explored here. In surveying these venues and the ways in which they create places for particular arts practice in New Orleans, we find that each one constitutes a place in New Orleans but also troubles understandings of place in the city. The Music Box is a fixed and secure structure but also open to the elements. It is a "permanent" venue, in a place that suffered significantly as a result of Katrina, in which the *impermanence* of structures, specifically homes, was acutely apparent. The building sits at the end of a street, just up from a line of houses yet directly across the tracks from an abandoned military base, now home to those who find themselves homeless. The André Cailloux Center seeks to destabilize the apparent neatness of interior and exterior, street and venue. The City Hall situation room is both a place to observe and manage events in the city but is also separate from the city, a place that is removed, perhaps necessarily so, in order for it to fulfill its function.

For Rodin, fundamental to good resilience practice and thinking is the idea that "we should not want to make ourselves, our communities, businesses, and cities rigid and unchanging and forever fixed, but rather flexible, adaptable, and capable of absorbing disruptions and converting them into change that contributes to the system's overall functioning and purpose."[41] The places we discuss in this chapter are precisely contributing to such flexibility. Thus, to recognize a plurality of situation rooms in a city is to understand and allow that there are no singular views of a city: the city itself is different depending on the place and perspective one occupies in relation to it (at any given moment). While we have focused here on two performance venues as situation rooms and identified performance as critical to the operation of civic situation rooms, we recognize that this term may be productively applied to other critical sites and centers within a city. As such, we recognize the significance of accounting for multiple situation rooms, of not focusing solely, for instance, on perspectives from the arts without taking into account those of resilience professionals, or vice versa. Each of our case studies addresses highly localized conditions, grounded in the personal experiences of those who have brought the spaces into being and/or who operate (within) them. With Music Box, ACC, and No Dream Deferred, this is a process that has taken many years of iterative development and engagement with the city and previous projects in different locations in the city.

We understand the arts as fundamental modes by which cities understand, renegotiate, and remake themselves. From addressing these three sites, we are acutely aware that while arts and city stakeholders are fundamentally engaged in thinking through the city by testing ideas and practices of life in the city, the arts are not necessarily seen as *(re)making* the city. Nor is the potential for the arts to remake the city, to re-create the city in a single event or through multiple activities, being recognized, theorized, or contributing to resilience planning in the city. This is a missed opportunity in resilience planning, both in the particular context of New Orleans but also more broadly in cities elsewhere. The intention of our work is to highlight the potency of performance to resilience thinking. Additionally, we argue for a more nuanced look at what engagement with a city's resilience challenges might offer artists both as potential topics of focus and in terms of articulating the importance of their practice in relation to a city's pressing plural concerns. This approach offers significant potential to the future of the city by helping to recalibrate understandings of the usefulness of "the arts" to resilience professionals and of "resilience" to arts thinking and practice. That is, we are modeling the arts, and performance in particular, as central to nuanced understandings of a city's identity and to thinking through a city's specific resilience challenges.

For Nicolas Whybrow "cities are *made* by human beings" in interaction with objects, spaces, places, and each other.[42] Meanwhile, Amanda Rogers argues that "performance is integral to infrastructural geographies of the city . . . [and can] offer a way to conceptualise the city."[43] As our study of these situation rooms demonstrates, this conceptualization is not just confined to interrogations that performances might make of a geopolitical context through aesthetic practices. It also includes the ways in which performance practices embed themselves in the *operation* of the city. This is evident in the deployment of performance techniques as central to the very running of the city in preparation for and in the midst of crises or city-scale public events. The centrality and usefulness of performance can also be illuminated through the ways in which particular venues might accidentally or deliberately call attention to environmental challenges by bringing people to a place in the city previously abandoned or maligned as an edgeland. Equally, by approaching resilience challenges through performance, we can consider the ways in which architectural decisions are made in appropriating a building to speak to the communities that surround them, offering an invitation to use the building as gathering place, performance venue, impromptu workspace, or simply a place to people watch.

In thinking about these sites in this way, our intention is to help articulate and make clear that performance, as a critical practice and mode of analysis, can help cities realize what Rodin calls "the resilience dividend," the capacity for a plural approach to resilience to bring "benefits that are sometimes beyond what you can imagine." This enables faster recovery from crises *and* brings economic and sociopolitical benefits "when things are going right as well as when they go wrong."[44] This call for plural approaches to resilience suggests that the arts can be key to imagining the future of cities through the development of more nuanced and diverse situational awareness, so that they operate with a resilience dividend. However, the arts and arts venues have not yet been seriously considered in this context. In each of the case studies presented here, the situation room operates as means through which New Orleans is understood, renegotiated, and remade in some way. In calling for these spaces to be considered situation rooms, we are recognizing that each one looks out from its location to the local area and surroundings, be that by dint of its formal function or according to the stated strategic and artistic aims of the organization. Each offers a vantage point from and on the city that enables individuals and communities, city stakeholders and private citizens, to ask critical questions of the city and about the shocks and stresses it faces. These sites use performance as a key mode of intelligence gathering, reflection, and communication, facilitating opportunities to develop and refine means of response to multiple and at time overlapping, intersecting city challenges.

4

LIVING WITH WATER

Walking the Industrial Canal

It is March 2018, just before eight in the evening, almost sunset. We had been watching a dance performance at the Music Box Village. As we leave the venue and walk out through the car park, we see a few vehicles and a dumpster with the words YOU GO GIRL emblazoned upon it, bikes chained to a fence, the curve of a rail line, flanked by telegraph poles.[1] Farther on, we take in the long, low, grass-covered bank of the Inner Harbor Navigation Canal, more commonly known as the Industrial Canal, which connects the Mississippi River both to Lake Pontchartrain and out to the Gulf. We stand there for a while, settling back into the world after the performance. We become aware of the sun slowly dropping in the sky, and we turn and climb the slope of the canal bank.

From the top of the bank, we look down to the water only a little way below us, in stark contrast to the longer, lower slope that we climbed to get here. The canal bank is not busy, but there are others around us. We notice a family carefully allowing a small child to take a few well-managed steps on the bank. We might be at a park but for the scale of the water here and the bright, insistent lights across the canal across from us. The last of the daylight is fading; we are struck by how close we are to deep water, and we retrace our steps. Later, when we revisit this walk on a map, we become aware of the many roads that stop at one side of the canal and begin again on the other. The canal brings deep water, and deepwater traffic, to an area of the city otherwise comprising streets, businesses, houses, and gardens. This is not without risk, and the canal funneled water into the city with devastating effects after Hurricane Katrina in 2005 and, before that, Hurricane Betsy in 1965. This structure, which was intended to separate people from water, ultimately failed to do so on critical occasions. These failures contribute to long-standing established questions of the security of infrastructure in separating people from water, both in New Orleans and beyond.

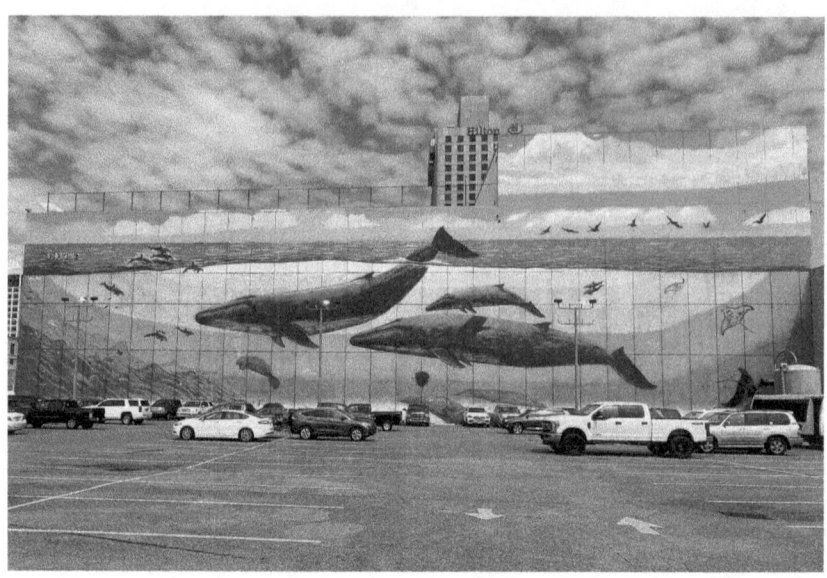

Robert Wyland's *The Blues Whales* mural on external wall of Hilton Hotel, 2022.

There is growing international interest in the ways in which we live with water in a changing world. In this context, the term *living with water* has become familiar in water management strategies and, particularly, for engaging communities in local water challenges, especially flooding. Here, we identify ways in which performance studies can reveal the significance of artistic and everyday practices of living with water. All too often, such artistic approaches do not sit within the familiar literature and practice of water management. In this chapter we identify novel ways in which three different arts projects contribute to emerging approaches to living with water. We focus our analysis on projects that address understandings, experiences, and practices of water in New Orleans, obliquely or directly. *Rising Tables* (2017) was an installation on the East Bank of the Mississippi, which was progressively washed away by the water. *Cry You One* (2013) was a walking performance in St. Bernard Parish, in Greater New Orleans, which reflected on the relation of water and land in the city, the region, and on the coast. The *Float Lab* (2022–) comprises a floating structure that can be employed as performance space on land or water; this experimental project responds to and enables reflection on rising sea levels in the region.

While each artwork was performed in Greater New Orleans or the metropolitan area, each looked beyond the "city," situating and conceiving of New

Orleans in terms of the state, region, and Delta. In all cases, the works offered new perspectives on the city and its wider relationship to the region. In addressing these artworks, we identify the ways in which artistic practices can enrich, rethink, and refine our knowledge of practices of living with water, both in New Orleans and in cities internationally that face water resilience challenges.

Managing Water

There is established academic research on issues of water management. In the United Kingdom, performance theorist Stephen Scott-Bottoms has long argued for performance as a critical means by which communities can make sense of water.[2] With landscape planner Maggie Roe, he has identified the importance of water as "a defining factor in the functioning and character of local environments and cultures." Scott-Bottoms and Roe explore increasing interest in community engagement in water management, through the creation of a "hydro-citizens" model. Here methodologies from performance were deployed to create a "generative, cyclical flow between private conversations, such as [specific] stakeholder meetings, and public creative outcomes." These "communities of practice" were central to the development of "site-specific performance presentations" that "engage[d] audiences with issues connecting the water environment, community and citizenship."[3]

Our sense from our own engagement with artists and with Hazard Mitigation staff in New Orleans, is that there is significant value in working with performance as a means of understanding and rethinking emergency management practices to address water. Indeed, while we have focused particularly on New Orleans, we have also done some exploratory work with arts and environment colleagues in Albuquerque to address the ways that arts practice can rethink issues of water scarcity. Eileen Julien has argued that arts and cultural production practices are a crucial means "to mediate and interpret diverse aspects of the urban experience *of others*."[4] At the same time, the United Nations has identified that "indigenous communities are key sources of knowledge and understanding on climate change impacts, responses and adaptation . . . [and] bear the brunt of both the impact and solutions to the most defining challenge of our time."[5] Taken together, these positions point to the critical importance of valuing diverse perspectives and, especially, the knowledge of communities for whom living with processes of environmental adaptation have been a way of life for many generations. In reflecting on specific arts projects here, we seek to show the kinds of questions and considerations that arts practice can contribute to water management in urban environments and their immediate geographic contexts.

There is both academic and professional interest in managing water challenges in cities, which can impose pressures, both in terms of hard infrastructure and the lived experience of a city. Water management can take varying forms that are particularly related to the local context. In New Orleans, issues include stormwater, risks of the Mississippi breaching the levees, the drying and shrinking of the land behind the levees, salt water flowing into the city's water systems, and the impact of coastal erosion on hurricane strength—to say nothing of the consequences of such erosion on coastal and low-lying communities. Necessarily, these issues intersect.

For Richard Campanella, water is "intrinsic" to New Orleans. The city, he reminds us, sits "entirely upon an idiosyncratic land form known as a fluvial delta." As he notes, the growth of the city involved acts of "reclamation, . . . subsurface drainage and artificial fill." As Campanella observes, the draining of the land resulted in the land dropping below sea level. Campanella identifies this as "the paradox of New Orleans: that the very water-manipulating devices needed to make this city prosper would also render it precarious." He has identified the acute public concern about contemporary challenges posed by drainage, specifically the "potholed streets and persistent floods." As he looks to the future, Campanella proposes that we rethink this practice of drainage that has been so fundamental to the city: "If water in New Orleans is truly a condition and not an abnormality, then assumptions underlying the city's centuries-long dewatering need to be reexamined—starting with the very notion of *dewatering*." Campanella identifies a clear opportunity to rethink long-established strategies of managing water in the city. He reads this particularly from the work of the cross-disciplinary design practice Waggonner and Ball, which has worked on a series of projects in the city, in part through a model of "Dutch Dialogues," which involved conversation with colleagues in water management in the Netherlands.[6] We are struck by the potential of transforming the ways in which New Orleans understands and manages water, and, indeed, the ways in which such practices might be productively shared internationally.

At a time of climate change, there is a pressing need to rethink ways of living with water. We are drawn to the importance of artistic and cultural practices of water in the city, as critical means of addressing local understandings of water challenges, principally flooding. There is increasing interest in the ways in which the arts and humanities can speak to the uncertain times in which we live and which may become increasingly more acute. For Jukka Mikkonen, a philosopher focusing on environmental aesthetics, "a growing number of artists and art scholars have proposed that art could help us in our encounter with climate change and adopting [sic] to [the] future. After all, science has told us what it knows; exploring the experiential and affective dimensions of climate change—what it will be like to be a human being in a radically different world—has been delegated for art and humanities."[7]

For Mikkonen, arts practice offers powerful means of imagining a changed environment in the future. While Mikkonen recognizes the value of arts and humanities in addressing critical questions, we are interested in going further here. There is also potential for artists, and arts scholars, to discover and share the potential to begin an alternative set of conversations with science and resilience management that extend beyond the experiential and affective. These would address structural opportunities and needs in the present. Our conversations with colleagues in resilience management to date suggest this is a timely, vital opportunity.

Performing Water

Perhaps unsurprisingly, artists in New Orleans have done considerable work to explore the relationship between water and land. New Orleans Airlift, which formed in 2009 and which owns, developed, and curates work at Music Box Village, has long explored understandings and practices of water in and outside the city. In 2017 Airlift staged *New Water Music*, a free, open-air, public performance on Lake Pontchartrain, with audiences gathered along the bank of the lake. The event echoed the first performance of Handel's *Water Music* (1717) on the River Thames, in London, with spectators on the shore and in boats on the water. *New Water Music* was composed by Yotam Haber, performed by the Louisiana Philharmonic Orchestra and volunteer musicians and directed and produced by New Orleans Airlift. Contributors included local fishermen, who performed "a shrimp boat ballet"; coastal advocacy organizations; fish fryers; and speakers from the Houma Nation and the Point-au-Chien tribe. This collaboration of different voices, cultures, and practices of living with water offered a complex examination of the city's relationship to water—at once a life source through food production, a place for recreation, and a source of fresh water.

The performance also raised difficult questions about climate change and the challenge water poses to ways of life in New Orleans and surrounding areas.

Film projects allow artists to reveal the condition and practices of the Mississippi River and the changing coastline of Southeast Louisiana. In *Eternal Flow: Mississippi River Views from Louisiana* Kevin McCaffrey, a New Orleans filmmaker, identifies a series of discrete but intersecting perspectives on the river that passes through the city and which gives New Orleans its "Crescent City" moniker. The film is a reflection on the river and also a document that reveals contemporary processes of river management and perspectives from those who work on, live with, and study the river. The film, which is available online, can be watched as a single project or in separate sections, allowing viewers to find their own way through the work.[8] McCaffrey's project resists offering a neatly secured, singular reading of the river. His work points to the extraordinary body of water that passes through the city and the ways in which this river intersects with the delta. The film draws close attention to the practices by which the river is held at bay, in ways that limit the movement of the river through the delta. While films can reveal contemporary readings of water in the city, they also provide situated readings of water at particular moments in time. In *Trouble the Water* Kimberley Rivers Roberts reflects on her experience of Katrina, from her position living in the Lower Ninth Ward. The growing archive of films on water in the city, especially those in which filmmakers in the city reflect on their situated understandings of it, chart and record local readings of water in ways that are less easily documented in live events. Individually, these films and live projects reveal considerable creative and critical labor in reading a situation at a particular time. Together—and alongside the many other works on water in the city—these projects present an archive that thinks and rethinks water in the city. With increasing attention being spent on finding new ways to live with water, it becomes problematic not to turn to this archive for perspectives, practices, and perhaps answers.

Aside from individual artworks, a number of sites for making and sharing work are located on or close to the water. A Studio in the Woods is part of the ByWater Institute at Tulane University. It comprises an area of almost eight acres of bottomland hardwood forest in Lower Coast Algiers, close to a levee and the Mississippi. It was once native land and subsequently a sugar plantation, with the challenging history of slavery this entails. The contemporary site is used for residencies by artists and Tulane scholars, and it provides a critical site for residents to find new perspectives on art and environment. Farther along the river, on the opposite bank, Crevasse 22 | River House is a sculpture garden and site for arts events. Beyond venues, the Prospect Art Triennial, which developed after Katrina, often includes a series of temporary or more permanent artworks being installed across the city, at times placed in or on—and thereby in dialogue with—the Mississippi.

Through performance, artists in the city, whether inhabitants or visitors, find ways of making meaning of water and land here. Too often, the knowledge from arts practice remains in the work and in the minds and bodies of those who made or attended or discovered the work afterward. Too often, internationally, artists' creative ideas, strategies, and practices that address life with water and land are not part of strategic conversations on the ways in which a city or geographical area develops management plans. In our own work in the city, we have found a particular passion for developing precisely these connections, both in the city and as a model for water management beyond New Orleans.

Alongside arts practice, new and hybrid approaches to water have developed in the city, as part of an international shift away from hard infrastructure to recognize individuals and communities in future planning and preparedness, which is particularly evident in practices of community codesign. In some cases, this work engages creative practitioners at points in a project's development and/or completion. The St. Anthony Green Streets Project in Gentilly District involved redesigning and retrofitting green infrastructure into an area of approximately ten blocks. While this was a major infrastructure project, the work also involved creative practices in its public opening, specifically a lantern walk, public artworks, and events. In part, the arts practice invited public consultation, although the work also provided means of inviting residents to relocate themselves in the altered local context. Residents received hand-delivered packages with details of arts events, artists' cards, and activities, to invite engagement with "the themes of water, ecology, resilience, and neighborhood history."[9] This project deploys arts practice in a particularly resilience-focused way that is perhaps further from our primary focus in this book. Nevertheless, such fusing of creative practice and hard infrastructure development is indicative of the symbiotic roles arts and resilience practices can play in a place. The work was part of the Gentilly Resilience District (GRD), a series of initiatives to develop "a national model" for a resilience district. The GRD recognizes arts practice as a critical element of the work, including storytelling sessions on "climate change, resilience, and the history and culture of Gentilly."[10]

In other cases, arts practice is not directly involved in projects or the work of organizations, but there is a commitment to renegotiating the position of individuals in urban water management, and such work can be read to operate performatively to transform understandings of place. This is particularly critical in the context of people and communities who have conventionally not been centered in such work. Notably, Imagine Water Works develops multidisciplinary approaches to "climate justice, land stewardship, and disaster readiness and response." The organization works to "hold space for conversation," particularly for communities who are "too often pushed out," and also to develop hazard mitigation plans for the city and nation."[11] Relatedly, the Water Leaders Institute provides training and support for city residents to develop and grow community initiatives. While the work is not directly engaged in arts practice, the project does collaborate on arts-engaged activities. Civic Studio, a cross-sector planning cooperative, collaborates with Blue House on *Mixed Media,* which addresses critical issues through multidisciplinary civic dialogue. The development of the Lafitte Greenway is a linear park and site for water management, imagined and now programmed and promoted by the Friends of Lafitte Greenway, a nonprofit and formal partner with the city. Just outside the city, at Docville Farm, in Violet, the Meraux Foundation runs projects that are intended to "improve the quality of life in St. Bernard," many of which focus on coastal management and restoration. In each instance outlined here, there is a commitment to engage local people in developing local innovations in existing contexts, resisting top-down approaches.

Beyond arts and organizational practices, other, more everyday performances negotiate land and water in the city, particularly when areas of the city flood. At a workshop in 2019, we were told of an evening when parts of the city flooded and so motorists, rather than get stranded in the water, pulled up on the neutral ground between carriageways of a road to wait for the water to recede. Those fortunate to be near a particular bar constituted an informal gathering of impromptu patrons, and so the bar took orders and began floating drinks across the flooded land in chest coolers. A performance of hospitality, of living with water: an everyday performance of resilience. Areas of the city do flood, requiring certain actions in the moment to take shelter, to find a way through or around. It is trite to say that New Orleanians make the best of floods, for what else is there to be done in the moment? And it is worse, as has been said too much, to applaud the resilience of the population (particularly when the population in question is Black) rather than fix the problems.

From situating arts practice, and our analysis, in the context of a series of existing and related ideas, practices, and projects in the city, we now move to look at specific projects. *Rising Tables, Cry You One,* and the *Float Lab* are examples of ongoing artistic and performance engagement in the environment. Taken together, and in the context of established reimagining of water in the city, we identify ways in which the works reveal continuing locally situated engagement in the climate emergency and demonstrate the significance of local bodies of knowledge and practice in response to the global challenge of flooding.

Rising Tables

Walking through Crescent Park in April 2018, we happen upon an installation on the batture, the space between the Mississippi River and its levees. Stacked high upon one another in decreasing size, from a large, robust-looking dining table to a small, single-stemmed circular side table, the installation comprises a series of domestic tables rising uncannily from the fast-flowing waters of the river. When we encounter the work, only one of the original three towers remains, the others washed away by the force of the river in the intervening period from their installation.

At this time of year, spring, the batture is part of the river, submerged beneath water that has swollen the Mississippi as a result of melting snow and ice far upriver. *Rising Tables* (2017), by Jennifer Odem, was part of Prospect.4, the fourth iteration of the international contemporary Prospect Art Triennial, New Orleans. Originally intended as a biennial and developed in response to the events of Katrina, Prospect is a citywide event that has now become a significant feature of the arts ecosystem of New Orleans, with growing international reputation and reach.

At first glance, the installation might have been constructed as a playful act of reclamation, picking flotsam from the river and playing a grown-up game of block stacking. At the same time, the towering tables offer more complex readings of life in the city and the potential challenges of living on the edge of the mighty Mississippi. As Odem reflects: "We share this place with the river . . . We know who's in charge."[12] The sculptural installation consisted of three towers of six or seven tables each, reaching some forty feet above sea level once installed into the original pilings of an old river wharf in what is now Crescent Park. Situated on the batture, it was always intended that the work

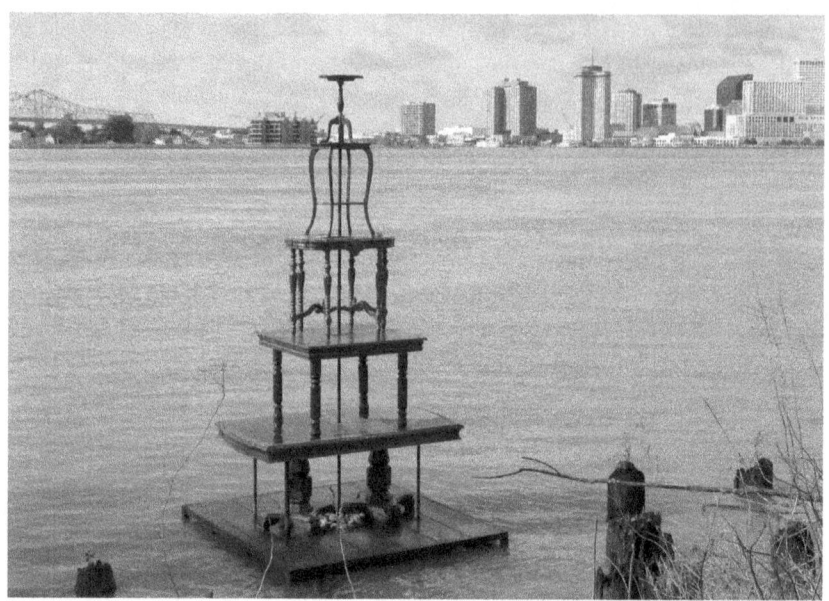

Photograph of the situated artwork *Rising Tables* (2017), by Jennifer Odem, 2018.

would engage physically with the rising levels of the river, the wake of the boats passing, and the force of floating debris caught in the flow, though it was not intended that towers be destroyed by this process. Opening in November 2017, Odem tracked the life of the artwork through the seasons and changing waters through photographs, regular visits to the installation site, and field note observations (all documented in the book of the project). What is interesting in having both observed the last structure in situ and exploring the book, and wider online documentation, is the ways in which the work can be read as a complex engagement with the water over the time of the installation, and its partial destruction, and a marker of place over time, a means of contextualizing and reflecting on the challenge of living with water in this city.

One crucial aspect of the work is its reflection on domesticity. In using domestic-scale tables, some grander than others, from different historic periods but all bought, donated, or gathered from within the city, *Rising Tables* operates to index that people live here. While this may not be a terribly complex reading of the semiotics of the piece, it is an important one: in a city so often exceptionalized, there is profound political significance in reminding people—especially tourists, who may be assumed to be in the audience of Prospect.4—that the city is also a domestic space, just like other cities globally. At a simple level, then, *Rising Tables* makes apparent the everyday reality of the city as a city at the edge of the Mississippi River, a place of homes and their residents.

Of course, the work is more complex than this too. In being site specific, the work operates also to track the rising and falling levels of the Mississippi River over the lifespan of the installation. In so doing, *Rising Tables* engages physically with the force and power of the river over an extended period of time. Beyond acting as a grand water gauge, of sorts, during the period of the installation, two of the table stacks were swept away by the river. A passing tanker, during a period of particularly high waters, caused a powerful wake carrying debris and heavy water flow through the installation. Never intended to be destroyed, the washing away might be read as performatively echoing the devastation caused to homes, businesses, and lives in the aftermath of Hurricane Katrina and other flooding events in the city.

Meanwhile, designed in part to reflect the process of stacking one's possessions on tables and furniture to raise them above the reach of floodwaters, the work, for Odem, "implies a rudimentary way to reach a higher place—in this case, simply above water."[13] The work performs an act of protection against the possible incursion of water; it stages the hope that some objects will survive. The act of stacking tables has been removed from any single home and further defamiliarized by being located in a park, which offers at least a partial framing of the work as public art. For the anthropologist Ian Hodder, "Things are inter-dependent."[14] In reflecting on Hodder's work in terms of artists who in varying ways "perform" home, Andrews writes that, the "ways in which artists reconfigure the connections between material objects in and of a place may reveal much about the ways in which they understand interdependencies between place, objects and people."[15] In *Rising Tables* Odem interrupts familiar interdependencies, speaking obliquely to preparations before a flood. While Odem might not have intended the work to be claimed by the river, and while it makes the work a more challenging project, *Rising Tables* also asks that we recognize that despite our protections, some things are lost. In terms of resilience, the washing away of the tables and the destruction of the towers performatively echoes New Orleans's relationship with water and with the Mississippi. *Rising Tables* acts as a means through which those who encounter the work over time can reflect upon the challenge of living in this place as it might be (re)claimed by the water.

As Odem recalls, the installation became something of a space for reflection, contemplation, and memorialization. For Odem the work not only speaks to her own histories of living with and around the Mississippi River but was also a mechanism through which others could reflect on theirs: "Throughout its course, I was greeted with stories, gifts, artworks, advice, critiques, and offerings almost daily." For instance, shortly after the piece's opening, Odem discovered offerings left on and around the sculptures; letters, wreaths, stacked stone sculptures, were left on an almost daily basis.[16] In inviting spectators to gather at the site to encounter the traces of individual interactions, *Rising Tables* activates deliberate contemplation of the relationship between land and water, Crescent Park and batture. This operates in a model akin to Robin Bernstein's concept of "scriptive things," in which "things [objects] prompt, structure, or choreograph behavior."[17] Yet where Bernstein theorizes the way in which individual objects, like a knife or a camera, create "repetitions of acts," this work prompted personal, emotional, and reflective responses, rather than repetitious movement. Touchingly, after the installation officially closed, Odem was preparing to take the last sculpture down but encountered someone standing almost at the top of the tower scattering the ashes of a loved one as a small funeral ceremony unfolded. *Rising Tables* operated to reflect the complex situation of the city and its, and its residents', relation to water.

Cry You One

Where *Rising Tables* was an installation that sat in position for a time, we turn now to a performance that investigates the relation of New Orleans to the water that surrounds it, not only the Mississippi. *Cry You One* (2013) was an "outdoor performance that journeys into the heart of our disappearing wetlands."[18] Alongside the performance itself, an online archive was developed to document elements of the performance and house video recordings of stories from people in southeastern Louisiana.[19] *Cry You One* was developed by Mondo Bizarro and ArtSpot Productions, two established theater ensembles in New Orleans, and directed by ArtSpot's Kathy Randels.[20]

During the live performance, audiences gathered to walk an area of St. Bernard Parish, in Greater New Orleans, and reflected on the land on which they walked, the disappearing coast, and the proximity of land loss to the city. The performance included varying forms, particularly music, song, and dance, with audiences being encouraged to participate in the event, which was framed as an act of farewell to the coast.[21]

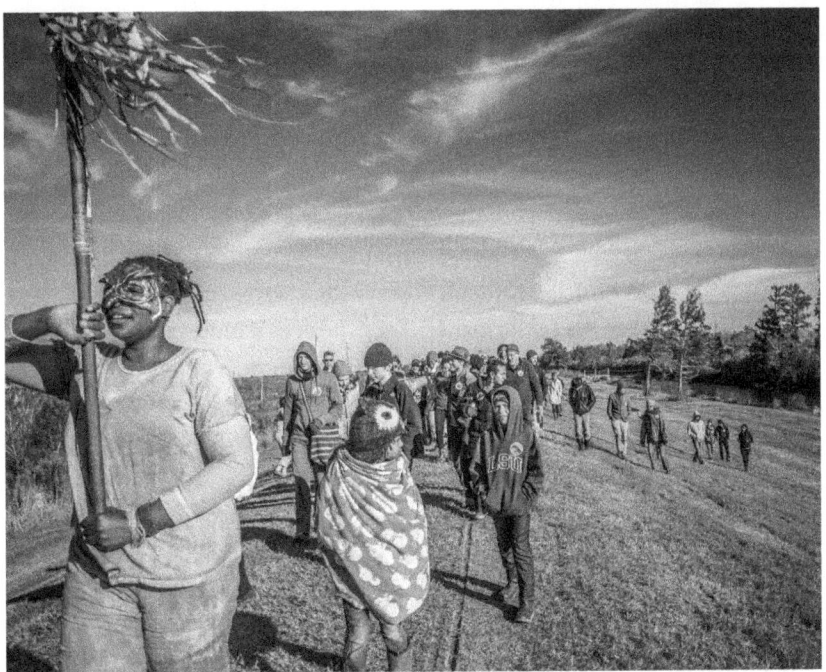

Performance image from *Cry You One*, 2013. Photo by Melisa Cardona.

Walking the Wetlands

Three performers, one woman and two men, each holding a fiddle, climb a slope of grass. They are dressed in clothes that have each been dyed the same shade of blue-green and marked with patches of yellow, green, and black. The performers each wear half-masks that suggest animals, but each mask resists easy definition. The woman's mask has yellow-and-black stripes, appearing feline. The masks of the two men have piglike snouts and sharply pointed ears, one at least has a row of what may have been painted upper teeth that sit above the man's mouth.

It is ten years after *Cry You One* (2013). We are watching *Work Sample—St. Bernard,* a video showing sections of the live performance, very much wishing we had seen the live event. The performance was situated over two and a half miles in the Central Wetlands in St. Bernard Parish, to the east of the New Orleans Metropolitan Area.[22] One of the men begins speaking, while the other two performers take up their fiddles, one playing with a bow, the other plucking the strings. The man who is speaking holds his bow aloft and waves and gesticulates with it to mark and accentuate his words, as if both conducting and accusing: "This marsh extends all the way to the back door of New Orleans. Bayou bienvenue-welcome. I wonder if they knew they'd have the Gulf washing up on their back porches. A few years ago they forced the 'Corps' to rock the mouth with gravel, but the salt snakes in. And the marsh erodes, and every year it gets wilder and wider."[23]

From the short film, it is difficult to place these speakers; they have slipped any broader frame of the performance. They speak as if removed from familiar notions of time, reflecting on the changing form of the land and the increasing impact of the Gulf Coast on the city. Perhaps these are creatures from this place, speaking back to the makers and inhabitants of the city, who have so changed this place. Yet while appearing removed from time, they also speak of practicalities, of front porches, of the Army Corps of Engineers. The work draws together the scale of a changing landscape and the practice of people here. At the same time, it draws together the practice of the city and the practice of the parish. The draining of New Orleans and the management of water in the city does not simply impact the city, but it alters the region.

The performers climb the bank slowly, swaying and taking steps in ways that echo their masks. As they climb, they approach both the camera and, as becomes clear, the loose line of spectators sitting along the bank. While the performers climb, the musicians play and repeat what might be the beginnings of a folk song. Around them the grass and shrubs through which the performers walk are shades of green, although there are also signs of dead grasses. Farther behind them, the green of the marsh is marked by the gray, dead trunks of trees.

As Mikkonen identifies, the arts and humanities are practices engaged in thinking through future scenarios. In *Cry You One*, albeit twelve years past, three performers were revealing, or certainly pointing to, a changed environment in what was then the present. The work invited audiences to look at the land that stretched to the city, imagining the waters of the Gulf finding their way across this land. The passage of water here is not neat. In 1935 large areas of the parish were flooded out of fear that the Labor Day hurricane might threaten New Orleans. In this moment, the verdant land and the stark dead trunks of trees speak of the impact of water on land.

While the arts and humanities may bring powerful perspectives to understandings of life through climate change, this is challenging work. In the case of

Cry You One, Rebecca Mwase, a theater maker in the city, has written on the difficulties she experienced as one of few women of color performing in the work: "Since *Cry You One* began in 2012, our ensemble has struggled with how to accurately tell the story of Southeast Louisiana. We are a predominantly white group, roughly half native Louisianians and all city dwellers. Our relationship to land deepened significantly through spending time out in the central wetlands, running, rehearsing, and creating this piece." Mwase identifies a similar kind of process in the experience of those who find themselves outside dominant narratives, modes, and roles. For Mwase: "This is what we who are artists, immigrants, activists, organizers and indigenous folk continue to find ourselves up against, struggling so hard to prove we belong that we can't find a way to see how our ways of belonging can complement and sustain us together."[24]

There may be power and opportunity in *Cry You One* to resituate ourselves in response to climate change, and this power and opportunity may continue by way of traces of the performance that continue into the present. Yet Mwase reflects that the process of making the performance was a challenge and that it raised issues of race politics and familiarity with city and coast. As Mwase reports, many members of Mondo Bizarro and ArtSpot lived in the city. In recognizing the contribution of *Cry You One*, we necessarily need to recognize the labor of those who made this work, who addressed unsettling issues and questions. The work of *Cry You One* was to rethink practices through which we attend to land loss; such processes of performance making about climate change are fundamental to the emergence of new knowledge and new practices. As such, artists working on the frontlines of climate change will, inevitably, deal with the multiple, layered injustices that are brought into sharp relief by the causes and effects of climate change.

Farewell

A man stands on the back of a truck. Nick Slie, codirector of Mondo Bizarro. We know him from our very first visit to the city, when we first spoke of this work. He wears bright-white overalls and a baseball cap, and he holds a microphone in one hand. We have joined the middle of a scene, and Slie is inviting the audience, gathered in a horseshoe around the truck, to find a partner, raise and hold their hands. There is laughter, at one point nervously and then more knowing when Slie recognizes some participants might be holding go-cups, the New Orleanian term for a take-out drink, most often an alcoholic drink.

When Slie determines everyone is in place, he continues: "Now, some of you mightn't remember this. This right here is what sets us apart here in Louisiana from everybody else, because we know how to say goodbye yeah, it goes like a-, a-one, a-two, three, a-one, two, three."[25]

To Slie's left, a woman—also wearing white overalls—lifts the violin she has been holding; the driver's door of the truck opens, and a man steps out with a guitar. The musicians begin, and we are in a dance, the camera in the midst of performers and spectators. "That's right. You know how to do it, hold them close."[26] As Slie speaks, the audience stands out of the shot, and it is not quite clear if Slie is noticing that these people *do* know how to dance this farewell or if he is in fact revealing to each of them how they do in fact know the way to do this dance. The argument of the performance becomes clear here: of course the participants remember; of course they recognize that local cultural practices can help address this moment. The image cuts away to other moments in the performance, although the music continues, running on over these other scenes. It seems appropriate that we are dealing in fragments here, moments from a past place and time. This is a work that speaks—sings even—of loss of the whole.

The loss of the wetlands has long been known and discussed in scholarly, professional, and public-facing contexts, not least in the Nova documentary *Goodbye Louisiana* (1982). Somehow we know all this, and yet it continues. Writing on theater, performance, and climate change, Lisa Woynarski reflects that theater and performance offer "moments of resonance, reflection, thoughtfulness, pleasure, fear and anger."[27] We recognize such a multiplicity of sensations and perspectives in *Cry You One*. This is not a singular work but, rather, a set of layered forms and practices. It is a site-specific performance, a national tour, a web archive, a CD, a project shared in presentation and conversation. As Slie reflects in one such talk on the project, the live performance itself is "part theatrical eco-tour, part song, part poetry, part story, and always featuring the land where we are." This multiplicity becomes important in the context of dealing with a crisis, for it resists easy routes to a conclusion. It offers means of attending to the multiple dimensions of a loss. For Slie: "We believe that the way we engage this disappearance [*sic*] says a lot about who we are as a people. And, who we are, as a people, in Louisiana is that, for centuries, we've used joy and vulnerability and a lot of celebration to deal with our loss."[28] In speaking to ideas of joy and celebration as means to address loss, Slie positions the performance in relation to the idea of a jazz funeral: "We were thinking of doing a jazz funeral for the land . . . We wanted some sort of processional."[29]

Yet, fellow performer Monique Verdin reflected, this was not a funeral. As Rachel Lee notes, citing Verdin, while "there is an element of 'communal mourning', there will also be celebration and the generation of solutions. *Cry You One* is part parade and part nature walk, at the end of which the audience is 'brought into a collective visioning space.'"[30] While articulating slightly different readings of the work, both Slie and Verdin identify a sense of the performance as attending to grief, land loss, and the complexity of the climate emergency through communal embodied engagement with mourning and celebration, sorrow and joy. *Cry You One* drew together a series of approaches to land loss, recognizing the importance of farewell but resisting singular readings of this loss. In the context of rethinking resilience, by pointing to the creation or "generation of solutions," Verdin demonstrates the opportunity for performance to prepare actively to address an unfolding challenge. The performance constitutes an internationally important modeling of how communities might mourn productively and, as such, can be seen as an exemplar of the potential for performance to offer new means of responding to and new means of thinking through the climate emergency.

Float Lab

As with *Cry You One, Float Lab* (2022–) is a work of multiple parts. The lab consists of a low wooden platform, mounted on a welded metal catamaran structure. On water *Float Lab* lies low, the frame barely visible. The structure floats comfortably on the water, and there are large blue barrels at either end, over which the deck extends. The deck includes five sections: a rectangular middle and four additional panels that are hinged. On land these panels can be raised to create the walls of a "room," albeit without a roof. With its side panels raised up, it can be loaded onto a trailer and towed on land. The structure has been designed to be highly adaptable and to be used in varying configurations and for changing purposes.

Float Lab was developed by Monique Verdin with Jayeesha Dutta, the Delta Collective and Another Gulf Is Possible. It is intended as "part field station for community engagement, part performance venue, the Float Lab will serve as an activation site to bring our ancestral, cultural and physical knowledge of the wild, free-flowing past into the present."[31] *Float Lab* is part of *Invisible Rivers*, a collaboration between Mondo Bizarro and the Land Memory Bank, and is described as a combination of "music, theater and boat-building."[32] We know

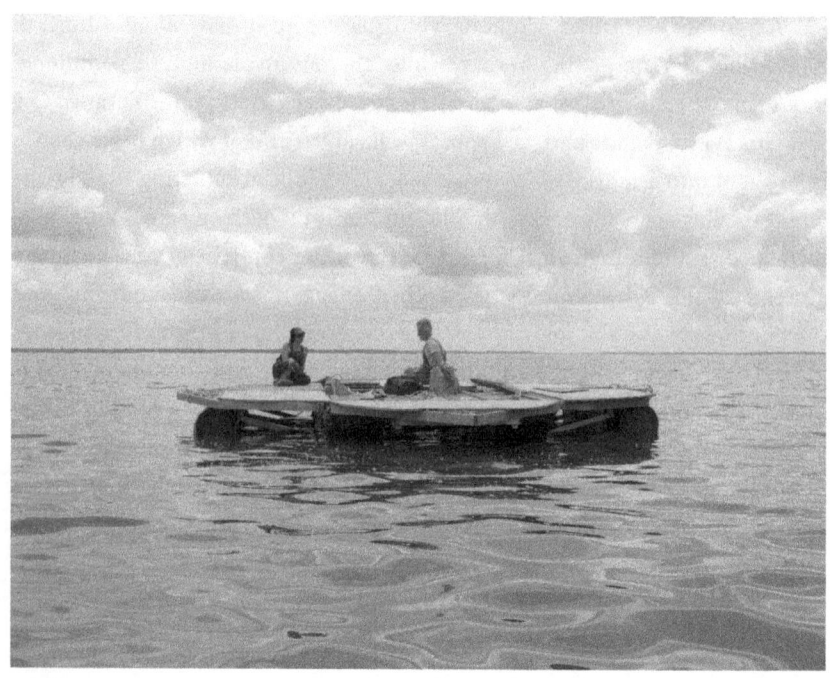

Project image from *Invisible Rivers*, 2021. Photo by Nick Slie.

of *Float Lab* through images and texts, although we have not seen the structure itself. Yet we are aware that *Float Lab* is often known through representations, rather than always being installed in situ; it is often revealed in images when on water. As such, this is a work that is often experienced at a remove, from watching on the shore, in a gallery, or online. This, then, is a project in which the form of the "work" shifts and adapts according to particular contexts and situations. This productively unsettles any sense that the work is ever final or finished; its form and process is as important as the "product" of the piece itself.

Boatbuilding

The beginnings of *Float Lab* are evident in an image in Verdin's exhibition and book, *Return to Yakni Chitto*.[33] In the Mobilian Trade Language, an Indigenous language, *Yakni Chitto* means "Big Country." Among the black-and-white images of the book, there is one taken in a workshop, where two men stand, smiling, between the two troughs that run the length of *Float Lab*. The image, from 2019, was taken in Bayou Pointe-aux-Chenes (Point of Oaks) in Terrebonne Parish, the name of which, as Verdin notes in her book, emerges from the French for "Good Land." In and beyond her arts practice, Verdin writes and speaks on the Houma. Her photography is both a creative practice and critical documentation of people, land, and loss. She describes the Houma's move to the bayous as a place of safety and, in the present, the need to move back in the face of the encroaching water. From this point of land loss, and until the need for relocation, she writes of the Houma, "We will continue to make our last stand on sinking land."[34]

For Verdin, *Float Lab* begins from a context of family. She explains: "In Terrebonne Parish, many of my cousins are welders who have worked in the oil field and at sugar mills while still carrying on the tradition of boat building. Our ancestors carved flat bottomed pirogue boats out of ancient cypress; now they have mastered the building of Lafitte Skiffs, a flat-bottomed fishing boat."[35] Verdin recognizes the dual skills of boatbuilding and industrial manufacture. By commissioning her cousin and his son to weld the structure of a boat, based on the pirogue boats, Verdin was bringing these practices together. This focus on the pirogue boat structure is important, as it reworks a design that is familiar but less widely used in the present. The effect is to repurpose the familiar to address changing times. In describing the project, Verdin frames this work as exploratory, a "lab" to test solutions, a transformative space enabling food sovereignty, a place of sharing and collecting. In the context of a pronounced pace of environmental change, the need to explore, to understand, and to be ready are key.

There is particular contemporary work on Indigenous practices of adaptation to climate change. Shanondora Billiot (Houma United Nation), Soonhyung Kwon, and Catherine Burnette report that tribal communities observe the challenges of passing on cultural knowledge in the context of "environmental changes through repeated disasters, chronic land loss, climate change, and pollution," together with "structural and persistent discrimination." They recognize that such changes can powerfully impact people's experience of place attachment, writing: "The transformation or loss of interaction with the environment is expressed as trauma for those whose traditions, memories, and resources are dependent on the environment."[36] In this context, travel by water, and the development of infrastructure that is appropriate to the specifics of a local context and to local communities, becomes compelling. Verdin's work reveals how local practices of making and sailing boats may help address the changes to place. Where journeys on land are replaced by journeys on water, there are opportunities to engage creatively in the form and infrastructure of those journeys, as part of a process of finding some agency amid a complex and long-standing context of land loss.

Alongside the significant impact on traditions, memories, and resources, there can also be very significant costs associated with adapting to climate change. These costs are not limited to communities in coastal Louisiana but are felt by Indigenous communities internationally. Kristen Green, Anne Beaudreau, Maija Lukin, and Larry Crowder document that fishing communities in Arctic Alaska have needed to purchase and sail boats to reach fishing grounds, where the loss of sea ice has restricted the use of snow machines. For Green and coauthors, the costs of this change can be prohibitive.[37] While this financial impact on individuals and communities may be substantial, Billiot, Kwon, and Burnette recognize that "the slow onset of global environmental changes limits funding for research and planning due to lack of sudden crisis."[38] Further, the costs and the time taken to implement adaptations may well severely restrict any opportunities for more exploratory or experimental practices. This poses a significant challenge given that the scale and pace of land loss has been extraordinary. In the context of this challenge, work such as Verdin's becomes all the more important, where practical investigations might open up critical opportunities to attend to local experiences, understandings, and attachments to place, particularly in the context of likely continuing effects.

Life on Water and Land

Despite the histories of boatbuilding practice that underpin the construction of *Float Lab*, this work is not identified as a "boat." The title of the piece speaks more of the activity of the work than the form of the structure, and it resists definition, perhaps because this would order expectations and understandings of what the work is and what it might do. If we begin from the proposition that this is a work premised on exploration, on asking questions, then we approach it in these terms, asking how it might enable investigation, where this investigation might unfold. Critically, by evading neat definition of form, *Float Lab* works on land and water.

For Verdin: "The Bayouside is everything for the Houma Nation. Our sense of sovereignty is tied to food security. We are just as much a water people as we are a land people."[39] To frame *Float Lab* in terms of water or land would undermine this core understanding of the Houma being people of water and land. As the water washes away land, as the salt water reaches farther into the wetlands, as the salt threatens the vegetation, so the bayou side is challenged, so new models of life on water and land are required. *Float Lab* is an artistic, performative attempt to investigate such new modes of living in this changing environment.

There is increasing interest in means of living between water and land and what this practice reveals about our identity and sense of self and place in the world. In terms of arts practice, the 2016 exhibition and catalog *Radical Seafaring* documented the ways in which artists were rethinking life on water and land, particularly through floating artworks that, as with *Float Lab,* resisted conventional forms.

While *Float Lab* speaks directly to life on the bayou side, representations of the lab have been very present in art spaces along the Mississippi (Studio in the Woods and Crevasse 22 | River House) and, recently, in an exhibit at the Contemporary Arts Center and outside the André Cailloux Center for a climate conference held by Mondo Bizarro in June 2023. These images bring the water and land of the wetlands and coast to the city and, necessarily, bring Indigenous understandings of place to the city. This is particularly critical as it carries with it Indigenous terms for the area that is New Orleans, principally, "Bulbancha."

Jeffery U. Darensbourg, a writer and researcher on Indigenous culture, writes that in the Choctaw language, *Bulbancha,* "the place of many languages," or "the place of many tongues," is the original name for this area. In bringing together people and places, *Float Lab* necessarily engages in the race and economic politics of past separation between land and water, urban spaces and bayous. Verdin's work values those who have too often been held apart from the center of thinking, planning, practices, and strategies. By drawing attention to Bulbancha, *Float Lab* wears away at the security of New Orleans, the predominant name by which many understand this place. Indeed, in *Bulbancha Is Still a Place,* Darensbourg identifies "Five Indigenous Names for This Lovely Place the Invaders Have Unsuccessfully Attempted to Rename 'New Orleans' (with Sources)."[40] As Imagine Water Works observes of its own work: "We honor the fact that people who have been pushed to the margins are the exact same people who know how to build a better future for themselves and their communities, even when the future feels uncertain."[41] In enacting connections between people and place, *Float Lab* honors those it draws together in journeys and in stops along the way. Whether on water or on land, *Float Lab* returns

Bulbancha to its place, albeit one that has been changed in substantial ways. At a time when the infrastructure of New Orleans is often regarded to be in such a parlous state, the return to reading the land as Bulbancha invites a critical conversation on the form and performance of this place.

In writing on the significance of art for the field of geography, Harriet Hawkins finds that art can "produce extensions in understandings and even possibly transformations of knowledge or subjects and of worlds." Rather than arguing for art's capacity to generate "expansive transformations," Hawkins finds that art "move[s] us in some way beyond, or outside of, the familiar and accepted horizons of our existing knowledge and practices."[42] Practically, *Float Lab* moves in and beyond familiar boundaries. It draws together water and land, coast and city, art and the everyday, art and climate emergency. In so doing, like *Rising Tables* and *Cry You One*, it invites those who encounter the work to move in conceptual ways, to shift thinking, to question the security of neat separations between water and land, the borders, boundaries, the three centuries of particular infrastructure agendas. In each of these arts projects, which rethink New Orleans in terms of its connection to the water, and thereby to the fragile wetlands and coast, we might well understand each one as contributing to paradigmatic change. This is most directly apparent in the work of *Float Lab* in contributing to understandings of New Orleans as Bulbancha. It is not only that the work remakes the city by its previous name, but it is evidence of the potential of arts practice to entirely remake the world.

We began this chapter reflecting on the infrastructure of the city, its impact on the land, its failings against the water. We end seeing the city in terms of the land on which it sits, the fluvial delta (described by Campanella). And we see the land and the water through the long and challenged practice of imposed order, wondering at what was lost through practices of drainage. The works here ask that we find new perspectives on the city, by asking searching questions about "looking back" at practices of the land that predate the city and looking forward to life in Bulbancha/New Orleans and surrounding areas in the context of climate change.

Without wishing to read the work reductively, *Cry You One* offers a model for attending to the losses of climate change, one that allows multiple points of engagement and reflection—even now, long years after the work first began.[43] And our contention is that the project of *Cry You One*, the expansiveness of the work—in terms of form and practice—is not over. The performance continues in our reflections here, in the impacts on those who made and who attended the work. On a visit in 2025, people still tell us about *Cry You One*, recognizing it as an important work in the recent history of performances in the city. What is critical is that this work was a chance for people in a place to find ways to enact a farewell, to take agency where so little agency for change was present, to find joy and celebration despite the need to mark a goodbye.

Float Lab revealed the ways in which Indigenous practices have focused more on adaptation than attempts at control. It reimagines Indigenous architecture as contemporary exhibition space and field station, as a flexible site to address climate challenges. *Float Lab* is a project grounded in family, in communities, in people, in practices of making that have been passed down through generations and passed on through embodied practice. Yet *Float Lab* is also about change, and, necessarily, it is in dialogue with forces of exclusion, specifically the writing out of Indigenous practices in contemporary understandings of Louisiana and in resilience practice more broadly. The work is small, a simple platform, yet it is also a complex, shifting work, designed to address life amid rising tides and to offer support when less mobile structures are threatened and lost.

Rising Tables is, similarly, an apparently simple work: tables placed upon tables and set in the water until they are no longer standing. And yet the work points to the fragility of domestic objects in the context of the Mississippi Delta. It recalls images and practices of piling up objects to survive a flood or for removal after a flood. It reveals tables that each emerge from a particular time period and which may impart connotations and worldviews from that period. *Rising Tables* offers an embodied encounter with objects that perform on the spectator in ways perhaps unpredictable in its design and construction. The piece calls people to account for and reflect on their lived experiences in this place and in living in similarly flood-threatened places. The project is both representationally about living with water and phenomenologically about encountering the water at a point marked for reflection and memory.

Through this work, and while we are only looking at three projects, we are struck by the ways in which these pieces sit together; several artists worked on each project, and the works reveal emerging local inquiries into and understandings of place and climate change. We wonder at the ways in which these growing, shifting debates might be captured, aware that documentation of arts practice is always flawed, always expensive, always difficult to manage in the tight limitations of arts projects. Yet to miss the work of artists remaking New Orleans, particularly as Bulbancha, is to miss acts that have international relevance as we struggle to hold onto and at times release the places that we love.

These three projects take us out of the city and back again. *Cry You One* was performed in St. Bernard Parish, outside the city limits, but fundamentally speaks to the city and its relation to the neighboring parishes and coastline. The work invites and enacts performances of farewell—powerfully, personally, politically. Often the loss of land is experienced by others, elsewhere, it is not made present in the here and now. *Cry You One* called attention to the here and now, marking the moment, lest it slip by. As Campanella finds, and as we argue here, the Greater New Orleans area is valuable when thinking of the geography of the land, for it reveals the situation of the city. These works bring this situation into being; they reflect upon it, from within and without. Indeed, in exploring the intersections of water and land, *Rising Tables, Cry You One,* and *Float Lab* ask that we rethink the "security" of separation between water and land in definitions of this city set on a delta.

5

PANDEMIC PERFORMANCES

Beyond Response and Recovery

"Post"-Pandemic New Orleans

It is Mardi Gras season, 2022. We're on the corner of Euterpe and St. Charles Avenue in Central City, wishing we'd brought folding chairs and a drinks cooler. Families sit on either side of St. Charles. As we wait for the parades to begin, children cycle along the street and chase one another on the neutral ground. Following restrictions on conventional parades in 2021, this is the first Mardi Gras in which floats once again roll down the streets. We value the delight, the joy, of being with others here, after so many challenging months of being apart. We are aware that some performers, police, and spectators are wearing pandemic face coverings, some that carefully match outfits. Many, us included, are not masked. Yet the pandemic is not over here: we wear masks when attending meetings, in taxis, and when entering, moving around in, and leaving restaurants. We hear someone check about mask mandates in a grocery store, and negotiations of "to mask or not to mask" are common public performances. In certain places, at certain times, practices of managing the pandemic remain clear.

Many artists in cities are engaged in addressing those cities, their communities, and challenges. They were, therefore, ideally placed to help understand and respond to the COVID-19 pandemic and face future crises. Performance offers a vital mode of making and researching arts practice in a city in order to understand how practitioners conceive of and respond to critical challenges. It can reveal innovative ways of practicing places, even during strict population controls, and be used to investigate both artistic and everyday practice and points where these intersect. When understood as "strategic interventions" in cities, such practices can be useful to the development of pandemic-focused emergency planning policy and strategy.

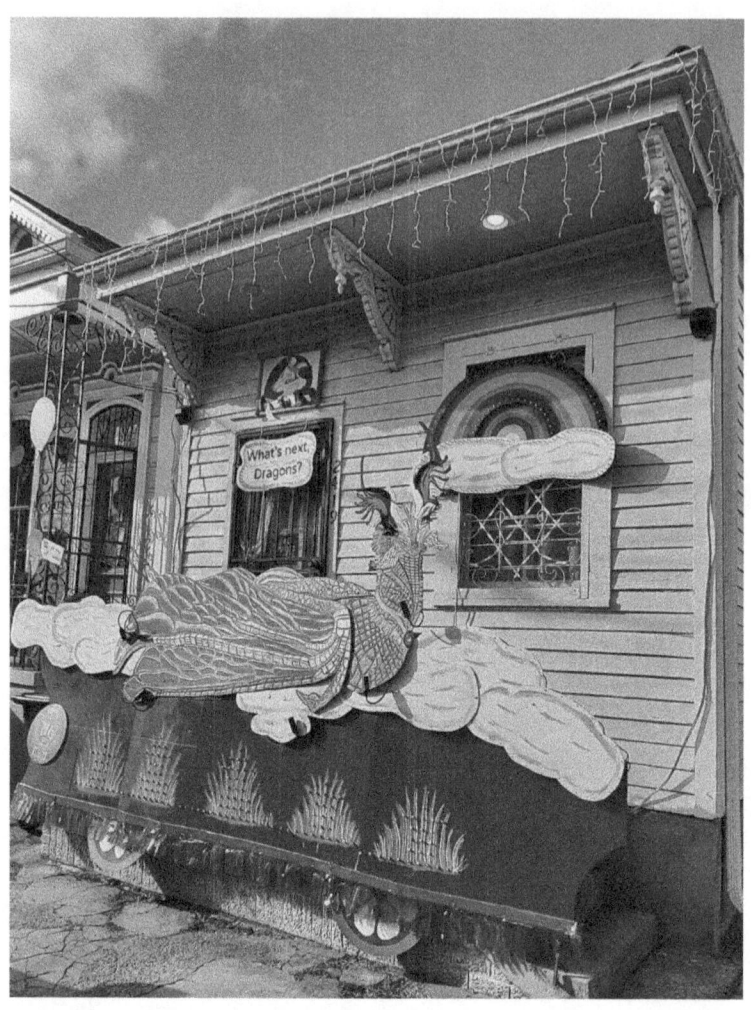

What Next, Dragons? house float in the Marigny, 2022.

In this chapter we are interested in the ways in which arts and culture organizations in New Orleans responded to the pandemic as it manifested in the city. We seek to understand ways we might productively read these interventions in the context of conventional practices of pandemic management. Internationally, the pandemic was addressed in the context of established practices and protocols of emergency management and the Disaster Risks Management Cycle (DRMC): Mitigation, Preparedness, Response, and Recovery.[1] Yet in reflecting on the pandemic, scholars in emergency management have identified that this cycle does not easily fit the pattern of a pandemic. The neat quartet of "mitigation, preparation, response, and recovery" is more suited to immediate emergencies, rather than ongoing and fluctuating conditions. In the context of the COVID-19 pandemic, we are particularly interested in the difficulties of defining response and recovery and determining the point at which a place is understood to have moved from acts premised on maintaining safety to something that resembles a return to everyday life.

The complexity of this transition, and the long-form slipperiness of these terms, was reflected back to us when we met artists and Indigenous leaders at the multi-arts and incubation space Catapult in June 2023.[2] At that point, we were quite some months after the pandemic was seen to have "ended" in New Orleans and almost a month to the day the World Health Organization (WHO) declared the pandemic over globally. Despite these seeming end points, as we reflected on our analyses from this chapter with artists and culture bearers, it was apparent that the pandemic (and its impact) will be far from "done" for many years.

Catapult: Voices across Arts and Culture

On the evening of Tuesday, 6 June 2023, we strolled from our apartment in the Warehouse District to Catapult on St. Ferdinand Street, where the Marigny meets the Bywater, very near JAMNOLA. A warm, sunny evening with the threat of rain seemingly passed, we were pleased to be walking. Our two-mile route paralleled the curve of the Mississippi and skimmed the edge of the French Quarter, and while we passed businesses and bars, we only caught glimpses of the river's edge; the city seemed quiet, the streets fairly empty. This was reflected back to us the next day as "the great exodus" having begun—some folks annually vacate the city in the summer to avoid the most intense heat.

Despite the quietness of the streets, a crowd of twenty to twenty-five arts and Indigenous cultural leaders, organizers, and cultural advocates have gathered at the venue for our event: "Pandemics: Performance as Response and Re-Familiarization." The event began casually, through the breaking of bread and sharing some wonderful food from a caterer called 1000 Figs. As people make up their plates, wise words from the then director of the Contemporary Arts Center, Neil Barclay, shared with us on the first day of our first trip in 2018 come back to us: food is essential when gathering people together in New Orleans.

The COVID-19 pandemic hit New Orleans hard, the consequences and aftereffects of it are still being processed: despite the pandemic being declared "over" by the WHO, it is nevertheless still a lived reality for many in this city (and globally). It is not over in anything but a technical sense, a sentiment that reverberates in the room as we share our research. Yet what becomes just as clear is the vital role that arts and Indigenous practices played in dealing with the immediate emergence of COVID-19 and its long-term impacts in communities across the city.

At this event, we offered research reflections on ways that we have found arts and culture to matter materially in the unfolding emergency of a pandemic. Not least in this is the way that arts and cultural leaders are very often *trusted voices* in many communities, especially in New Orleans: "Who folks do trust and hold in esteem and look up to for social guidance are the artists and culture bearers—the people in the community who make music, who make Indian suits, who are chefs and culinary artists or poets, spoken word artists, singers."[3] More broadly, while the pandemic had global impact and changed arts and everyday practices, arts practitioners and organizations turned to face the pandemic in dynamic and meaningful ways with incredible speed. At the same time, emergency planners globally turned to the DRMC in conceiving their responses to the crisis. But, we suggest, the neatness of "Mitigation—Preparedness—Response—Recovery" fails to account for the complexity of lived experience in a given place, at least conceptually. This is particularly the case in an "extended" crisis that unfolds over some years. The pandemic was not a swift nor neat event that could be easily compartmentalized; "response" and "recovery," in particular, are messy categorizations, to say nothing of how we might recognize when we move from one to the other. As such, we need new ways of thinking and new forms of practice in the face of events like pandemics. Our argument in this chapter is that performance offers new insights toward this.

In our discussion at Catapult, we offered an initial analysis of multiple performances that happened in the city responding to the pandemic to argue that performance and cultural practice offer means of "rethinking" the pandemic (and thus practices of emergency management). Taking this approach affords opportunities to think in new categorizations that might be seen to sit across and between those of the DRMC.

As organizations and individuals "flexed" with the unfolding of the pandemic, so they offered innovative means of understanding how to live productively within that context. In this chapter we reflect particularly on three key pandemic performances to consider not only what they reveal about performance's place in addressing the immediate crisis of a pandemic but also how these may help us prepare for future such events.

By attending to arts practice in New Orleans during the pandemic, we seek to think in new ways about key terms within the Disaster Risks Management Cycle and to think beyond the potentially misleading simplicity of response and recovery. That is: here we investigate performances that attend to the point between response and recovery and help us think in new ways about these existing terms. We argue that artistic and cultural performances offer pandemic management strategies that emerge from the artists and organizations organically (rather than instrumentally) but which can have profound impact on resilience planning and practice. Specifically, we introduce the idea of "re-familiarization" as a critical step in the journey from response to recovery.

Focused on processes of creative well-being, our first case study analysis explores *Jazz Festing in Place: An On-Air Festival* (April 2020), which was hosted by WWOZ, a music radio station in the city. After Mardi Gras, Jazz Fest is one of the largest festivals in the city. Following the governor's "stay at home" order, the first phase of which ran from 22 March to 15 May 2020, the managers of Jazz Fest ran the festival online, allowing people in the city, nationally, and internationally to tune in at a distance. Listeners were invited to engage remotely while also finding ways to mark and share their practice of the festival at home. The event ran early in the pandemic but was repeated, both later in 2020 and subsequently.

In January 2021, NOLA Ready launched *#SleevesUpNOLA*, a public information campaign to encourage vaccinations. NOLA Ready is the city's Emergency Preparedness Campaign, run by the New Orleans Office of Homeland Security and Emergency Preparedness (NOHSEP) Public Engagement Branch. A critical element of the campaign involved short films in which culture bearers in the city explained why they were getting their "shot." We are interested in the ways *#SleevesUpNOLA* grounded its vaccination communications strategy in local performance practices and the degree to which this work slips free of familiar municipal pandemic messaging that focused more on delivery of "the message" rather than the ways in which public health messages might land with people in the city.

Finally, theater company Goat in the Road held *Scavenger Hunt* on 17 April 2021. In thinking through this work, we are interested in the ways "the Goats" invited people to play in the streets after an uneasy year living with COVID. This sense of return to the streets was playful rather than simply practical and so reveals the ways in which the arts can engage communities in practices of moving beyond response.

All these works offer nuance and a productively "messy" understanding of how a crisis unfolds and is managed.[4] Yet the examples are not neat in and of themselves; for instance, while Goat in the Road used Catapult as the gathering spot for *Scavenger Hunt,* the venue was also a food distribution center, a staging point and setting for online performances, the host of an Indigenous pirate radio station, and critically, a "kitchen" for Indigenous medicines that were distributed to thousands across the United States. The hybridity, flexibility, and agility of artists, arts organizations, and cultural leaders afforded significantly more nuanced and dynamic responses to the pandemic than can be captured in a given management cycle.

Rethinking Pandemic Management

Emergency planning is a live discipline and practice, forever rethinking, reimagining, and revising approaches to better protect people and places. In our work, in all of our dealings with emergency planners in the United Kingdom, the United States, and Europe, we have been struck by their attention to questions of equity in the work they do while recognizing that it is a predominantly white, mainly male, profession (in those geographic contexts at least). In that complex situation, there has been growing interest in theorizing critical phases of the emergency planning cycle. In part this is vital to better understanding the phases and the cycle itself and to being alert to the potential for revisions and reinventions that might offer innovations in resilience and emergency management.

The number and precise definition of the four phases of the DRMC can vary, but internationally, they are regularly represented as operating within a cycle: one leading to another, and recovery informing future mitigation. This cycle is, of course, less neat than its diagrammatic rendering admits. For David A. McEntire, in *Disaster Response and Recovery,* the idea of phases is perhaps "misleading" because it is difficult to understand where one part of the cycle ends and another begins. Indeed, often some "aspects of phases may occur simultaneously," especially between response and recovery. Further, he finds that it is sometimes too "difficult to separate them conceptually."[5] This issue is particularly marked in the case of pandemics, in which, as B. S. Fakhruddin, K. Blanchard, and D. Ragupathy note, there is very scarce research exploring the transition between response and recovery, "forc[ing] us to think beyond typical emergency management structures."[6] Indeed, they recognize that pandemics may involve shifts from response to recovery and back again, until the development and rollout of a vaccine. Even then, we would argue, based on our previous pandemic research in the United Kingdom, it can be hard to determine which part of a pandemic management cycle a given place, or community in a place, sits in. Vaccination rates and personal risk tolerances vary considerably, and as COVID-19 made so painfully clear globally, different age and ethnic demographics are impacted more or less than others. So, while the DRMC is an appealingly neat construction, at the very least it needs to be recognized that the unidirectional progression through its phases limits the complexity of how a crisis may be understood, professionally for both emergency and resilience planners. Indeed, aspects of all the practices we look at in this chapter foreground the importance of fluidity in working between response and recovery. They allow, often playfully and creatively, for critical interrogation of what response and recovery might look and feel like in a place and for different people or groups in that place.

Beyond Response and Recovery

Fakhruddin and colleagues recognize that the pandemic led to significant rethinking of the conventional Disaster Risk Management Cycle, and they call for "an integrated cycle of prevention, preparation, response and recovery" in which multiple disciplinary areas come together to address the complexity of crisis management.[7] Their work, and broader rethinking of the DRMC, points to a need for new models to inform future planning and, particularly, to address the slow time of a pandemic, in contrast to the suddenness of shocks. Yet in our work, we are interested in the potential for practices that allow engagement with liminality. Liminality may initially appear unsettling in emergency planning, although it reflects the reality of a lived situation in pandemic times.

Our hope is that the performance practices discussed here might contribute to emerging learning on the pandemic and provide powerful models of practice through which to navigate the slippery complexity of shifting from, or *between,* response to recovery and as a means of judging how people in a place may be sensing their position in relation to moving from response to recovery. A critical area for such work is to resist structural exclusions. Writing on critical ethnography and storytelling, Kirk Leach and Jason Rivera recognize that "the effects on and experiences of historically marginalized communities" need to be investigated and reflected upon if resilience scholarship is properly to help combat "the overall social vulnerability of society." Crucially, they argue that "disaster recovery services provided by non-profit organizations, in addition to public organizations and community based organizations, have racialized and gendered narratives that have traditionally been missing in disaster and emergency management scholarship." While Leach and Rivera's work demonstrates that local personnel, perspectives, and practices can be vital in response, they also caution that it is vital to understand the politics of organizations that offer support in a disaster and the potential for some organizations, and thereby some communities, not to be represented in response efforts.[8] While no single book or research project can capture and represent fully the complexity of a city, this chapter explores the vital work of practitioners who are not normally considered as offering vital response, re-familiarization, and recovery work in and "after" the pandemic.

There is ample evidence that performance thinking and practice comprise powerful ways to understand what it means to live with and through crisis and that performance can and should be taken seriously in the context of city resilience and emergency preparedness strategy.[9] Meanwhile, colleagues within emergency planning are seeking innovative approaches. For instance, James Gillman, then interim head of service, Connected City, Bristol, has argued for the need to place a city's cultural offer at the center of its resilience planning.[10] Moreover, Gillman identifies the potential for performance to offer modes of conceptualizing, representing, and expressing the experience of risk (especially the pandemic) that can help cities process crises and plan for new ones.[11] Similarly, then head of resilience at Newcastle City Council, Helen Hinds has argued persuasively for the need to "expand" the disciplines "in the room" when developing emergency strategy.[12] For Hinds this responds to a need to develop "entirely new ways of thinking about the current [COVID-19] crisis" and future methods of emergency preparedness.[13] This call for innovative expansion of thinking in emergency planning is echoed in international professional and academic literature too. For example, in *Crisis Response Journal*, Emily Hough, Matthieu Langlois, and Patrick Lagadec argue that COVID-19 revealed that "in a systemic, hypercomplex and mutating context, no one should expect to be the central and unique focus point—the distribution of expertise, questions, perspectives, dynamics and operations has to be rapid and wide. The goal is not to find 'the' overarching and magical solution, but to navigate creatively within black holes amid huge disorder, where traditional maps have been lost, sensemaking is difficult and the horizons are shrouded or invisible . . . the way forward should be a collective endeavour, anchored upon intelligence, creativity and trust."

The COVID-19 pandemic presented us with a global context in which there are "no previously learned answers that can be applied." Building on our previous research, we would nuance this statement a little. SARS, MERS, Ebola, and the flu have all taught lessons. We might argue that during the COVID-19 pandemic, some policymakers were unable to transfer those lessons from one context to another: the maps were indeed lost. The situation requires creativity, complex problem solving, and critical thinking across disciplinary boundaries that are not necessarily (or not normally) part of the emergency preparedness landscape. Indeed, we might even go so far as to say, in the words of Hough, Langlois, and Lagadec, that "addressing the consequences of global destabilization *creatively* is a matter of national survival."[14] In our work, we are particularly interested in thinking through the consequences of such "creative" methods in the context of developing strategic approaches to response and recovery practice, and to understanding the transition between them. This has profound implications for how we understand, live, and work in a place in and "after" a pandemic.

The COVID-19 pandemic required new thinking and a reimagining of previous practices of emergency preparedness and response, laying bare what Alka Sapat argues was the discipline's lack of engagement in, and limited incentivization of, complex interdisciplinary collaboration.[15] As we have elsewhere argued, inclusion of arts, culture, and performance fields is vital for any such interdisciplinary endeavor to be successful.[16] This is because as professor of emergency management Jane Kushma observes, "significant gaps remain in knowledge and practice, [in emergency planning] . . . requiring deliberate and active learning, innovation, and a strategic management focus."[17] If, as Kushma also argues, "a disaster forever changes the landscape, literally and figuratively," and therefore the idea of "the new normal" has gained popular traction as a way of capturing post-disaster contexts, then cultural practices of reimagining life in a place are vital tools of response and recovery, not merely nice-to-have distractions. As the interim head of the Emergency Planning Society put it when reflecting on our research focused on the United Kingdom in 2022, there has been "a critical gap" in resilience thinking and practice not taking seriously the contribution cultural and artistic performances make to processes of emergency management. The performance examples in this chapter crystallize the strategic potential of that contribution, reflecting on the COVID-19 pandemic and revealing potential models of response for future comprehensive emergency management design.

Critical (Re-)Framing: Reimagining Local Pandemic Response

What constitutes a "response," and who should be responding? And what is next? Recovery? If recovery is framed as return to a precrisis context, then it is necessarily flawed because at the very least, this is to ignore the potential for a better postcrisis environment. Kushma argues that recovery mainly occurs "after the lifesaving and life-sustaining actions," focusing on rebuilding, restoring and/or (re)developing after the immediate need for response has subsided. For Kushma, planning for the recovery phase is critical in any resilience strategy or plan because it "allows for the development of a vision for the future that emphasizes the reduction of risk and negative consequences from disaster."[18]

This sense of futurity is encouraging, but as we have argued, the resilience mantra of "bouncing back" is retrograde in its fundamental logic. This is evidently the case in New Orleans, where contexts of racism, inequality, and inequity were not ones to desire bouncing back to. Indeed, presenting arguments for alternatives to precrisis contexts is especially critical because in not doing so, there is a perennial risk that crises will exacerbate previously existing political and social problems that have profound implications for the (negative or inequitable) lived experience of a place. Attending to the possible worlds enacted through performances of and about resilience reveals new ways of thinking about—and practicing—crisis response and thence moving into a new form of recovery.

Perhaps it seems a stretch to argue that arts and culture are suited to emergency response. Perhaps it makes more sense to look on them as the things of recovery, once the infrastructure of the "new normal," even the temporary new normal, is in place. Yet this is to remove the importance of the practices by which people make sense of a place. Further, the more that emergency management teams shift their practice to address local understandings of place and take up creative approaches to crisis response, the more it becomes critical to review the ways that people and organizations in a place contribute to multivocal responses to challenges faced by that place.

In any given context, pandemic response practices constitute performances of a place: be that the formal, civic management of streets and areas with signage and stay-home orders; the informal redistribution of food and other essentials via social networks and community groups; or artistic responses that reflect, critique, and imagine a future beyond the pandemic. While all equally vital in their own way, the importance of cultural production of differing kinds in daily life during the COVID-19 pandemic was internationally recognized in popular, journalistic, and academic arenas. Indeed, cultural policy scholar M. Sharon Jeannotte argued that there is significant global evidence that "cultural activities during the pandemic were highly valued, widely supported, and pursued resolutely despite the many obstacles placed in the way of both creators and consumers." Jeannotte's analysis focuses principally on the ways in which people turned to the consumption of cultural production as a means of escape and entertainment, alongside exploration of the "creative [ways cultural producers used] digital platforms, particularly social media, to try to recapture and connect with audiences and patrons."[19] As artists responded to COVID-19, they discovered ways of practicing life and work in our changed cities, flexing creative understandings of place, community, and audience with care and diligence. Indeed, artists are exceptionally well placed to help reveal, articulate, and encounter what emergency planning theorists referred to as the pandemic's "questions [that] have been overlooked, [that] are unseen."[20] Relatedly, performance analysis provides an innovative methodology to understand the creative ways those living and working in cities are reimagining and making sense of daily practices through pandemic measures, notably including mask wearing and social distancing.

Educationalist Laura J. Hetrick has argued that the arts are "a way of coping with discomfort, trauma, uncertainty, and a lack of wellness in life" and so must be taken seriously as a cornerstone of strategic responses to and planning for pandemics.[21] Moreover, the arts provide mechanisms by which communities and individuals can think through the complexities of a given situation or context. Performance, we suggest, can be a process of pandemic response and recovery and facilitate or enable a fluid, bidirectional transition between them through a process we will theorize as re-familiarization.

Pandemic Performances

The arts offer models of thinking through pandemics. There are critical international efforts to address the importance of creativity, such as the UNESCO

Creative Cities network. Yet there is limited work on the ways creativity, and the arts in particular, speaks to resilience planning and practice. In 2020–22 we ran a project in the United Kingdom and the United States exploring the ways in which artistic and cultural practice can directly inform strategies and practices of emergency planning. In a mid-project report prepared in 2021, we set out a series of "invitations to innovate." Our concern here was to reveal ways in which arts and culture in a city are already addressing resilience challenges in that place. We developed a set of actions by which emergency planners could engage with local arts organizations and venues, both short-term (in the midst of a crisis) and for longer-term capacity building.

A critical example of pandemic performance from that research was the work of Slung Low, a UK performance company and arts venue located in Holbeck in Leeds. Early in the United Kingdom's first lockdown, Slung Low curated a public exhibition of pictures made by local residents. Cable-tied to lampposts for people to explore during the once permitted act of daily exercise in public, the exhibition offered entertainment, distraction, and joy in a COVID-secure way. It was a small contribution to making physical distancing more sustainable. Later the company became a non-means-tested food distribution center and built a "volunteer army" to support the diverse and often at-risk communities of Holbeck.[22] In June 2020 the company produced a one-off theater performance for families, staged in its carpark. Actors performed from the back of a flatbed truck for family bubbles in individual tents, the audience listening through headphones. The performance offered the community something "to look forward to, a change of activity, a moment of respite."[23] This was performance as a mechanism for sustaining (social and cultural) life in lockdown.

These relatively small interventions offered opportunities for shared experiences within a local context, reflecting on the lived reality of the pandemic through art and performance. These actions were critical acts of response that adhere to the United Nations Office for Disaster Risk Reduction's understanding of response actions. They helped to reduce the health and well-being impact of the lockdowns and contributed to ensuring public safety by offering cultural engagement in safe ways.[24] But more than this, Slung Low's practices enacted a cultural subsistence that helped sustain social distancing, even while they helped meet the basic subsistence needs of people affected by becoming a non-means-tested food bank. The company made performance and cultural production central to its pandemic response, speaking to the local context in profoundly effective ways. It used the skills of cultural production and performance (stage and project management, communication and empathy, producing and fundraising, representation) to enact responses that were more "basic" but no less vital.

It would be difficult to map the ways in which people and organizations in a given city transformed their practice through COVID-19. While some work is documented online, or was made specifically for digital consumption, and some pandemic innovations continue, other acts were more ephemeral. Chalked words on streets, porch concerts, even the more everyday act of a wave, or a smile, across a street: these critical practices risk being undocumented. As history is always flawed, always partial, it seems likely that some of the most precious moments provided by arts and culture practitioners and organizations may go unrecorded. In seeking to think through practices here, we are interested in particular practices that might inform our reading of the art and culture of pandemic response, both now and for the future.

Indeed, New Orleans has imagined responses to infectious disease before. The 1950 film *Panic in the Streets* imagines efforts by the city's public health official and the police to track down a new arrival to the city who has brought a highly transmissible disease. More recently, and in work that we have analyzed ourselves, Goat in the Road Productions staged *The Stranger Disease,* which addressed the arrival of yellow fever to the city in 1878. Whereas *Panic in the Streets* was entirely fictional, *The Stranger Disease* (2018) shared a narrative that was grounded in the lives of people who had lived in the city.

The Stranger Disease was staged in Madame John's Legacy, an eighteenth-century house in the city, which is usually open to the public as a heritage site, although the building was closed to the public for renovation at this time. Scenes took place in various spaces in the building, often simultaneously, and spectators were able to pick out their own route through the event, following characters as they chose. As with *Panic in the Streets,* this performance spoke of the risks of infection arriving from the docks. As Duggan reflects in 2019, the performance was particularly distinctive both for being performed in the French Quarter, which is highly popular with tourists, and being about the impact of people from out of town arriving into the city. The work was strangely prescient, as COVID-19 arrived in the city two years later.

During the pandemic, Goat in the Road continued its work revisiting people's stories from the New Orleans of the past. In *Sick Notes: Letters from an Epidemic* (2021) the company used its emerging model of performing the past to create online performances based on imaged letters from characters in *The Stranger Disease*. The project was filmed at BK House, formerly Beauregard-Keyes House Chartres Street.[25] Spectators are able to access the work through videos and text, via an interactive online performance platform that enables viewers to plot their own journeys through the stories being told. Finding connections between characters and their shared experiences, the digital performance is both historic reconstruction and contemporary reflection. The work allows an opportunity to place the contemporary pandemic context into conversation with the (fictionalized, performed) lived experience of a historic antecedent.

In an alternate project, albeit one that also involved (this time actual) personal stories of a pandemic, the Historic New Orleans Collection (HNOC) recorded interviews with first responders and public health and emergency planning practitioners in the city, capturing their experiences of COVID-19. *From the Frontline: Narratives of the Covid-19 Pandemic in New Orleans* offers an online oral history of the COVID-19 pandemic as experienced by those most professionally exposed to it.[26] Some artifacts are films, some audio files; some are carefully managed, some recorded among the sounds of everyday life. The work records the ways in which professionals in a range of roles responded to COVID-19 in New Orleans, charting perceptions, decisions, and emotions. This is difficult work: people hesitate; they hold back tears. The recordings allow time for this. Through the recordings, it is acutely evident that professional practices and personal experiences were bound together through the response phase of COVID-19.

Aside from specific projects, organizations in the city created structural responses to the pandemic, to enable artists to continue working in the city. For instance, "Creative Response" was an initiative led by Antenna, Ashé Cultural Arts Center, and Junebug Productions to provide direct financial support to artists from the outset of the pandemic. Emerging from this financial response, Creative Response Network seeks to leverage the power of creative industries networks to "reimagine the region's arts landscape to one that centers on equity, justice, accountability, and sustainable livelihoods through the production, presentation, preservation, advocacy, and cultivation of art."[27]

Another pandemic innovation was the city's response to the canceling of Mardi Gras celebrations in 2021. Still in the throes of rest-in-place orders and wider COVID-19 control measures, the city mandated that the annual Carnival festivities could not proceed as normal; the city was ostensibly closed to visitors, and physical distancing mandates meant that having crowds on the street would be impossible. Wanting both to support the numerous artists who work to produce multiple aspects of New Orleans Mardi Gras, especially float design and decoration, and to enable some form of Carnival to proceed, 2021 saw the emergence of the "Krewe of House Floats" and so-called Yardi Gras.

House floats, as the name suggests, saw houses across the city decorated in Mardi Gras style in place of floats in the hope of delivering what tour guide and presenter Andrew Farrier described as "the vibe that we all know and expect out of this season."[28] Yardi Gras began with an initiative to "Hire a Mardi Gras Artist": using a crowdfunding model, a lottery was set up for residents to enter in order to win a commissioned artist to decorate their homes. Initially intended to cover approximately forty homes, the idea "grew exponentially" through online campaigns and eventually encompassed more than a thousand locations across all areas of New Orleans, the wider region, and even some international house floats.[29] The techniques used in the construction of these installations are those of parade float construction and artistry; as a result, the aesthetic echoes of Carnival "proper" reverberated across the city to celebrate Mardi Gras, but they also made explicit the absence of Carnival performances, crowds, music, and festivity normally associated with this citywide performance.

Nevertheless, in the number of house floats being taken up as part of the wider Mardi Gras "vernacular" since its inception in 2021, Yardi Gras was a "success." When we returned to the city in 2022, house floats provided a means of celebration in parallel to the "main" parades, enabling perambulatory exploration of areas beyond the central throng of activity. Yardi Gras, then, both deployed the city's cultural infrastructures and workers to galvanize communities' resolve in the face of continued lockdowns and offered the city and its inhabitants a new version of Mardi Gras that prioritized the local over the touristic.

The projects we have identified each focused on the value of attending to individual experience. Taken together, these works speak to the complexity of responding to an unfolding crisis and to the need for innovation in the face of shifting phases in a pandemic. While there are differences between personal testimony of professionals during COVID-19 and imagined narratives during yellow fever, there are also striking similarities. Each of the works reveals nuances of response—the journey through multiple micro-phases of response—rather than conceiving of it as a single monolithic process. They reveal actions of making sense of response. In investigating performance projects, we are interested in the detail of what they enabled in varying phases of the pandemic response and the ways the works may help us to understand, plan for, and find new ways of practicing pandemic response.

Together Apart

Digital models of gathering were not uncommon during the pandemic but often tended to operate as discrete one-off events, rather than in festival formats. For instance, in Bristol the performance and festival producers Mayk hosted a live "house party" via the music streaming platform Spotify.[30] The company invited people in the city to connect in a collective digital space, from their own domestic contexts. On one level, the work comprised a playlist, used by people across the city (and perhaps beyond) to create a shared, collective performance in the city. Yet Mayk augmented this playlist by running a live social media feed. The work reimagined a disco in simple, playful ways, enabling those "at the party" to join in as they chose. The work invited people to perform their home as a disco for a night in the city: "You can play it as loud or soft as you want. You can hide in the other room if you want. Dress up or down."[31] Within the scope of the evening the event was durational, allowing people to drift in and out, in concentrated or distracted ways over time. It allowed for individual responses and renegotiations of the event, as participants could "attend" with friends in other places in and beyond the city and curate their experiences through public or private chat messaging.

Mayk's house party aimed to engage people in the city of Bristol in a shared temporal and aural experience, but this was not an experience that was *about* Bristol's cultural performances. Although innovative, the house party was a small-scale intervention rather than the reinvention of a Bristolian institution for COVID times. In contrast, the moving online of New Orleans's Jazz and Heritage Festival (Jazz Fest) was of quite a different scale in both duration and reach.

Jazz Festing in Place

A family group from Wailua, Hawaii, smiles into the camera. They are standing outside in what appears to be a private garden, with inflatable pools behind them. In Old Lyme, Connecticut, a man and woman stand at a fireplace, holding a poster for the New Orleans Jazz and Heritage Festival, in which Dr. John walks on and almost above the clouds toward a grand piano, on which a series of drinks have been laid out. There are people holding food and drinks—a woman holds a beer can in a koozie, a fabric sleeve designed to keep cans cold.[32] Others hold or display merchandise from past festivals, as well as Jazz Fest products from this year. Two children are pictured on chairs outside, with a sign advertising FEST PARKING for twenty-five dollars. While some people are outside, others playfully reimagine the outside inside, sitting on folding chairs in their living rooms. These are images from a Flickr album of images submitted by listeners to *Jazz Festing in Place*, held on WWOZ in 2020.

The images place people together, people who might have bumped into one another at Jazz Fest but who are meeting in their homes, in parks, and at beaches. WWOZ invited festivalgoers to "pull out your festival shirts, hats, flags, chairs and *get ready to celebrate the best of New Orleans music* from your backyard, your front porch or your air-conditioned living room-anywhere in the world!"[33] At a first-order analysis, this was simply an audio experience, an act of listening to recordings at home. On another, it was entirely more playful, inviting people to contribute to a collective performance of a "festival" in a globally distributed network of participation, both through listening and in other more performance-like ways: costuming and scenography, cooking and cocktail making, and processes of calling or sending in evidence of that participation. As was evident in so many pandemic projects, people were together apart.

Listening from England

London was *hot* in late April and early May 2020. Really hot. New Orleans–in-summer hot, or so it seemed as we (the Duggan family) "locked down" with our two small children. Venturing out with the kids made us feel vulnerable in those earlyish days of the pandemic. On one occasion, my (Patrick's) son was ushered out of someone's way on the sidewalk by a hand being placed on the side of his head. Gently but firmly, he was guided around the other pedestrian. Visions of infectious contact on the narrow streets of East London's residential areas kept us from venturing too far from home. So we used to go for walks in the parched, tumble-down Victorian graveyard at the end of our street rather than risk longer walks to more pleasurable pastures. In hindsight this feels something of an overreaction, but the anxiety we felt was palpable when out with the children. As a result, we worked hard to find escape in home-based activity.

One weekend we "went to New Orleans," inventing our own Mardi Gras–style party by dressing up in homespun costumes, festooned with beads from past trips, listening to New Orleans jazz, cooking up jambalaya, and designing masks and imagined floats. Such one-off practices were vital but fleeting and, if I am really honest, a little energy sapping when coupled with wider work commitments and the other tasks of living. So, when WWOZ, New Orleans's "Jazz and Heritage Station," announced it would be running *Jazz Festing in Place: An On-Air Festival* with its local and global audience, we leaped at the chance to engage in a practice that linked us to others around the world in playful and engaging ways. As WWOZ put it:

> We are thinking of you and sending our best wishes!
> Here is a very special announcement we hope will lift your spirits.
> . . . The 8-day broadcast will . . . include interview segments highlighting the music, food, crafts and heritage of New Orleans and Louisiana to give the feeling of a wide-reaching cultural festival. We will also be sharing recipes for some of your favorite Jazz Fest cuisine, and also help you connect with local festival food and craft vendors.[34]

Analytically, the commitment to multiple days and hours, mirroring the hours of the in-person festival, allowed a dipping in and out over time that made the festival experience accessible in and around other commitments. Accompanied by discussion and description of the way others around the world were "festing" and a Twitter (now "X") hashtag to follow (#jazzfestinginplace), the experience felt genuinely a way of being together apart, a way of reconciling the experience of global lockdown through shared experience, a familiar experience of collective listening and enjoyment in the defamiliarized COVID-19 world.

For two long weekends (22–25 April and 29 April–2 May), *Jazz Festing in Place* provided a means of marking time in something of a celebratory way. Time differences prevented our engaging as completely as we might have done had we been at an in-person festival, but in a way that was the point. In bringing the festival to a global, locked-down, in-place audience, WWOZ invited people to engage in a participatory practice of listening, sharing, celebrating, cooking, and dressing up that allowed for collective experience of multiple

kinds at whatever level of engagement people felt able to muster. For the Duggan family, this ranged from preplanned cocktails with games and dancing
in the garden to incidental moments of simply needing to change the energy.

Jazz Festing in Place had a structure that responded precisely to the needs
of the occasion. Jenny M. Groarke and colleagues identified that, in the United
Kingdom, "rates of loneliness during the initial phase of lockdown were high"
and that rising "rates of loneliness . . . may increase prevalence of mood disor-
ders, self-harm, and suicide, and exacerbate pre-existing mental health conditions."[35] Elsewhere, Joanne Ingram, Christopher Hand, and Greg Maciejewski
found that "even relatively short-term social isolation—specifically reduced social contact with those outside the household—has a negative impact on cognitive abilities/executive functions." They suggested that "if lockdown conditions
continue to be used in the fight against the COVID-19 pandemic, strategies
to alleviate cognitive decline during prolonged restrictive conditions should
be considered."[36] WWOZ's digital festival offered one such strategy. Operating within the regular Jazz Fest structure, the event offers a familiar temporal
experience of place in structure as well as in the music itself. While of course
not being the same as a live, in-person festival, the digital offer operated to
connect people globally through cultural practices of New Orleans. Moreover,
given the cultural importance of Jazz Fest, *not* to have had the festival, even in
digital form, would have been to disregard the wider sociocultural importance
of the event in the city.

Creative Re-Familiarization: Goat in the Road's *Scavenger Hunt*

Whereas the New Orleans Jazz and Heritage festival moved online to support
collective cultural experience in lockdown, performance company Goat in the
Road's *Scavenger Hunt* (April 2021) afforded participants an opportunity to
return to the streets, playfully exploring the Marigny-Bywater area of the city.
Replacing an annual Bingo Night fundraiser that supports the company's educational programs, the poster for *Scavenger Hunt* framed the event as if it were
a couple of hundred years old:

> Do not be alarmed for coming to your very own neighborhood is a delightful,
> fortifying, stupefying
>
> FAMILY FRIENDLY SCAVENGER HUNT!

hosted by Goat in the Road Productions for the benefit of all persons.

WIN PRIZES! WITNESS ART! EAT SNACKS!

CRAFT GOAT HORNS ON SITE! ENJOY YOUR LIFE![37]

Given that much of Goat in the Road's contemporary theatrical practice is focused on reenactments in, and of, the city, this project might indeed have been
the restaging of a scavenger hunt from the 1800s. Yet the language of the poster
was playful and very much grounded in the present. Performed in 2021, after
the city had lived through a year of COVID-19, the simple pleasures of winning
prizes, witnessing art, and, particularly, enjoying life were still relatively unfamiliar in public places. As such, the work invited people in the neighborhood,
the city, and beyond to engage playfully in the streets through a performance
of re-familiarization with Marigny-Bywater.

Artistic practice is often understood and valued for *defamiliarizing* that
which is familiar, for inviting us to look at the world in new ways, from new
perspectives. There are roots of this term in Victor Shklovsky's term *Ostranenie*
and also in Bertolt Brecht's term *Verfremdung*, both of which have been understood as "defamiliarization."[38] In ordinary times, art can productively unsettle the familiar, enabling us to take new perspectives, ask new questions, and
look to new ways of remaking the familiar. This can be particularly valuable
in addressing challenges that are bound up in the familiar, particularly where
the familiar world results in negative, exclusionary, and otherwise deleterious
conditions.

During a shock or an underlying stress, ordinary times are already unsettled, if not entirely upturned. In such circumstances, it becomes critical to
understand the operation of arts practice. In the context of the COVID-19-
driven defamiliarization, artists began to engage in practices that we might
understand as re-familiarization. For some this was an explicit engagement in
and reflection on re-familiarization; for others it was more implicit, grounded
in the local conditions and experiences of the world having been unsettled. For
Goat in the Road it was rooted in the traditions of street performance (social
and aesthetic), of costuming, parading, and decorating in the place.

Re-familiarization is relatively under-theorized, which is curious given the
degree to which people experience removal from, and return to, a place. Aside
from some engagement in the arts, it has been discussed in fields including

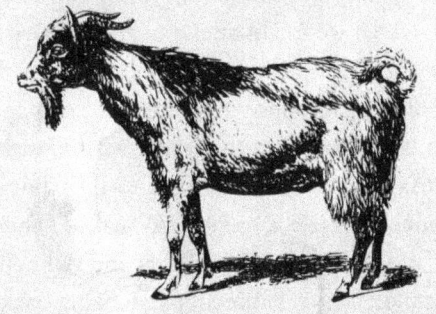

GOAT IN THE ROAD PRESENTS...

A SCAVENGER HUNT!

Do not be alarmed for coming to your very own
neighborhood is a delightful, fortifying, stupefying

FAMILY FRIENDLY SCAVENGER HUNT!

hosted by Goat in the Road Productions for the benefit of all persons.

WIN PRIZES! WITNESS ART! EAT SNACKS!
CRAFT GOAT HORNS ON SITE! ENJOY YOUR LIFE!

*Without doubt the spectacular event will improve all senses: taste, touch, smelling,
hearing, and visuals. Do not delay in buying your tickets. It shall and will take place.*

SATURDAY, APRIL 17TH, 2021. 1-7PM. $10-$60.

THE HUNT STARTS AND ENDS AT 609 ST. FERDINAND STREET.
STAGGERED SIGN-UP TIMES. COSTUMES ENCOURAGED. MASKS
REQUIRED FOR CHECK IN. FOR FURTHER INFORMATION:

www.goatintheroadproductions.org

Promotional poster, designed by Chris Kaminstein, for Goat in the Road Production's *Scavenger Hunt*, 2021.

social care and urban planning. In his work preparing for the future of urban design, Mark C. Childs finds that re-familiarization returns images and symbolic expressions to a codependent system of cultural and symbolic production and thus reveals things we have known but have forgotten.[39] This perhaps suggest the idea of revelation in order to return to a previous state, echoing the problematic narrative of bouncing back in resilience theory. There are risks in "returning": to resituate ourselves in familiar habitats and habits, to reconstruct places and practices as they once were, is to lose an opportunity to reimagine places and the structural exclusions they perpetuate. By returning to a preexisting normal, we return to the comfort of established exclusionary structures.

In their exhibition *Refamiliarization* (2021), Justin Berner and Julia Irwin considered the ways in which we might attend to re-familiarization after the pandemic. For Berner and Irwin, the pandemic "effected a thoroughgoing sense of defamiliarization"; in response, they suggest, the pandemic obliges us to assess what must be recast and resisted and what, if anything, may be recovered with care.[40] As people were restricted to their homes during the pandemic, there was hope, and talk, of a new normal, which we might read through Childs's work as a *new* system of cultural and symbolic production, a mode of re-familiarization that is bidirectional, looking back and forward. Re-familiarization should not (by default at least) involve returning to the way things were. Rather, it is a process of recognizing the familiar within a changed context; it is partial, limited, and a process of situating the familiar within the new. To return for a moment to the DRMC, for us, then, re-familiarization offers an additional step in the cycle between response and recovery. But whereas the DRMC is seen to operate unidirectionally (respond then recover), the bidirectionality of re-familiarization allows for attention and reverberation between both. Re-familiarization can be a process precisely of engaging in a moment of both response *and* recovery.

Berner and Irwin's exhibition was an inquiry into the idea of re-familiarization rather than an effort to engage in a practice of it; nevertheless, the work productively suggests that actions after a pandemic may incorporate multiple responses to the familiar, in varying and perhaps multiple forms and combinations. In this next section, we investigate how artists engage in re-familiarization practice, how they manage the risk of "just" returning and the discoveries they make and share through this process.

"Things to Spy"

Participants for Goat in the Road's *Scavenger Hunt* registered online, in groups of up to six. The event began and concluded at Catapult, on Ferdinand Street. Start times were staggered between 1:00 and 7:00 p.m., to maintain physical distancing. Marketing for the event explained, "Goat in the Road is replacing its popular Bingo Night with a socially distanced, fun-for-the-whole-family, Scavenger Hunt. Family and friend groups can sign up to follow clues around the Marigny and Bywater, explore the art and murals of the neighborhood, and spend a Spring day outside with a light dusting of competition."[41] On check-in, participants were given a sheet of paper with the heading THINGS TO SPY!! on which were printed sixteen images to be found during the event.[42] The *Scavenger Hunt* invited people in (and perhaps beyond) the city to return to the streets and, particularly for those living or working in Marigny-Bywater, to relocate themselves in the neighborhood. While the event was framed for friends or families, the focus on families was particularly marked. The sheet of images explained, "If you spy any of these things, tell your grownup and they'll mark it on the map!"

The task required either good knowledge of the area or commitment and a keen eye, most likely a little of both. One image depicted a painted advertisement on the brick wall of a building: HOME OF THE FAMOUS CREOLE TOMATO. In another, purple, green, and yellow stars had been stuck to the front of a blue painted wood-paneled building, and another showed a pink dumpster. Each of the images depicted an addition to a place: painted surfaces (murals, a door, a telegraph pole, the dumpster), objects hanging or affixed to a place (stars, crocheted flowers, a ghostly sheet), or an object temporarily installed in a place (a carriage but no horse).

The *Scavenger Hunt* was premised on temporary creative engagements with place. The work, then, spoke of individual engagements with a place, as opposed to institutional creative endeavors. As a survey of Marigny-Bywater, this spoke of and to the people of the area and the ways in which they had commented on, shaped, and reimagined the material structures of this place. Whereas many pandemic projects, in the United Kingdom at least, invited people to put art in their windows, this work revealed the scale of art that was already in and around buildings and animated it through instructional performance practices and, for some participants, through costume. In returning performing bodies to the streets of the Marigny-Bywater in playful, family-orientated ways, with a clear and explicit attention to people's safety both practically and in terms of the event's marketing, Goat in the Road used performance-making strategies and well-understood participatory models to enable re-familiarization, even as the world was changed and changing because of the pandemic.

Writing on contemporary archaeology, Dante Angelo and coauthors recognize "the fleeting materiality of local responses to a global pandemic."[43] The pandemic provided a context for Goat in the Road to reveal the relatively fleeting materiality of local responses to place *and* the ways that such fleeting material interventions are critical to making and understanding places for the long term. That is, while murals are not exactly fleeting, paint suffers over time—it can discolor and chip or too easily become unfixed from the surface beneath, while that surface may itself degrade. And yet, in weathering over time, the mural signals the place of its staging. Paper stars on a wall or knitted flowers on a tree are more easily identifiable as fleeting interventions, yet when understood as an iterative performative expression of place, they can cohere into a long-term *performance practice of place.* This is important because it begins to signal a way that calling attention to these practices, such as facilitated by instructional performance, can reveal both established and emerging place identities (and their relation to surrounding places, especially in a city of neighborhoods like New Orleans).

Rebecca Solnit reflects on the importance of maps for cities in her Atlas Trilogy of books of maps and texts of cities, of which *Unfathomable Cities* (produced with Rebecca Snedeker) focuses on New Orleans. Solnit and Snedeker's work recognizes the multiple maps and meanings that may be made of a city, across different media and forms. Here, in *Scavenger Hunt,* the scale was smaller, an area of a city, a neighborhood. The work performed a hyperlocal mapping yet one that spoke to similar creative practices throughout the city. Here Goat in the Road was mapping the area in which its company members, and presumably some audience members, lived and worked. This was a pandemic mapping, when so much of the city was off-limits for periods of time, when it became important to understand what matters locally. In focusing on the signs of people in places just as pandemic restrictions were being relaxed and people were enabled to return to those places, the work valued the human, the relatively temporary, the quirky, and the colorful to re-familiarize participants with being in the streets again and to signal the possibility of renewal and reinvention through creative expression.

The Incongruity of Goats in the Road

For many participants, engaging in a live event in early 2021 may have been a fraught experience. Mardi Gras had been canceled, tourism numbers were enormously down, the city's streets emptier in both everyday (commuters, shoppers, restaurant goers) and performance terms (no parades, no second lines, no tourist tours). Certainly, as an event, this was framed to be welcoming, to be navigable at a distance from others. In advance of the *Hunt,* Goat in the Road shared an image of how Catapult would be set up for the event. The picture showed the front gate, the building, and the sky above. Labels had been attached to features of the image: the "garage door will be open," the "sky will be still be up here," "snack table here," and "check-in table goes here." The image allowed potential participants to gauge the safety of the space in advance. The event was outdoors, the space appeared uncluttered, and the staggered starts would help separate participants. This aside, the gap between the entrance gates looks narrow, lending potential participants to be concerned about proxemics of entry and exit.

Images of the event from Goat in the Road show families on the trail of their sixteen quarries. A woman holds a clipboard, with the page of images attached and a bag of what may be sweets. Three children, each in a mask, gather for a photo by a stone ornament of a goat, perhaps in a front garden they found on their travels. Three others, also all in face masks, pose for a photo together, holding out their arms as if they are goat forelegs. One is dressed in leopard skin leggings and what may be a faux fur top. On her head, she wears long gold fabric horns, flowers with white tendrils; another is dressed in gold short trousers, a brightly colored top, and wears purple foam horns, again with flowers and tendrils. While the headwear may have been made during the check-in process, the clothing demonstrates planned preparation for the event. Afterall, the publicity proclaimed, "Costumes Encouraged," reflecting the wider importance of costuming and masking as a cultural practice of New Orleans.[44] From the suits of Black Masking Indians, social aid and pleasure club outfits, and the costumes of Mardi Gras krewes and spectators to dressing up for Halloween, Pride, and Gay Easter, making and wearing costumes in the city is a marker of place and identity.[45]

Tourism scholar Haywantee Ramkissoon argues that in the context of a pandemic, "an important discussion to bring to the table is the need to promote interventions for people to cope with the pandemic and to adjust to the post-pandemic world. Promoting affective attitudes toward place can foster well-being outcomes." They go on to argue that this can have important positive impact on healthcare systems and in equipping people with coping mechanisms during and beyond a pandemic.[46] Ramkissoon recognizes the value of place affect as a means of enabling people to engage in the post-pandemic world and to generate health and well-being effects, identifying place affect as a "sub-dimension" of place attachment. Arts practice, we argue, can comprise

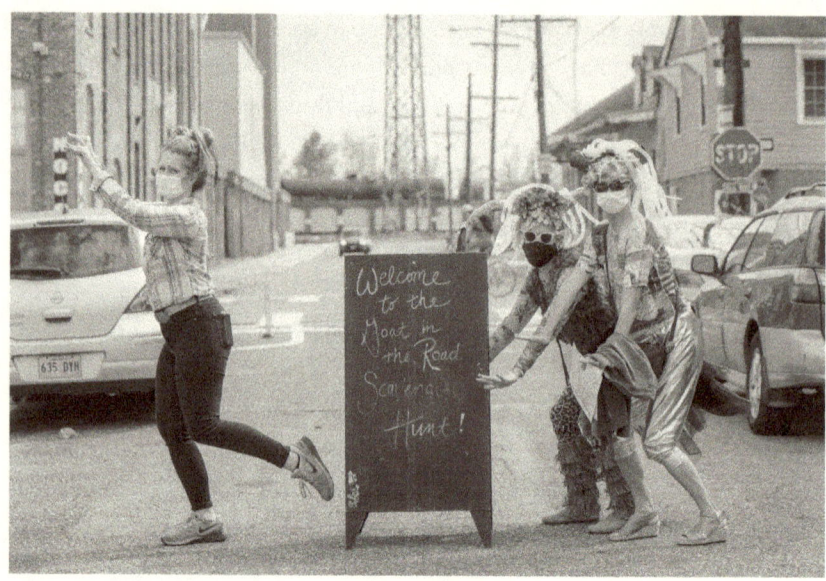

Costumed revelers dressed for *Scavenger Hunt,* 2021. Photo by Joshua Brasted.

intervention and operate to engage people with places, and so grow place affect. In the context of a pandemic, when being in places beyond the home is perceived as dangerous, practices of performance, including costuming and instruction, offer means of framing those places and the ways in which people can engage in and generate affect from them.

Costumed performances are a familiar feature of life in New Orleans, notably during Mardi Gras but also events such as White Linen Night (and Dirty Linen Night, a week later), in which participants wear white linen to echo past use of the cloth in the heat and humidity of the city. While some instances of dress are celebratory, playful, others point to the politics of the city, and at times these run together. As Pravin Shukla reflects, "The Mardi Gras Indians of New Orleans wear flamboyant beaded and feathered 'suits' to raise awareness of the discrimination they have suffered in the city."[47]

Scavenger Hunt, then, was not simply an act of returning to the streets, if such an act is even "simple." After many New Orleanians had sheltered in place through phases of the pandemic, the *Scavenger Hunt* offered a means for people to return to *these* streets. To re-familiarize oneself with streets in New Orleans requires an element of dressing up, playing up, playing out. Moreover, the *Scavenger Hunt* calls on familiar practices of place and performances in it. In his captivating history of Mardi Gras beads, Doug MacCash explores the "thrill of the throwing game," in which parade goers call up to float riders for a "throw," a gift distributed from the parades to the crowds. This is most commonly a set of beads, though krewe-branded toys, doubloons, and other "merch" are regularly hurled to competitively outstretched hands. Among this cornucopia are the rare, handmade gifts that krewes more sparingly pass out along their parade route, causing parade goers, as MacCash illustrates, to try everything from deploying the "cuteness" of their children to "faux disability" in an attempt to secure this precious treasure. It is for this reason that behavioral scientist Patrick Bordnick describes the process of attending a parade as being like "a treasure hunt" in which one has to work out how best to connect with krewe members as they pass by, grabbing their attention and favor.[48] In a way, then, the practice of hunting for clues among (admittedly thin) "crowds" of others is a familiar embodied practice for those attending Goat in the Road's *Scavenger Hunt*. This is not only important in its capacity to re-familiarize and reorient people back to the city "post"-pandemic, but it also signals the wider importance of performance practices in understanding place and social connections in and beyond the pandemic moment.

From Response to Recovery

The *Scavenger Hunt* was a threshold event. Images show some participants with masks, some without; the conditions separated people, and yet the event as a whole brought people together. As an activity, the *Scavenger Hunt* revealed how participants felt about the pandemic and their levels of comfort with others, recognizing that sensations of unfamiliarity in being out with others in public may remain long after one's sense of risk has diminished.

While scavenger hunts were fairly widely used during the pandemic, offering relatively safe outdoor opportunities for collective experience, many of them were framed around fine arts practice, in which artists left artworks for participants to find.[49] Aside from the pandemic, artists have explored scavenger hunts as a mode of arts practice. From 2000 to 2008 the artist Joshua Sofaer ran a series of events entitled *Scavengers* (in Germany, the UK, and the United States). During these events, teams of participants were given one hundred clues to places in a city, where "information or an item has to be gathered, recorded or made."[50] The project comprised the hunt and a gallery exhibition and a series of related events. In San Francisco this included a symposium on "found objects" and a discussion between Sofaer and participants. The San

Francisco Museum of Modern Art, which hosted *Scavengers* in 2006, held a scavenger hunt based on the photographs of Walker Evans, whose images document the Great Depression in the United States. Participants were invited on a "walking adventure around the city" to solve clues to Evans's work. A version of the event was held again in 2018, in response to the wildfires in California that year. What marks the Goat in the Road project is its profoundly local, performance-oriented engagement with place at a time when people in the city, and the city itself, were each determining their position on the pandemic and how they felt to be "emerging" from it in the spring of 2021.

Although not framed explicitly as a re-familiarization event, *Scavenger Hunt* invited people to return to the streets of Marigny-Bywater, to experience objects of cultural and symbolic production in this part of the city by "playing the goat." The company name Goat in the Road was selected when the company founders had once looked out of the window at a New Orleans street to see a lone goat standing in the road. The incongruity of the scene stood out and piqued their interest. Some years and a pandemic later, the company released its own "goats" into the street, replaying the feelings and degrees of incongruity, replaying the unfamiliar in the familiar through performance.

The risk of a scavenger hunt is that it is too easily understood, with the implication that it may be easily introduced and used as a future pandemic strategy. While potentially valuable in this context, there is a risk that the nuance of a local place and local understanding of a phase in the pandemic could become lost. To recommend scavenger hunts as productive modes of re-familiarization is to recommend close attention to that which is hunted and what this says of the place, the people within it, and the ways in which the place is lived. It is to invite sideways perspectives on the place, as a part of the place, a delicate, lived, situated negotiation of defamiliarization and re-familiarization.

The selection of places in the Marigny-Bywater, the curation of them as a physically distanced but playful event, and the invitation to dress up in a city so *au fait* with costuming reveal careful attention to the ways in which we might rediscover and value a place after having been away for a time. Of course, many in Marigny-Bywater will not have been away but, rather, limited in how much time they might spend outside in the area or in how they viewed this place in the context of the pandemic.

Goat in the Road demonstrated that re-familiarization does not "simply" constitute a return to once familiar places and practices; rather, we argue here for re-familiarization to be understood as a creative practice of curation, framing, and performative attention to particular places and practices. A post-pandemic scavenger hunt offers a frame through which participants are enabled to practice re-familiarization. As Berner and Irwin identify, re-familiarization can involve questions, rather than answers, the practice of resituating oneself in a place can draw attention to this act of resituating as a critical practice. While this is not the same form of protection as a vaccination, it is leveraging place affect as a means to transition between response and recovery.

Leveraging the Power of Creative Local Response

It is tempting to read vaccination as a point of recovery. Vaccination is a practice of securing inhabitants of a city, an act that will limit hospital admissions and death rates. Yet vaccination raises similar challenges to testing; it asks people to engage with systems that previously have not been without challenges. We are, internationally, increasingly understanding the challenges of health inequity. Given the potential for lack of take-up, it may be more productive to understand vaccination as a means of response, or certainly a practice that remains cuspal, an act of response that is necessary to reach a point of recovery. Helene-Mari van der Westhuizen and colleagues observe of mask wearing: "During the COVID-19 pandemic, wearing face coverings is being rapidly introduced as a public health intervention in countries with no cultural tradition of doing so. For successful uptake, such interventions need to be grounded in the social and cultural practices and realities of affected communities, and campaigns should not only inform, but also work to shape new sociocultural norms."[51] We need more properly to understand signs as cultural artifacts, as a critical part of the place in which they are situated, speaking to people who use that place. Thus, we need to develop messaging that directly addresses those people, encouraging and enabling them to incorporate restrictions into their daily experiences and modes of being in the city.

To understand vaccination in New Orleans, it may be useful to reflect back to testing in the city. New Orleans opted to be one of the first cities to pilot federal testing facilities. The system was an out-of-town drive-through. Thoumi and colleagues reflect on this approach, taking New Orleans as a case study in their report on vaccination strategies in the United States, and find that the city's initial approach to COVID-19 testing centers led to "disproportionately low COVID-19 testing rates in areas with high social vulnerability and minimal access to transportation."[52] More important, especially in the context of the city having lived through an extremely militarized response in the immediate aftermath of Hurricane Katrina, was the reflection by the director of the New Orleans Health Department, Dr. Jennifer Avegno, that the pilot system "wasn't going to cut it for a lot of people right? You know, the first person you saw was a guy in fatigues with a gun."[53]

Avegno describes pushing back, explaining, "This isn't going to work, let us do it locally." "We realized the virus was disproportionately hitting residents of color . . . generally on the lower income end, so we had to bring the testing to them." A local walk-in scheme became the way, and having developed "hyperlocal" testing centers, New Orleans built on this strategy for the distribution of vaccinations. A hotline was established and call centers set up, initially staffed by employees of the Health Department. Subsequently, "local community members, volunteers, and native Spanish, Vietnamese, and other language speakers staffed the call centers," affording local knowledge and language expertise that enabled the centers more properly to reflect the communities they were trying to reach.[54] Vaccination sites were located in places that were accessible to local communities, and the city developed partnerships with local businesses to run vaccine events that very often had free food and music. The conjoining of local expertise, community voices, food, and cultural practice began to seed the way for what would become a highly successful vaccination drive.[55]

#SleevesUpNOLA

It is well understood that voluntary or nonemergency management organizations play a critical role in emergency management, particularly response and recovery. Yet there is less work on the importance of performance to this context or the potential for conversation and collaboration between emergency and more everyday practices in emergency management. We lack understanding of locally situated and locally significant approaches to emergency management.

This lack of research is a critically significant absence in emergency response. Where emergency managers prepare for, train, and rehearse emergency response, local creative practices of response often constitute innovations in the moment. These are activities that take place during a response phase, often as innovations or restagings or revisions to existing practices. They may fill in gaps in response, risk duplication, or even appear to work in opposition to planned, mandated, and rehearsed practices. This can lead to risks of misunderstandings, conflicting aims and practices, and, in short, appearing to be well-meaning but "in the way."

Our interest here is the potential to connect up emergency response and local response practices, and indeed to look to the possibilities for both collaborative practices and new innovations that ground emergency strategy in local practices. Indeed, we focus on *#SleevesUpNOLA* as a compelling case study of locally situated emergency creative planning. While this innovation emerged through the pandemic, it was grounded in understandings of the vital importance of local cultural performances that predated the pandemic. The more we build understandings and capacity for shared concern by stakeholders, the more we seed potential for collaborative, creative thinking in mitigation phases, in advance of a pandemic, and in the moment of active response.

The cultural identity of New Orleans is founded on embodied practices—it is part of how the city functions, part of how the city is. This is not glib essentializing of culture in the city but a belief that is profoundly held by people in New Orleans. For example, at the height of the pandemic, culture bearer Cherice Harrison-Nelson, the Big Queen of the Guardians of the Flame Mardi Gras Indians, described New Orleans's cultural practitioners as "spiritual first responders."[56] This idea of cultural practitioners as "first responders" is an interesting one, but where Harrison-Nelson sees the value of cultural practice in offering "spiritual" connection and engagement (understood broadly) across communities, we want to argue that an analysis of the public health video campaign *#SleevesUpNOLA* reveals performing bodies in Carnival, parading, and other forms of New Orleans's street culture as a "cultural first response" with material impact on COVID recovery.

In July 2021, NOLA Ready, "the City's Emergency Preparedness Campaign," the public-facing communication effort on emergency planning, released the *#SleevesUpNOLA* campaign and video across social media platforms (we encountered it via Twitter, now X, through the @nolaready account). The video aimed to use New Orleans–specific performance forms to dispel vaccination hesitancy and encourage uptake.[57] Over twenty-eight seconds, we are told that this is "our shot" at returning to the things and people we love in New Orleans. In particular, cultural performance forms associated with Mardi Gras, and wider parading culture, and cultural leaders from within them are deployed to encourage us to roll our sleeves up and get the jab: Baby Dolls, Black Masking Indians, besuited social aid and pleasure club members, and the Krewe of Red

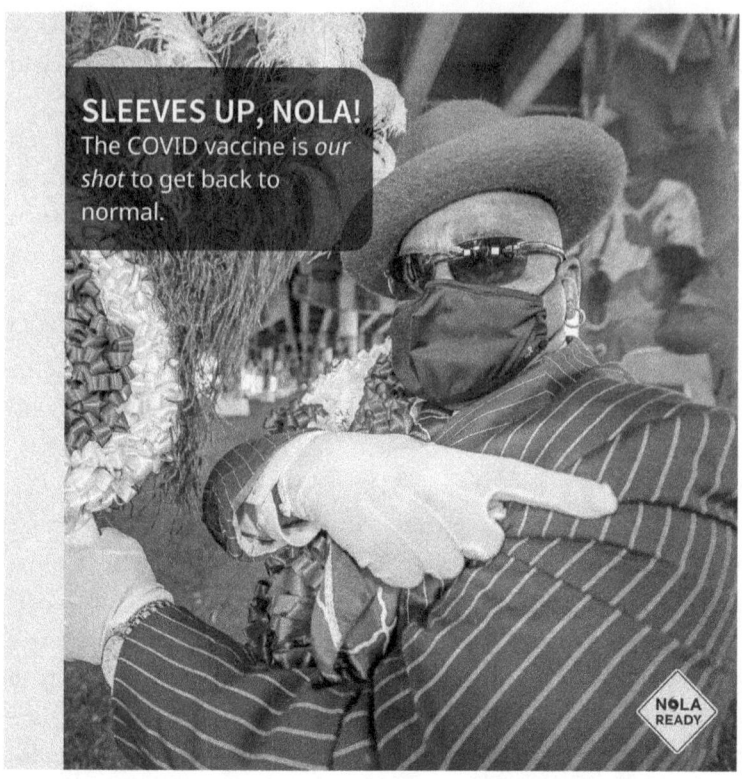

SLEEVES UP, NOLA!
The COVID vaccine is *our shot* to get back to normal.

NOLA READY

Promotional image for COVID-19 vaccination, 2021. Photo by Crista Roc.

Beans "explain why the COVID-19 vaccine is our shot to get back to normal." *#SleevesUpNOLA* is a complex performance of New Orleans culture as public health message, as celebratory call to (get jabs in) arms, and as advertisement for the city—after all, it is these (sorts of) performances people come to the city for. There is a very deliberate deployment of cultural performance as a means of pandemic response, an understanding that these particular local performance forms can help manage perceptions of risk and benefit in vaccine take-up.

Questions of perception and trust are critical to pandemic preparedness and response. If the risk of vaccination or fear of the people administering it outweigh the perceived risk of the virus, then it is reasonable to expect limited engagement and significant anxiety about any "rollout" of a vaccination administered by authorities that present as militaristic in their approach to community outreach and engagement. By contrast, performance offers a means through which to represent communities back to themselves and to return embodied experiences to public perception of pandemic management. In the

#SleevesUpNOLA campaign, cultural performances are used to represent vaccination as being part of the city's culture and identity. That is, New Orleans deployed social, cultural, and aesthetic performances as pandemic response, embedding what Asali DeVan Ecclesiastes, of Ashé Cultural Arts Center, referred to as the esteemed, trusted voices of artists and culture bearers.[58] Such foregrounding of these cultural performances positions them as at once what people come to New Orleans for (the cultural performances of the place) and a powerful means through which New Orleans reflects itself to itself in a moment of existential thereat and crisis.

By attending to the contribution of arts and culture to planning for response and recovery, we can identify processes and practices that might underpin more nuanced future action than (current understandings of) the DRMC allows for. Not only that, but these practices pluralize the voices included in established responses to a crisis, representing vital knowledges from different communities and (attempting to) synthesize them as vital, strategic resilience contributions. Indeed, if we value the contribution that arts and culture made to one or more phases of comprehensive emergency management, we must document and build that knowledge into future phases locally, nationally, and internationally. The more that arts and culture are embedded in emergency management, the more that perspectives from these fields will be routinely sought in revising practices.

Left unchecked, emergency plans and innovative local creative responses will operate as they do at present, in varying forms of parallel practice. At times, innovations, people, contexts, will allow for connections and productive collaboration. As a crisis unfolds, there is a risk that local creative practices of response may be seen to "get in the way" rather than offer obvious solutions. However, as our case studies here have shown, arts and culture offer dynamic, novel approaches to problem-solving that can be valuable to individuals, communities, neighborhoods, and the city. In that context, one critical, "easy" next step could be for artists and resilience and emergency professionals, collaboratively, to document and take account of the innovations arts practitioners across New Orleans took during COVID-19. In doing this work, as we have done here, they should ask what models exist from COVID-19 practices that could be set out for future pandemics and how these might fit into and benefit the execution of phases of the resilience cycle.

While the innovations explored in this chapter expanded the practice of pandemic response in New Orleans, they also expanded definitions of local practices in the city. This is critical given Thomas's critique that much of local residents' sense of place and personal attachment to their city has been framed by tourism. There is, then, value in reclaiming practices and reshaping them at times of challenge, though it may be little comfort. This said, each of these practices reimagines the familiar, the known. It introduces new forms and new modes of engagement. This approach offers the potential to disperse audiences and change modes of participation. *Jazz Festing in Place* develops and values association with the city and its music at one remove. *Scavenger Hunt* asks people to look in new ways at the city and at art in the city.

While we have focused here on response, we are acutely aware that this phase is conventionally followed by "recovery." Indeed, Goat in the Road's *Scavenger Hunt* pointed to a form of recovery, a moment when play in the streets would feel comfortable *again.* The ease of use of the term *recovery* suggests a return to the conditions that may well have constructed, contributed to, or compounded issues in the first place. While it may be possible to rebuild, to re-create spaces, the people who inhabit those spaces are likely changed. This is addressed in the ways in which recovery has been bound up with the phrase *bouncing back.* In part this chapter has argued that the introduction of re-familiarization into the DRMC would alleviate this tension by enabling smoother, bidirectional transition between response and recovery.

Internationally, artists, arts organizations, and culture bearers responded to the pandemic, sometimes entirely transforming their working practices. Some of these practices will become part of the continuing culture of a place. In New Orleans house floats may continue during Mardi Gras (they have done so each year to 2025), providing a model for managing future shocks. Yet many of the innovations that proved vital in a moment in the pandemic run the risk of being lost. If we are to rethink resilience, we need to document and analyze the work of arts and culture during a crisis to be ready for related shocks in the future. There is a real question over the funding for such documentation and how it might be done to best effect. On one level, we might document a list of artistic and cultural actions, yet a principal risk of such an approach is that it separates arts and culture from strategic practices in a city. Where arts and culture addressed unmet needs in a city during the pandemic, then "after" the pandemic, it is vital that we plan to avoid such unmet needs in future events.

The case studies analyzed in this chapter reveal the degree to which the pandemic led to arts and culture practitioners "rethinking" practices that might conventionally be understood as recovery. In so doing, they present recovery as a potential crisis: the return to normality inherent or implied in much resilience theory not only runs the risk of banalizing a crisis through narratives of having bounced back or being "recovered," but it also profoundly risks reaffirming and perpetuating preexisting systems and structures. There is a danger that attempts to "bounce back" in New Orleans will be motivated by a desire to "return" to the neatly commodified version of the city that we critique in chapter 1. In contrast, the ways in which artists and culture bearers reimagined familiar practices in the city during the pandemic might be read productively as a call to resist such familiar, often commercialized, framings of New Orleans. The reframing of some Mardi Gras practices with house floats and enabling Jazz Fest for an online global audience demonstrate that even very well-known traditions in the city's annual calendar are live, shifting practices that can actively take account of events in the contemporary moment. In thinking through the pandemic via cultural performances that emerged during its unfolding, we hope to have revealed the significance of arts and culture workers in crisis response.

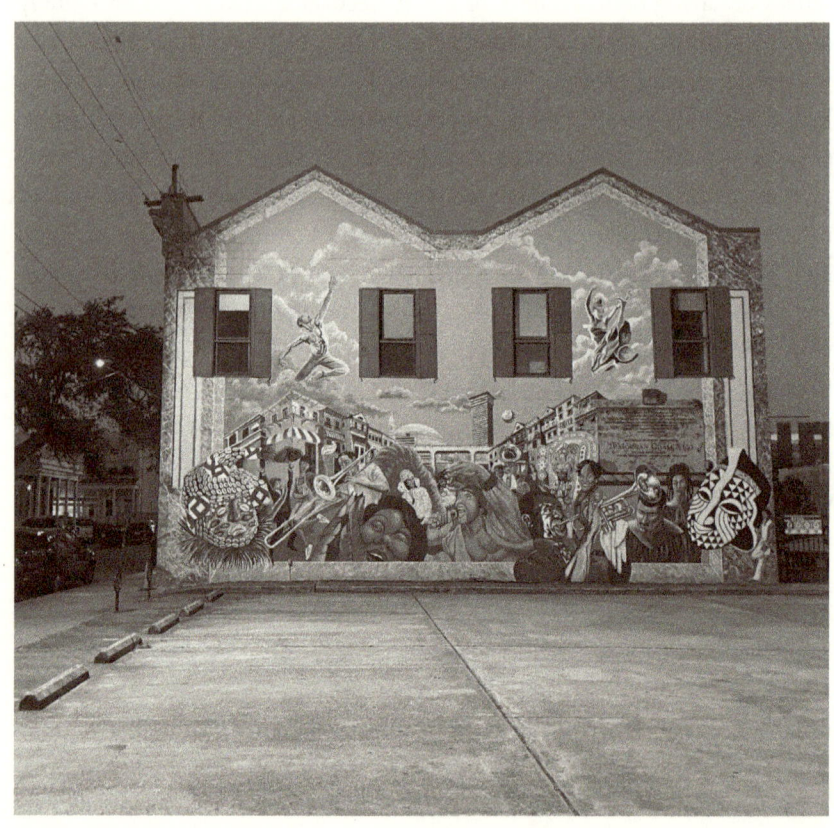

Ashé Mural, close to Ashé Cultural Arts Center, Oretha Castle Haley Boulevard, 2022.

CURATING CONNECTIONS

By Way of Conclusion

Close your eyes and imagine New Orleans.
What comes to mind? What do you see?

In our work in the city, we have been struck by the different ways in which cultural practices across the city are engaged in reimagining what New Orleans is, both as a place to live and work and in terms of its position within the cultural imaginary. New Orleans is very often represented in the world through popular and touristic narratives. The work of the practitioners and organizations discussed in this book is more complex, nuanced, and profound. What is most important here are the ways in which we understand, identify, and grow conversations between the practices this volume discusses and the understandings and strategies that might be developed as a result of those conversations.

Where artists and researchers curate connections, so, too, do inhabitants of the city, in their practice of the city, particularly their creative practice. In dancing in the streets, in dressing up for Mardi Gras or Halloween or a scavenger hunt, in dropping into "deep gras," in busking and performing in Jackson Square, in decorating their houses, people speak to streets, neighborhoods, and the city about the city. Much of what we have analyzed thus far in the book has been specific venues, events, and activities, sometimes small incidental things, sometimes grander and more permanent entities. In each instance, the chapters have drawn connections between perhaps seemingly different or disparate practices to illuminate the ways they can attend to particular challenges in the city: overtourism, infrastructure and streets, managing events and crises in the city through situation rooms, living with water and the role of adaptation and performance in doing so, responding to a pandemic by re-familiarizing people with their city. As we conclude the volume, we want to attend to other practices of connection that not only reveal the value of curated connection but speak also to the great breadth of practices in the city that we have not had space to analyze as individual chapters but which speak to questions of resilience.

We are aware in signaling the curated nature of these connections that there is a politics at play, that curation is not a neutral act. In a sense, in including *curating* in the title of the conclusion, we are deliberately calling for a political reading of the book and, much more important, of the work we have put into conversation in these pages. For curator-scholars Mørland and Amundsen, contemporary curatorial practices deploy deliberately political methods that constitute "radically new way[s] of working." This moves the political from the preserve of the content alone to "activat[ing] art's political potential through curatorial form and structure as well." In this way, they argue, curation "affords the means to agitate, speak, and to be listened to" so curation is no longer about the politics of shaping the art world but a powerful practice "for political purposes, aiming to change societal structures."[1] We do not argue that this book will change societal structures per se, for that is best done by stakeholders in the city working in locally determined, equitable, and mutually beneficial conversations and collaborations. Rather, in this book, we identify that each of the case studies we discuss has very real potential to transform societal structures, understandings, and strategies of resilience both individually and especially in connected conversation across familiar disciplinary divides.

The Art and Politics of Representing New Orleans

New Orleans, as all major cultural cities, has an established set of venues that present the city back to itself. While the focus of this book is not on major arts institutions, it is valuable here to explore the role and function of two such organizations in relation to city-facing exhibitions they curated: first, the Historic New Orleans Collection's *Art of the City: Postmodern to Post-Katrina* (2019); and second, Ashé Cultural Arts Center's *Art of the Black Experience* (2022). These exhibitions, and through them the organizing institutions, speak to politics of place in both the artistic content of the works and, especially, through forms of performative engagement beyond the walls of the exhibition.

ART OF THE CITY: POSTMODERN TO POST-KATRINA

In 2019 artist Jan Gilbert curated *Art of the City: Postmodern to Post-Katrina* in the Historic New Orleans Collection's newly purpose-built space for contemporary art in New Orleans at 520 Royal Street, in the heart of the French Quarter. The exhibition initially emerged from HNOC's desire to showcase some of the hundreds of items in its holdings, with a focus on the urban landscape of the city. While the final curation included thirty-five pieces directly from HNOC, Gilbert insisted the exhibition be multidisciplinary and, crucially, include programming that was outside the building itself.

The exhibition had significant visibility in the city due to its prominent location and through striking event branding across different neighborhoods in New Orleans. Such marketing was enabled by Helis Foundation funding and the relative security that comes as a large, landowning organization.[2] The HNOC is located the French Quarter, and with citywide marketing, the exhibition explicitly sought to engage tourists and locals alike. With that in mind, Gilbert's curatorial insistence that *Art of the City* needed to include exhibits, artifacts, and events from beyond the collection's holdings and physical space is key to the politics of the work.

The exhibition comprised multiple forms across a number of spaces and areas of the building; from framed, formal paintings to installations, sculptures, and interactive digital pieces. While significant in scope and scale, the exhibition was a beginning point of the wider curatorial practice and hence the wider point of the project. *Art of the City* included formally staged and curated bicycle tours that could be self-guided or joined at predetermined moments of collective experience as "bike rolls" during the May to June of the exhibition's run. The tour is also a legacy artifact of the project, as it exists now in digital form for people to download and undertake.

Similarly pushing beyond the exhibition space, *Art of the City* also included public art, events, discussions, and acts of mapping in its careful, deliberate attempt to bring the beautifully curated fine artworks of the exhibition into explicit conversation with areas across the city. For instance, *Stoop Stories* comprised "a series of informal gallery talks with artists featured in the exhibition, inspired by the kind of neighborly conversations held on front porches throughout the city."[3] This work frames and stages a common conversational practice of the city, of neighborhoods in the city, in which people sit on their stoops and watch the world go by or talk with their neighbors. As a performance framing device, *Stoop Stories* enables live conversation about the importance of different modes of arts practice and the ways they represent and rethink New Orleans for New Orleanians and for visitors. In a small way, the intervention brought a familiar practice from the city into an institution.

Reflecting on the form of the work, Gilbert suggests the exhibition was curated through a "joyful irreverence" that deliberately railed against chronological or logically ordered approaches. This was to ensure *Art of the City* "feel[s] like the city, like you're wandering through this wonderful, chaotic city," where the politics of exploring the impact of Katrina on the city becomes "interwoven, interspersed because as we know, Katrina comes back."[4]

Within a curatorial frame that seeks to offer an embodied and intellectual encounter that reflects the experience of being in the city, it seems critical that such work reaches as wide a swathe of New Orleans residents as possible. To assist in this, as well as installing aspects of the exhibition in different neighborhoods across the city (from the Quarter to City Park, Algiers to the Industrial Canal), all aspects of the exhibition were free. While not a surefire way to ensure engagement, this at least removes a financial barrier, meaning people can participate no matter their personal circumstances.

In *Art of the City* there was a range of activities happening that curated connections across the multidisciplinary aspects of the exhibition. Thus, HNOC was embroiled in a swirl of activities rather than presenting a straightforward, traditionally understood institutional exhibition. The entanglement of free live events, building-based installation and exhibiting, bicycle tours, and public art afforded opportunities for this work to performatively engage in representing and rethinking New Orleans across multiple sites over a significant swathe of time (April–October 2019).

ART OF THE BLACK EXPERIENCE

Where *Art of the City* might be understood as a "finished" project in multiform conversation with New Orleans, *Art of the Black Experience* presented a different means of reflection and representation on and of the city. At one level, this was an extraordinary exhibition of Black art and artists from across New Orleans, housed in one of the most important artistic and cultural venues of the city. That is, of course, enough in and of itself. However, the work was made more extraordinary in its collaboration with Arts Council New Orleans to ensure that viewer-selected works would make their way back into the public domain: "Ashé Cultural Arts Center in partnership with the Arts Council New Orleans presents Art of the Black Experience: A Call for Artwork for the City of New Orleans Percent for Art Collection. Up to $100,000 of artwork will be purchased to become part of the city's permanent collection."[5] As the title and focus of the exhibition made very clear, the project was intended to center lived experiences of Black identity in the city and the importance of these experiences to the wider place identity of New Orleans. These works being taken into the city's permanent collection ensures the exhibition's political legacy and connects the exhibition, artists, and artworks to longer-term understandings of New Orleans. The deployment of these artworks across municipal spaces in the city offered an opportunity for "the City" to center, understand, and deploy the cultural knowledge represented within these works. Artist and Ashé chief equity officer Asali DeVan Ecclesiastes put it more clearly:

> **Black art** matters because . . .
> **Black art** shatters boundaries of imagination and limiting social projections
> **Black artists** are crafters of dream-filled futures and unflinching social reflections
> **Black art** captures the depths and the heights of humanity's aspiration
> **Black artists** gather resources out of ether, magic for your appreciation
> **Black art** enraptures, helps align worlds that might otherwise splinter
> **Black art** matters because Black artists make movements rather than push margins.[6]

Art of the Black Experience continues the long legacy of Ashé as an active force in the city, claiming space for Black knowledge and for Black arts, culture, and communities and ensuring that this is taken seriously at the level of city decision making.

Art, Food, Family, and Social Justice

Exhibitions constitute a particular kind of curatorial practice of the city. It is not too much of a stretch to suggest that the restaurant Dooky Chase, an established Black-owned restaurant in the Tremé, has, for a very long time now, curated a series of interwoven activities across: art, cuisine, business, and activist practices. The "restaurant" has become a long-standing place of understanding and representing the city and of rethinking the nation.

We have been to Dooky Chase a few times now. On each of our trips, and while we are uncomfortable with visitor itineraries, it is one of the things people tell us we must do while in the city. On each of our trips to Dooky Chase, we were delighted to meet with Edgar Chase III. On our first trip, Chase was passing between tables, welcoming and chatting with diners. He sat with us for a while, we talked a little bit about our research, and he let us know that his niece, Chase Kamata, was studying theater in London. He took a photo of the

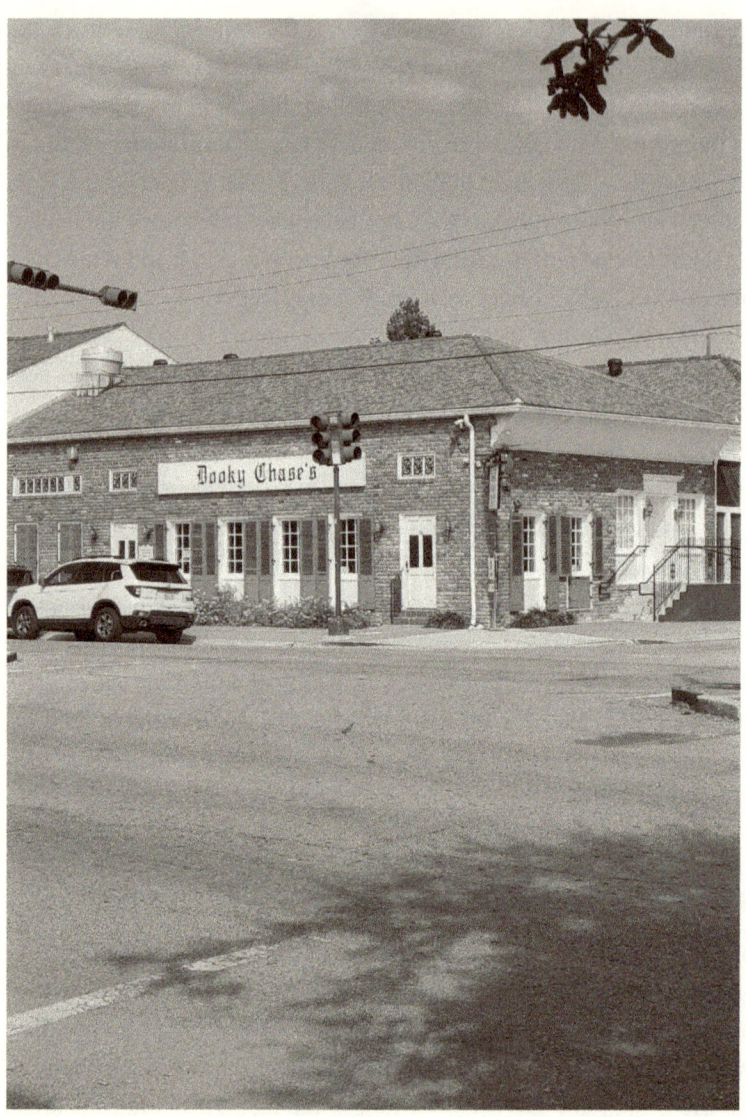

Exterior of Dooky Chase restaurant, 2022.

three of us and sent it to Kamata. The second time we visited, Chase was there with Kamata, who, by coincidence, was back in the country. They kindly joined us for the evening. We spoke about theater, arts, the work of the restaurant in the city, and Chase's and his niece's own experiences of the city. Chase reflected particularly on the art collection at the restaurant. There is art throughout the restaurant, some framed works, some sculptures. We had been aware of this collection on our previous trip but had not known that Leah Chase, Edgar Chase's mother, had a particular desire to introduce art into the restaurant. At Edgar Chase's prompting, Kamata revealed work she had created and which hung in the space. Our 8:30 p.m. booking and spirited conversation meant that time passed, the restaurant emptied, so Chase and Kamata showed us around the space as one would go round an exhibition.

Dooky Chase is a familiar restaurant in the city, the country, and internationally. It was a critical meeting place for activists during the civil rights movement; it was a safe place to eat when, in Mia Bay's words, "traveling Black."[7] More recently, it was here that Leah Chase chided Barack Obama for proposing to add hot sauce to a dish. Chase tells us about the gallery level that was then being newly developed and about the project to celebrate Black New Orleanians in pavers on the sidewalk. This is a place where on any given night, people are made welcome, where the act of having a meal is more than the consumption of food. The established history and practice of Dooky Chase in the Tremé and in the city, its growth and development, its creation of a vital space for African American art, resist neat definitions as a singular place in the city. We are reminded of Asali DeVan Ecclesiastes's reflection that while communities may distrust certain city departments or officials, "who folks do trust and hold in esteem and look up to for social guidance are the artists and culture bearers—the people in the community who make music, who make Indian suits, who are chefs and culinary artists or poets, spoken word artists, singers."[8] Dooky Chase draws together people who are trusted. As Leah Chase herself reflected of the early days of the restaurant: "After high school proms, Dooky's was the only place parents would allow their daughters to go. For that matter, it was often the only place Black youngsters of the day, male or female, were allowed to go."[9] While such trust is valuable in itself, it can also operate powerfully within the community and city. Dooky Chase operates on multiple, interconnected fronts as arts venue; living room, lounge and dining room; heritage site; a place of lively political debate, action, and activism. It has historically been, and in its contemporary interventions in the city continues to be, a powerful, energetic site of situational awareness. Dooky Chase is all the things that resilience should be. It is the very definition of a site that brings together multiple forms of resilience practice. Dooky Chase rethinks resilience knowledge and disrupts hegemonic associations of neoliberalism associated with that term. In doing so, this institution redistributes knowledge from those practices back into the city and beyond.

Decoration and Repair in a Changing City

In our visit in February 2022, we are aware that we are visiting the city only a few months after COVID-19 restrictions were lifted and after Hurricane Ida, the most significant hurricane to hit the city since Katrina. We speak to the artist and curator Jan Gilbert and her husband, the filmmaker Kevin McCaffery, about living in the city during Ida. We were already aware that by the time Ida had become a category 4 storm, there had not been time to evacuate the city. At 150 miles per hour, Ida was just 7 miles an hour below a category 5 hurricane. The city lost power. Gilbert and McCaffery tell us that this time they had not fixed wooden boards to their windows. They describe waking in the night, going downstairs, and realizing their windows were at risk of being blown in and how they stood in the dark, their hands outstretched, holding the large plate glass sliding windows against the storm, looking out as the trees bent in the wind. We wonder how long they stood there. They talk, joke a little. We wonder at the practice of bracing against a storm.

When we speak with the director of hazard mitigation, Austin Feldbaum, he mentions, "Y'all will see a lot of blue tarps in the city."[10] And he's right—we see them everywhere. This wasn't Katrina-level devastation, but the impact is absolutely clear: houses have been impacted, roofs breached, trees felled. While we did see blue tarps in the city, we also watched the city building up to Mardi Gras day. We passed trees increasingly festooned with beads and "house floats," an innovation developed during COVID-19 in which parades were banned and so people decorated their houses as stationary "floats." We stopped at a house dressed for Vax Fest, with swags of oversized beads hanging from a balcony and a sign promoting take-up of the COVID-19 vaccine. On another house, its front steps and porch decorated with mismatched plant pots and greenery, a bright-yellow NOLA Ready SLEEVES UP NOLA! sign declaims that "THE COVID VACCINE IS THE WAY OUT OF THE PANDEMIC." To the left of the sign, a pink plastic flamingo has been perched, jauntily, on a plant pot. In the context of house floats, and the cancellation of Mardi Gras a year earlier, the decorations alone speak to the challenges of the pandemic. Yet these decorations find playful means to share messages that governments internationally had found difficult to promote. Here, whether set among precisely crafted displays or more eclectic assemblages, the formality of vaccine messaging is woven into performances of homes in the city.

Beyond COVID-19 specific guidance, homes gift other messages to the city. For instance, on a yellow house, hanging from a wrought iron porch pillar, is a painted image of a rat holding a sign that advises: "Keep ya head up NOLA." By November 2022 we're aware of far fewer tarps, although we still see them at points across the city. The Halloween decorations are still up. Gigantic spiders crawl across the webs that wrap around a house on Magazine Street. Skeletons play a steely game of cards; flags in the gold, purple, and green colors of the city blow in the breeze. Practices of decoration inform how people live in the city. Approaches to decoration vary from the complex, whole-house installations to seemingly more minor, playful interventions, such as painting a stoop sea blue and carefully, deliberately placing a small plastic yellow duck at the center of this expanse of color. No matter the scale or complexity, these decorative interventions are performative iterations of place identity. They offer expressions of belonging that ground these homes in shared practices of the city that help to resist catastrophized narratives of the city. They celebrate New Orleans, even as it faces considerable challenges.

Resisting Catastrophe: A Last Point

In analyzing processes of cultural production in New Orleans since 2017, we hope to have reflected on changing and plural practices in the city, to reveal different ways of performing city resilience at multiple scales and in different areas of the city. While there is a range of work here and a good period of time covered, however, the book will only ever offer a snapshot in time. Almost inevitably, given the speed of change in any city, but in New Orleans in particular, there is a risk the book will be out-of-date by the time it is published. Yet in offering examples and case studies that reveal models of rethinking resilience that emerge from and with cultural practices of the city, we hope the book will stand the test of time.

Not all practices in a city are documented in perpetuity, and yet if we lose documentation of them or if we do not pay enough attention to their importance and impact at the time of their happening, we run the risk of losing their resilience potential. This book then is both a reflection on a city over an eight-year period, from 2017 to 2025, but also a set of models of practices, understandings, and approaches that can be explored in years to come and in contexts beyond New Orleans. We are not arguing that the examples we analyze are the only ways of enacting a rethinking of resilience but that they provide means of thinking and practicing that might be adapted, refracted, and rethought.

Ultimately, in all our work on New Orleans, we have been interested to reveal diverse performances that resist or challenge dominant paradigms of how the city is understood and so address new ways of practicing resilience that resist all-too-familiar narratives about the place. Our research began with a hunch: that performances in a city reveal the ways in which a city thinks through the challenges that it faces. The work has revealed a need for new means of facilitating dialogue between these performances in a city. For stakeholders in New Orleans, our work on the ground, through conversation and workshops, has offered means of rethinking familiar ideas and practices. Indicatively, the city's Hazard Mitigation team has embarked on what they call "a long-term path of embedding arts and cultural practices in [its] strategic planning."[11]

Alongside touristic representations of the city, New Orleans is often subject to catastrophizing narratives (indeed "catastrophe" was the theme of the American Society for Theatre Research conference in New Orleans in November 2022). COVID-19 has further contributed to catastrophized narratives of the city. Yet with campaigns like #SleevesUpNOLA, the city has once again responded with and through performance. As we write in the "post"-COVID moment, it is vital to ask pressing questions of the risks, rewards, possibilities, and limits of performance in and of the Crescent City. Too often, New Orleans is described as a city of catastrophes—flooding, hurricanes, poverty, racism, tourism, violence—without critical attention to wider understandings of the city, particularly as made manifest in social and aesthetic performances. Just as we would not necessarily assume that the tourist experience of New Orleans offers a real sense of the place, so we must not get caught up in narratives that continue to catastrophize it.

As with all performative acts, to discuss the city in these catastrophic terms means and does something in and beyond the city; just as tourism drives understandings of place identity and practices of place, so, too, catastrophe can be written into understandings of the city in reductive and banalizing ways. By contrast, we hope this book reveals some of the richness of the city's cultural and civic performances, those that are "beyond" all too habitual representations of the place. In so doing, the arguments here seek to illuminate different ways that New Orleans's performance cultures move us beyond catastrophizing narratives about the city.

This book reveals different perspectives on this city that you may or may not be familiar with, illuminating perspectives, practices, and understandings of New Orleans from specialists, *key* voices in the cultural economies of the city—people who, we would argue, are senior "city strategists," whose work directly relates to the resilience of New Orleans. Their professional practices and personal understandings of the city help navigate, understand, and position the city in relation to the "challenges" that it faces. Our research demonstrates that cultural performances from New Orleans offer models of thinking about cultural production in other locales that can be valuable in resilience thinking internationally.

One reason why we wanted to write this book is because catastrophized narratives of New Orleans dismiss the importance of performance practices here and suggest that there might not be anything more to be learned through the analysis of performances in and of this city. In a city facing significant challenges but supported by such incredibly rich, diverse, and powerful cultural practices, it is vital that we recognize that arts and resilience practitioners are all engaged in addressing the ways that we move beyond catastrophe in New Orleans. The city's cultural infrastructure not only reflects the place, its histories and stories, but in imagining possible futures from multiple perspectives across multiple media, performances of New Orleans are world making. They playfully address the city's future and resilience challenges in dynamic, positive, and creative ways.

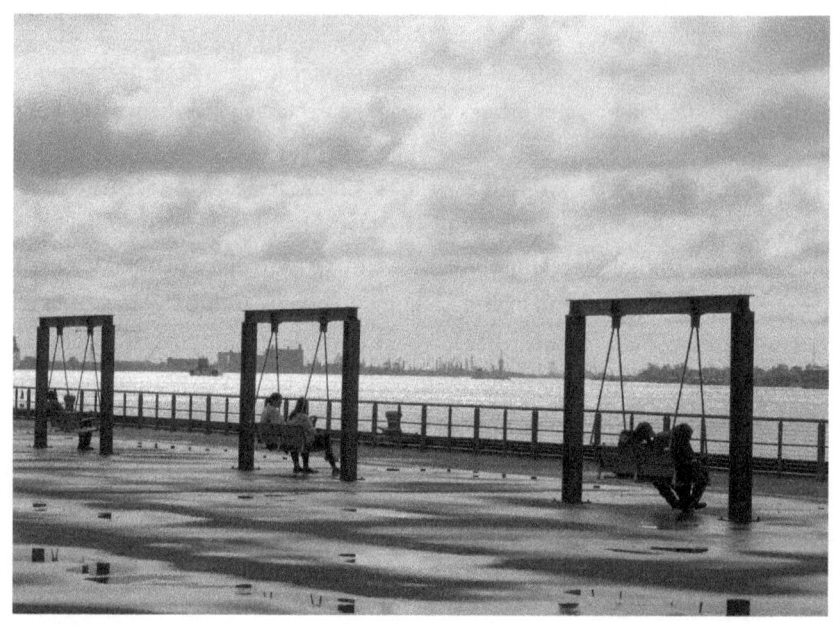

Swings at Crescent Park, 2019.

LAGNIAPPE

On Not Being Done with New Orleans

We almost did not do this work. If we had listened to several established scholars in our field, we might well have believed that there was nothing more to say about New Orleans in terms of arts and performance. Despite the tendency for academics in arts and humanities to work alone, we found, and continue to find, strength in thinking, working, and writing together. "Perhaps," we were told early on, "only one of you needs to go back"—the implication being that to pursue the research, especially collaboratively, was something of an extravagance. When we spoke with cultural practitioners in the city and told them the story of the journal editor who had rejected our work because we were "done" with New Orleans, they bristled, the injustice and racism of such positions echoing over time flashed across their faces. When we recounted the same story at the American Society for Theatre Research in 2022, there was a collective intake of breath throughout the room.

The trouble with many understandings of New Orleans is that they are simplistic and reductive, and they resist the richness of the city. We hope that in drawing attention to the work of critical practitioners in the city, we have unsettled any such troublingly simplistic readings. Reductive approaches to the city are particularly curious once we allow for lagniappe. This is a city where "a little something extra" is bound up in the practices of city life. It is critical that scholars of the city understand the ways in which local practices offer *something extra*. Indeed, this is to recognize that such practices speak powerfully to contemporary challenges in New Orleans, and present "gifts" to those living, working, and managing challenges beyond the Crescent City.

Although not always immediately clear from the institutional positions they occupy, resilience and emergency planners in the United Kingdom, the United States, and Europe were, throughout our conversations, concerned with ensuring that the work they do addresses inequity and dismantles systemic forms of racism and oppression. Although there are no neat and easy means to enact these objectives, the fact that equity sits centrally in the minds of colleagues in emergency planning and resilience is compelling. Similarly encouraging is the fact that many colleagues highlight, often publicly, that the resilience profession is generally white, often male, and highlight this as a condition requiring change.

In this context, we must recognize that New Orleans has much to offer global communities of arts and resilience practitioners and scholars, especially in terms of understanding critical challenges and addressing inequities. Given the embedded nature of cultural production in the city, it is surprising that the city's knowledges, processes, and practices are not taken more seriously internationally. It is, indeed, perplexing that the city is regularly dismissed as only a party town or the site of catastrophe. The city is at least as culturally important as Beijing, Cape Town, Havana, London, New York, Paris, or Tokyo.

When we began our work in the city, we understood this place as being New Orleans, in part framed by familiar articulations of the city. The removal of Indigenous names of places decenters and devalues Indigenous peoples, their ancestors, and their understandings, experiences, and practices of place. As with a growing list of places in the United States and internationally, in New Orleans there is significant, albeit relatively recent, attention being paid to the need for organizations and people to recognize Indigenous lands. The challenges of this city are bound up with those of the Mississippi Delta, and the impact of actions taken to protect the city ripple outward. The growing effort to identify this place as Bulbancha is both a critical, necessary recentering of peoples of this place and a means of committing to a more equitable future.

The research undertaken for and presented in this book demonstrates the need for municipal, resilience, and emergency planners to identify where decisions by marginalized communities are made and celebrated. The knowledge emerging from these communities' choices and priorities needs to be acknowledged and taken seriously; decisions enacted with these perspectives in mind will be more sophisticated, more nuanced, and more impactful as a result.

We must become better at reflecting on, framing, and planning for tourism in New Orleans. There is incredible work being done by individuals, organizations, companies, and departments, in buildings, on streets, by communities across the city—work that helps to understand long-standing extraordinary, and sometimes overwhelming, challenges. After too long living with the idea of New Orleans constituting three-and-a-bit days in a party town, it is time to take account of the scale, subtlety, breadth, and significance of performances of New Orleans.

New Orleans is a globally important city; taking its cultural productions seriously matters.

It is not possible to be "done" with New Orleans.

NOTES

"Come Back Often": By Way of Introduction

1. See Marigny Opera House, https://marignyoperahouse.org/history-community.

2. Montano, Disasterology.

3. See Kershaw, "Practice as Research through Performance."

4. See, for example, Carrico, *Dancing the Politics of Pleasure;* Dessens, "New Orleans, Where the Stage Is the Street"; Sakakeeny, *Roll with It.*

5. Magelssen, *Simming,* 116.

6. "Where to Build the Walls That Protect Us."

7. Stephen Hodge, personal telephone correspondence with Duggan, 30 June 2017.

8. Winterson "With His Manchester Poem, Tony Walsh Found Words."

9. A video of the performance of the poem at the Manchester vigil is available on YouTube: BBC, *Poem about Manchester: "This Is the Place,"* accessed 21 September 2018, https://www.you tube.com/watch?v=PszMmYpQjPo.

10. DeFrantz and Gonzalez, *Black Performance Theory,* 6.

11. Ibid. Here DeFrantz writes as "Male-Identified Queer High Yellow Duke University," by which he positions himself and his reflections on theorizing research.

12. The book draws on a series of visits we made to the city (six fieldwork trips from 2018 to 2025, each lasting between eight and twelve days), alongside research at a distance between visits (from 2017 onward, but especially through 2020 and 2021, as the COVID-19 pandemic prevented us from doing research in the city).

13. See Liu and Burnett, "Insider-Outsider."

14. For the purposes of full disclosure, we had forms of in-kind support for a public symposium at the Contemporary Arts Center. Other organizations generously engaged with this work and its development, including access to venues, offices, and sites for the purpose of meetings, workshops, and fundamental research.

15. Aimée Hayes, interview with authors, Roosevelt Hotel, New Orleans, 31 March 2018.

16. Ecclesiastes, conversation with authors at *Brass on the Boulevard,* 23 February 2022.

17. Young, *Theatre and Race,* 67, 68.

18. See NBC News, "New Orleans Now Nation's Murder Capital."

19. Rodin, *Resilience Dividend,* 4.

20. See Birch and Carney, "Regional Resilience."

21. Cited in Rodin, *Resilience Dividend*, 43.

22. Manyena, "Concept of Resilience Revisited," 434.

23. Tierney, "Resilience and the Neoliberal Project," 1333.

24. See Chandler and Reid, *Neoliberal Subject*.

25. See Duggan, "Rethinking Tourism"; and Kang, "'I Have a Right Not to Be Resilient.'"

26. Harvie, *Theatre and the City*, 7–8. Early research on arts and contexts of resilience includes Andrews and Duggan, "Situation Rooms"; and Brown, Eernstman, Huke, and Reding, "Drama of Resilience."

27. Godschalk, "Urban Hazard Mitigation," 136.

28. Morris and Kadetz, "Culture and Resilience," 251, 234.

29. Chandler, "Editorial," 1.

30. 100 Resilient Cities, "Frequently Asked Questions (FAQ) about 100 Resilient Cities," accessed 21 September 2018, http://www.100resilientcities.org/faq (website no longer exists).

31. Walker and Salt, *Resilience Thinking*, 114.

32. Chandler, "Editorial," 1.

33. See, for example, Nield, "Tahrir Square EC4M"; Nield, "There Is Another World."

34. We note here Amanda Rogers's use of the term *co-constitutive* as a valuable term to reflect on the interrelation of performance and cities. Rogers, "Geographies of the Performing Arts."

35. Chandler, "Editorial," 1.

36. Dodd, "Creative Cities."

37. Shepherd and Wallis, *Drama/Theatre/Performance*, 223. See also Butler, *Bodies That Matter*; Austin, *How to Do Things with Words*.

38. See Schechner, *Between Theater and Anthropology*; Roach, "Dreaming New Orleans."

39. Swain and King, "Using Informal Conversations in Qualitative Research," 3.

40. This approach went through research ethics processes at Brunel University London and Northumbria University (2020–25) and the University of Surrey (2017–19).

41. Twardowski, "They're Tryin' to Wash Us Away," 15, 16.

1. After Overtourism

1. New Orleans Sustainable Tourism Task Force, "Abstract."

2. Thomas, *Desire and Disaster in New Orleans*, 3.

3. Werry, *Theatre and Tourism*, 10.

4. Sloane-Boekbinder, "African Symbolism."

5. See New Orleans Sustainable Tourism Task Force, "Abstract."

6. World Tourism Organization (UNWTO); Centre of Expertise Leisure, Tourism & Hospitality; NHTV Breda University of Applied Sciences; and NHL Stenden University of Applied Sciences, "Overtourism," 3.

7. Ali, "Genesis of Overtourism."

8. For a comprehensive discussion of definitions of *overtourism*, see Nilsson, "Conceptualizing and Contextualizing Overtourism."

9. UNWTO; Centre of Expertise Leisure, Tourism & Hospitality; NHTV Breda University of Applied Sciences; and NHL Stenden University of Applied Sciences, "Overtourism," 5.

10. New Orleans Sustainable Tourism Task Force, "Abstract."

11. Roach, "Dreaming New Orleans," 18.

12. Patrick Duggan, personal field notes: New Orleans, 26 March 2018.

13. We searched on Google for "tourism AND French Quarter AND New Orleans," 3 March 2023.

14. Atkinson, "New Orleans Music," 249; Bălan and Bordelon, "Role of Water and Tourism Management," 273.

15. Coady, "New Orleans Rhythm and Blues," 97, 100.

16. Crutcher, Tremé, 7.

17. Thomas, Desire and Disaster in New Orleans, 14.

18. Ibid., 5.

19. Bălan and Bordelon, "Role of Water and Tourism Management," 273.

20. Rodin, Resilience Dividend, 257.

21. Ibid.

22. See, for example, Bălan and Bordelon, "Role of Water and Tourism Management"; Thomas, Desire and Disaster in New Orleans; Souther, New Orleans on Parade.

23. See Souther, New Orleans on Parade.

24. Cited in Kaplan-Levenson, "Why New Orleans Leaned into Tourism."

25. Levendis and Dicle, "Economic Impact of Airbnb on New Orleans"; Hernborg, "40+ New Orleans Tourism Statistics, Numbers and Trends"; New Orleans & Company, "About NewOrleans.com," https://www.neworleans.com/about-us.

26. Doug MacCash, interview with authors, Mojo Coffee House, Magazine Street, New Orleans, 2 April 2018.

27. Mahn et al., "Personalising Disaster," 166.

28. See, for example: Fields, Wagner, and Frisch, "Placemaking and Disaster Recovery"; Dudley and Duffy, "Tourism Discourse and Surveillance"; Gotham, "Touristic Disaster"; Miller, "Disaster Tourism and Disaster Landscape Attractions after Hurricane Katrina."

29. Mahn et al., "Personalising Disaster," 168–71.

30. See Thomas, Desire and Disaster in New Orleans; and Clark et al., "Confederate Reckoning."

31. See "Things to Do in New Orleans," Tripadvisor, https://www.tripadvisor.co.uk/Attractions -g60864-Activities-New_Orleans_Louisiana.html; "The Best Things to Do in New Orleans Right Now," TimeOut, accessed 24 November 2023, https://www.timeout.com/new-orleans/things-to-do /best-things-to-do-in-new-orleans.

32. See, for example, Travel Bunny, "3 Days in New Orleans—What to See and Do in the Big Easy" (sixth entry in a Google search for "top to-dos in New Orleans," 16 March 2023), in which eleven of the fourteen suggested activities are based or start in the French Quarter: https://the travelbunny.com/3-days-in-new-orleans-travel-guide.

33. Rough Guides, "New Orleans Travel Guide."

34. NewOrleans.com, "New Orleans Signature Drink Recipe."

35. Pakan and Purwandani, "Itinerary, Information, Denial," 885, 898.

36. Ella Mingazova notes James Buzard's (1993) work on the traveler-tourist dichotomy, observing that "while travellers sought to gain in-depth knowledge of places, of the land, tourists looked at the landscape and remained on the surface." While Mingazova notes that the dichotomy has subsequently been reimagined, "the traveller/tourist dichotomy has not disappeared from contemporary travel writing but simply become more subtle." Mingazova, "Slow Travel Writing," 182.

37. Wade, Roberts, and de Caro, *Downtown Mardi Gras*, 7.

38. Ibid.

39. New Orleans Sustainable Tourism Task Force, "Abstract," 7.

40. New Orleans Sustainable Tourism Task Force, "Culture Misunderstood."

41. UNWTO; Centre of Expertise Leisure, Tourism & Hospitality; NHTV Breda University of Applied Sciences; and NHL Stenden University of Applied Sciences, *"Overtourism,"* 8.

42. A version of this section was first published as a blog entry on 23 February 2022 for Performing City Resilience during field research in 2022: https://performingcityresilience.com/2022/02/23/carnival2022.

43. UNWTO; Centre of Expertise Leisure, Tourism & Hospitality; NHTV Breda University of Applied Sciences; and NHL Stenden University of Applied Sciences, *"Overtourism,"* 8.

44. Ibid., 6.

45. Formally, the New Orleans Convention & Visitors Bureau (NOCVB), New Orleans and Company exists to ensure "that the tourism industry benefits all residents of New Orleans, as it continues to benefit our members and our visitors, to nourish and sustain the culture of our city which makes New Orleans a world-class travel destination and the world's greatest place to live, for those of us lucky enough to call it home." Accessed 30 November 2023, https://www.neworleans.com/about-us/about-new-orleans-and-company.

46. Music and Culture Coalition of New Orleans, "Reallocation of Tourism Revenue.".

47. See Performing City Resilience, "Resisting Catastrophe."

48. Music and Culture Coalition of New Orleans, "Good Visitor's Guide to New Orleans."

49. UNWTO; Centre of Expertise Leisure, Tourism & Hospitality; NHTV Breda University of Applied Sciences; and NHL Stenden University of Applied Sciences, *"Overtourism,"* 3.

50. Originally taken from the website of Kermit's Tremé Mother-in-Law Lounge (https://www.kermitslounge.com), the web page has since been updated. However, photographer Mark Roberts recalls the same citation at FineArtAmerica, accessed 30 November 2023, https://fineartamerica.com/featured/mother-in-law-lounge-mark-roberts.html#:~:text=Featuring%20daily%20food%20made%20by,the%20grill%20going%20out%20back.

51. Oswell, "Kermit's Treme Mother-in-Law Lounge."

52. See JAMNOLA website, accessed 21 February 2022, https://jamnola.com.

53. JAMNOLA, "Costume Closet" signage seen by authors, 21 February 2022.

54. Young and Markham, "Tourism, Capital, and the Commodification of Place," 276, 277.

55. Ibid., 279.

56. Ibid., 281.

57. See JAMNOLA website, https://jamnola.com.

58. UNWTO; Centre of Expertise Leisure, Tourism & Hospitality; NHTV Breda University of Applied Sciences; and NHL Stenden University of Applied Sciences, *"Overtourism,"* 3.

2. Playing in the Streets

1. See, particularly, @lookatthisfuckinstreet, accessed 24 November 2023, https://www.instagram.com/lookatthisfuckinstreet/?hl=en.

2. Carrico, "Un/Natural Disaster and Dancing," 34.

3. Dinerstein, "Thirty Nine Sundays," 107.

4. Roach, *Cities of the Dead*, 14.

5. Dinerstein, "Thirty Nine Sundays," 107, 113, 112.

6. See Greene, "'Masking Indian—Practising Africa.'"

7. Sakakeeny, *Roll with It*, 34.

8. Elam, *Taking It to the Streets*, 73–74.

9. Landry and Bianchini, *Creative City*.

10. Shand, *Creative Arts of Governance of Urban Renewal and Development*, 2.

11. Source10, *Ideal City*.

12. Davis, *Caring City*, 10.

13. Bertolini, "From 'Streets for Traffic' to 'Streets for People,'" 749, 750.

14. Riggs, *End of the Road*, 1, 2, 10.

15. Thorpe, *Owning the Street*, 5.

16. Ibid.

17. Sadik-Khan and Solomonow, *Streetfight*, 3.

18. Thorpe, *Owning the Street*, 5.

19. See, for instance, Benjamin, *Arcades Project*.

20. Montgomery, *Greening the Black Urban Regime*, 143–44. The Cass Corridor is an area of Detroit.

21. Hunter, Pattillo, Robinson, and Taylor, "Black Placemaking," 51.

22. Playable City, "About," https://www.playablecity.com/about.

23. See Playing Out, "An International Movement," https://playingout.net/nearby-you/an-international-movement.

24. Playful City, "Build a World of Play: A Playful Street," https://www.aplayfulcity.com.

25. Playable City, "Playable City Sandbox."

26. Campanella, "Why Prytania Jogs at Joseph," 19.

27. Thomas, *Desire and Disaster in New Orleans*, 159.

28. McKinney, *New Orleans*, 24; cited in Wade, Roberts, and de Caro, *Downtown Mardi Gras*, 22.

29. Wade, Roberts, and de Caro, Downtown Mardi Gras, citing Dikec, *Space, Politics and Aesthetics*, 3.

30. Iveson, Lyons, Clark, and Weir, "Informal Australian City," 12, 18.

31. See, particularly, Mukhija and Loukaitou-Sideris, *Informal American City*.

32. Iveson, Lyons, Clark, and Weir, "Informal Australian City," 24.

33. Running from Florida to California, the I-10 at this point in its journey is most regularly referred to as the Claiborne Expressway or the overpass. We use both interchangeably, and at times we use "the I-10" to recognize the scale of infrastructure running through a neighborhood.

34. "300 Unique New Orleans Moments: Construction of the Interstate Highway System in Louisiana."

35. Schneider, "Why Is It So Hard to Kill This Freeway?"

36. Blankenhorn, "Resilience of Tremé."

37. Campanella, "Why Idyllic Claiborne Avenue Was Undone by Expressway."

38. Bay, *Traveling Black*, 3.

39. Archer, "White Men's Roads through Black Men's Homes," 1330.

40. Schneider, "Why Is It So Hard to Kill This Freeway?"

41. White House. *Fact Sheet: Historic Bipartisan Infrastructure Deal,* 28 July 2021.

42. Schneider, "Why Is It So Hard to Kill This Freeway?"

43. Ecclesiastes, cited in ibid.

44. Khalaj, Pojani, Sipe, and Corcoran, "Why Are Cities Removing Their Freeways," 1.

45. Department of Parks and Parkways, "Neutral Grounds."

46. Reckdahl, "Divided Neighborhood Comes Together."

47. Dessens, "New Orleans, Where the Stage Is the Street," 17, citing information on the project at New Orleans African American Museum, http://noaam.org.

48. Dessens, "Remembering in Black and White," 134.

49. See Lazar, "Brandon 'Bmike' Odums."

50. WWNO, "'The Monster.'"

51. Diana Nawi, in Keith et al., *Prospect.5,* 49.

52. "About the Krewe of the Rolling Elvi," *Mardi Gras New Orleans,* accessed 23 December 2023, https://www.mardigrasneworleans.com/parades/marching-clubs/krewe-of-the-rolling-elvi.

53. In referring to this as a gathering phase, we recall Richard Schechner's use of *gathering* in early forms of theater. See Schechner, *Performance Theory,* 176.

54. LeJeune, "Deep Gras."

55. Shusterman, "Bodies in the Streets and the Somaesthetics of City Life," 1.

56. Radice, "Creativity, Sociability, Solidarity," 4.

57. Bordnick, cited in MacCash, *Mardi Gras Beads,* 104.

58. Coerce, cited in MacCash, *Mardi Gras Beads,* 104.

59. Cited in Kezia Setyawan, "What Goes into a Handmade Mardi Gras Throw."

60. Erdely, "Masking COVID, Crafting Community," 407.

61. Ibid.

62. Cited in Setyawan, "What Goes into a Handmade Mardi Gras Throw."

63. Wade, Roberts, and de Caro, *Downtown Mardi Gras,* 7.

64. Errol Laborde, who claims to have coined the phrase, defines "super krewes" as those with very large numbers of riders who roll in parades that are "visually impressive" and in which each float is "a sensory experience." These krewes are "awash with celebrities" and have distinctive and "distinguished signature elements" throughout. See Laborde, "Defining a Super Krewe."

65. Sheehan, "(Re)working Subjectivities."

66. Rodin, *Resilience Dividend,* 265.

3. The Art and Performance of Situation Rooms

1. When we conducted the research in 2018 and subsequently wrote "Situation Rooms," the building that is now the ACC was being developed into a performance venue to "home" the Southern Rep Theatre. Much of the argument we advanced in the 2019 article was reflecting on the *potential* of the space and the ideas underpinning it (as articulated to us at the time). Subsequently, the Southern Rep Theatre has dissolved and acknowledged its complicity in systemic racism and potentially alienating practices. This chapter reflects on the original arguments we made, many of which are even more pertinent to the work ACC is conducting, and brings them more fully up-to-date.

2. Anderson and Gordon, "Government and (Non)Event," 160, 174.

3. Rodin, Resilience Dividend, 207–8.

4. Bohn, *Nerve Center,* 22.

5. "Inside the Situation Room."

6. Split Britches, *Situation Room.*

7. Fuel Theatre, *Situation Room.*

8. Cited by Quinn, "Los Angeles Has Its Own Situation Room."

9. See also Rimini Protokill, *Situation Rooms.*

10. Gardner, "Going Off-Script."

11. Magelssen, *Simming,* 3, 17.

12. See de Certeau, *The Practice of Everyday Life.*

13. Rogers, "Geographies of the Performing Arts," 68.

14. Ryan Mast, interview with authors, City Hall, New Orleans, 2 April 2018.

15. NewOrleans.com, "New Orleans Second Line History."

16. Manyena, "Concept of Resilience Revisited," 446.

17. Returning to the venue in June 2023, we were struck by the extent to which the outside area had been landscaped, with hardcore used to lay more discernible paths into the venue that are clearly identifiable from the street leading up to it.

18. New Orleans Airlift, "Music Box Village."

19. Delaney Martin, interview with authors, Music Box Village, New Orleans, 3 April 2018.

20. Anderson and Gordon, "Government and (Non)Event," 174.

21. Aimée Hayes, interview with authors, The Roosevelt Hotel, New Orleans, 31 March 2018.

22. Southern Rep Theatre, "Southern Rep Theatre."

23. Southern Rep Theatre, "New Home for Southern Rep".

24. Hayes interview.

25. American Theatre Editors, "Artistic Director Aimée Hayes to Leave Southern Rep."

26. Southern Rep Theatre, Facebook statement.

27. See Bayou Road Business Association website, accessed 30 November 2023, https://www .bayouroad.com.

28. André Cailloux Center for Performing Arts and Cultural Justice, "About Us."

29. No Dream Deferred, "We Will Dream".

30. André Cailloux Center for Performing Arts and Cultural Justice, "History."

31. André Cailloux Center for Performing Arts and Cultural Justice, "About Us."

32. No Dream Deferred, "Home."

33. No Dream Deferred, "Our Mission."

34. Wynne and Riedy, "Precinct-Scale Innovation and the Sharing Paradigm," 25.

35. Meeting with authors, Old Road Coffee, 2024 Bayou Road, New Orleans, 8 June 2023.

36. Bayou Road Business Association, "Black Bayou."

37. Wynne and Riedy, "Precinct-Scale Innovation and the Sharing Paradigm," 35.

38. Gooden, *Dark Space,* 18.

39. hooks, "Architecture and Black Life," 18.

40. Rodin, Resilience Dividend, 274.

41. Ibid., 52.

42. Whybrow, "Introduction," 12.

43. Rogers, "Geographies of the Performing Arts," 68.

44. Rodin, *Resilience Dividend,* 9, 320.

4. Living with Water

1. We learn, later, of the work of Hugo Gyrl, a queer graffiti artist, in and beyond the city, whose You Go Girl artworks intervene joyfully in the city.

2. See Scott-Bottoms, "Rise and Fall of Modern Water."

3. Scott-Bottoms and Roe, "Who Is a Hydrocitizen," 273, 279.

4. Julien, "Introduction to Arts of Survival," xiii.

5. United Nations, "On the Frontlines of Climate Change."

6. Campanella, *Draining New Orleans,* 271; for "Dutch Dialogues," see 276–87.

7. Mikkonen, "Aesthetic Appreciation of Nature and the Global Environmental Crisis," 58.

8. See Restore the Mississippi Delta, *Eternal Flow.*

9. "Gentilly Resilience District Launches Lantern Walk."

10. City of New Orleans, "Gentilly Resilience District Creative Engagement and Communications Plan."

11. Imagine Water Works, "Who We Are."

12. Odem, *Rising Tables,* 3.

13. Quoted in E. Wilkerson, "Along the River," in ibid., 8.

14. Hodder, *Entangled,* 3.

15. Andrews, *Performing Home,* 31.

16. Odem, *Rising Tables,* 13, 18.

17. Bernstein, "Dances with Things."

18. Mondo Bizarro Productions, *Cry You One.*

19. The archive was available at www.cryyouone.com, although it is currently offline.

20. The project was the third piece in a trilogy of works on and about water and environment in Louisiana: *Beneath the Strata / Disappearing* (2006) and *Loup Garou* (2009–10).

21. We focus here on the online documentation of the live event and short films that recorded stories in the online archive.

22. Creative Capital, "Mondo Bizarro Presents *Cry You One.*"

23. Mondo Bizarro, *Cry You One (Work Sample—St. Bernard),* YouTube, 16 May 2020, https://www.youtube.com/watch?v=pnM7kq3z3LU&list=PLke1_9NotAlk6QC8Jn6wlP6ujELcXfIEB&index=3.

24. Mwase, "Culture of Belonging."

25. Mondo Bizarro and Artspot Productions, *Cry You One.*

26. Ibid.

27. Woynarski, *Ecodramaturgies,* 222.

28. Nick Slie, cited in Creative Capital, "Mondo Bizarro Presents *Cry You One.*"

29. Nick Slie, cited in Coviello, "Preview: *Cry You One.*"

30. Lee, "*Cry You One* Lets the Land Speak."

31. Contemporary Arts Center New Orleans, "*Float Lab.*"

32. U.S. Department of Arts and Culture, "Mondo Bizarro and The Land Memory Bank."

33. The exhibition was held at Newcomb Art Museum, Tulane University, New Orleans, and the book was published with the Neighborhood Story Project. See "Monique Verdin: Return to Yakni Chitto," accessed 30 November 2023, https://newcombartmuseum.tulane.edu/port folio-item/return-to-yakni-chitto.

34. Verdin, "Ebb and Flow," 24.

35. Verdin, *Return to Yakni Chitto.*

36. Billiot, Kwon, and Burnette, "Repeated Disasters and Chronic Environmental Changes," 23, 24.

37. Green, Beaudreau, Lukin, and Crowder, "Climate Change Stressors".

38. Billiot, Kwon, and Burnette, "Repeated Disasters and Chronic Environmental Changes," 24.

39. Water Leaders Institute, Building a Home in the Delta.

40. Darensbourg, quoted in Scheer, *Bulbancha Is Still a Place.*

41. Imagine Water Works, "Who We Are."

42. Hawkins, *For Creative Geographies*, 246.

43. Indeed, the importance of *Cry You One* as a key performance engagement with resilience has been highlighted to us from colleagues in both arts and resilience on each visit we have made to the city, including in March 2025.

5. Pandemic Performances: Beyond Response and Recovery

1. The "Disaster Risks Management Cycle" is common in most emergency management approaches internationally but see, for example, FEMA, *Emergency Management in the United States.*

2. Duggan, "Catapult."

3. Ecclesiastes, quoted in Ivry, "New Orleans Creatives Get to the Heart of the Matter.".

4. Law, *After Method,* 2.

5. McEntire, *Disaster Response and Recovery,* 5.

6. Fakhruddin, Blanchard, and Ragupathy. "Are We There Yet," 1–2.

7. Ibid., 4.

8. Leach and Rivera, "Dismantling Power Asymmetries in Disaster and Emergency Management Research," 338, 348.

9. See, for example, Duggan and Peschel, *Performing (for) Survival;* Andrews and Duggan, "Towards Strategy as Performance in Hazard Mitigation".

10. James Gillman, letter of support, AHRC/UKRI Covid-19 Rapid Response grant application, 2020.

11. James Gillman, interview with authors, 27 April 2021.

12. Helen Hinds, meeting with authors, 18 August 2021, Newcastle upon Tyne.

13. Helen Hinds, letter of support, AHRC/UKRI Covid-19 Rapid Response grant application, 2020.

14. Hough, Langlois, and Lagadec, "Leadership in Terra Incognita," 16–17; 16; our emphasis.

15. See Sapat, "Transboundary Disasters and Nongovernmental Organizations."

16. See Andrews and Duggan, "Towards 'Strategy as Performance' in Hazard Mitigation"; and Andrews and Duggan, "Situation Rooms."

17. Kushma, *Case Studies in Disaster Recovery,* li.

18. Ibid., xlix.

19. Jeannotte, "When the Gigs Are Gone," 5, 4.

20. Hough, Langlois, and Lagadec, "Leadership in Terra Incognita," 17.

21. Hetrick, "Embracing Uncertainty through Embracing the Arts," vi.

22. Alan Lane (Slung Low's artistic director), interview with authors, conducted online, 13 April 2021.

23. Alan Lane, cited in Morton, "Slung Low Stage a Treat for Local Families."

24. The UNDDR defines response as "actions taken directly before, during or immediately after a disaster in order to save lives, reduce health impacts, ensure public safety and meet the basic subsistence needs of the people affected." See UNDRR, "Response."

25. Further information about the house and its complex history, including its role in the slave trade, can be found at "Beauregard-Keyes House," Wikipedia, accessed 19 February 2023, https://en.wikipedia.org/wiki/Beauregard-Keyes_House.

26. Historic New Orleans Collection (HNOC), *From the Frontline: Narratives of the Covid-19 Pandemic in New Orleans,* accessed 10 December 2024, https://www.hnoc.org/research/front-line -narratives-covid-19-pandemic-new-orleans.

27. National Performance Network, "Creative Response Network," accessed 10 December 2024, https://npnweb.org/contact/creative-response-network; also see Creative Response, "About," accessed 20 October 2023, https://creativeresponse.works.

28. Farrier, "Mardi Gras (Yardi Gras) 2021."

29. Rosefeldt, "Alternative Mardi Gras 2021," 74.

30. MAYK, "This Is Not a Party."

31. Ibid.

32. WWOZ New Orleans, "Festing in Place 2020," Flickr album, accessed 1 March 2023, https://www.flickr.com/photos/wwoz/albums/72157713877114722/page7.

33. WWOZ, "WWOZ Presents Jazz Festing in Place."

34. Ibid.

35. Groarke et al., "Loneliness in the UK during the COVID-19 Pandemic," 1.

36. Ingram, Hand, and Maciejewski, "Social Isolation during COVID-19 Lockdown," 945.

37. Goat in the Road, "Goat in the Road Presents."

38. See Shklovsky, "Art as Device"; Brecht, *Brecht on Theatre.*

39. Childs, *Foresight and Design,* 45.

40. Berner and Irwin, *Refamiliarization.*

41. Goat in the Road, "Goat in the Road's Scavenger Hunt."

42. Goat in the Road, Scavenger hunt instructions, provided to the authors by the company in 2022.

43. Angelo, Britt, Brown, and Camp, "Private Struggles in Public Spaces," 163.

44. See, for example, Grams, "Freedom and Cultural Consciousness."

45. See NewOrleans.com, "Costume and Masking Culture."

46. Ramkissoon, "Place Affect Interventions during and after the COVID-19 Pandemic," 2.

47. Shukla, *Costume,* 257.

48. Bordnick, cited in MacCash, *Mardi Gras Beads,* 103.

49. See also *Spread Art Not Rona* by JC Bruckmann, Cody Smith, and Olivia Lemmons, accessed 10 December 2024, https://eu.lcsun-news.com/story/news/2020/07/09/coronavirus-new -mexico-covid-19-las-cruces-events-instagram-art/5390790002; and Palo Alto Public Art Pro-

gram's temporary installations of artworks, accessed 10 December 2024, https://www.paloaltoon
line.com/arts/2021/03/03/creativity-and-joy-palo-alto-hopes-to-combat-the-ongoing-pandemic
-blahs-with-new-public-art.

50. Sofaer, *Scavengers*.

51. Van der Westhuizen et al., "Face Coverings for COVID-19".

52. Thoumi et al., "Hyperlocal Covid-19 Testing and Vaccination," 9.

53. Historic New Orleans Collection, "COVID-19 Oral History: Dr. Jennifer Avegno".

54. Thoumi et al., "Hyperlocal Covid-19 Testing and Vaccination," 9.

55. For data on vaccination rates in March 2022, see NewOrleans.com, "New Orleans COVID
Safety Plan," last updated 19 April 2022, https://www.neworleans.com/blog/post/new-orleans-covid
-safety.

56. Levin, "Attempt at Mardi Gras".

57. NOLA Ready is "the City of New Orleans disaster preparedness campaign, managed by
the Office of Homeland Security & Emergency Preparedness." See https://mobile.twitter.com/nola
ready/with_replies.

58. Ecclesiastes, quoted in Ivry, "New Orleans Creatives Get to the Heart of the Matter."

Curating Connections: By Way of Conclusion

1. Mørland and Amundsen, "Political Potential of Curatorial Practice".

2. The Helis Foundation is a private Louisiana-based foundation with the stated aim of "advancing access to the arts in New Orleans"; see https://www.thehelisfoundation.org/about. Established in 1966, the Historic New Orleans Collection is museum, research center, and publisher
"dedicated to the stewardship of the history and culture of New Orleans and the Gulf South"; see
https://www.hnoc.org.

3. Historic New Orleans Collection, *Art of the City*, promotional flyer.

4. Beyond Bourbon Street, "Art of the City," episode #90.

5. Ashé Cultural Arts Center, "Art of the Black Experience: About the Exhibition," accessed
18 February 2022, https://www.ashenola.org/art-of-the-black-experience.

6. Ibid.

7. Bay, *Traveling Black*.

8. Ecclesiastes, cited in Ivry, "New Orleans Creatives Get to the Heart of the Matter."

9. Chase, *Dooky Chase Cookbook*, 8.

10. Austin Feldbaum, interview with authors, City Hall, New Orleans, 18 February 2022.

11. Ryan Mast, letter to authors, "Impact Statement on NOHSEP Engagement with Performing City Resilience," 2019.

BIBLIOGRAPHY

Ali, Rafat. "The Genesis of Overtourism: Why We Came Up with the Term and What's Happened Since." *Skift*, 14 August 2018. https://skift.com/2018/08/14/the-genesis-of-overtourism-why-we-came-up-with-the-term-and-whats-happened-since.

American Theatre Editors. "Artistic Director Aimée Hayes to Leave Southern Rep." *American Theatre*, 9 September 2020. https://www.americantheatre.org/2020/09/09/artistic-director-aimee-hayes-to-leave-southern-rep.

Anderson, Ben, and Rachel Gordon. "Government and (Non)Event: The Promise of Control." *Social & Cultural Geography* 18, no. 2 (2017): 158–77.

André Cailloux Center for Performing Arts and Cultural Justice. "About Us" and "History." Accessed 30 November 2022. https://www.accneworleans.com/about-us And https://www.accneworleans.com/history.

Andrews, Stuart. *Performing Home*. London: Routledge, 2019.

Andrews, Stuart, and Patrick Duggan. *Performance as City Pandemic Response: Invitations to Innovate*. Report. Newcastle, UK: Performing City Resilience, 2021. https://performingcityresilience.com/publications.

———. "Situation Rooms: Performing City Resilience in New Orleans." *Liminalities: A Journal of Performance Studies* 15, no. 1 (2019): 1–23.

———. "Towards Strategy as Performance in Hazard Mitigation: Reflections on Performing City Resilience in New Orleans." *Research in Drama Education* 26, no. 1 (2021): 187–201.

Angelo, Dante, Kelly Britt, Margaret Lou Brown, and Stacey L. Camp. "Private Struggles in Public Spaces: Documenting COVID-19 Material Culture and Landscapes." *Journal of Contemporary Archaeology* 8, no. 1 (2021): 154–84.

Archer, Deborah N. "'White Men's Roads through Black Men's Homes': Advancing Racial Equity through Highway Reconstruction." *Vanderbilt Law Review* 73, no. 5 (2020): 1259–1330.

Ashé Cultural Arts Center, in partnership with the Arts Council New Orleans. *Art of the Black Experience*. "About the Exhibition." Accessed 1 December 2023. https://www.ashenola.org/art-of-the-black-experience?rq=Art%20of%20the%20Black%20Experience.

Atkinson, Connie Zeanah. "New Orleans Music: A Reappraisal." PhD Diss., University of Liverpool, 1997. Midlo Center Publications. Paper 3.

Austin, John L. *How to Do Things with Words.* Oxford: Clarendon Press, 1962.

Bălan, Nina Aurora, and Bridget M. Bordelon. "The Role of Water and Tourism Management in Venice and New Orleans." *International Journal of Research* 15 (2021), http://dx.doi.org/10.21463/shima.120.

Bay, Mia. *Traveling Black: A History of Race and Resistance.* Cambridge: Harvard University Press, 2021.

Bayou Road Business Association. "Black Bayou." Accessed 26 November 2023.https://www.bayouroad.com/black-bayou.

BBC News. "Poem about Manchester: 'This Is the Place.'" YouTube, 24 May 2017. https://www.youtube.com/watch?v=PszMmYpQjPo.

Benjamin, Walter. *The Arcades Project.* Translated by Howard Eiland and Kevin McLaughlin. Cambridge, MA: Belknap Press, 2002.

Berner, Justin, and Julia Irwin. *Refamiliarization, Platform Artspace and the Worth Ryder Gallery.* University of California, Berkeley, 29 September–1 October 2021. https://www.refamiliarization.org.

Bernstein, Robin. "Dances with Things: Material Culture and the Performance of Race." *SocialText* 27, no. 4 (2009): 67–94.

Bertolini, Luca. "From 'Streets for Traffic' to 'Streets for People': Can Street Experiments Transform Urban Mobility?" *Transport Reviews* 40, no. 6 (2020): 734–53.

Beyond Bourbon Street. "Art of the City, Postmodern to Post-Katrina." Episode #90, 22 May 2019. https://beyondbourbonst.com/art-of-the-city-postmodern-to-post-katrina-episode-90.

Billiot, Shanondora, Soonhyung Kwon, and Catherine E. Burnette. "Repeated Disasters and Chronic Environmental Changes Impede Generational Transmission of Indigenous Knowledge." *Journal of Family Strengths* 19, no. 1 (2019): 1–29.

Birch, Traci, and Jeff Carney. "Regional Resilience: Building Adaptive Capacity and Community Well-Being across Louisiana's Dynamic Coastal–Inland Continuum." In *Louisiana's Response to Extreme Weather: A Coastal State's Adaptation Challenges and Successes,* edited by Shirley Laska, 313–40. Extreme Weather and Society series. Cham, Switzerland: Springer, 2020.

Blankenhorn, Grace. "The Resilience of Tremé: The Fight to Reclaim Claiborne Avenue." *Krewe Magazine,* 2 May 2023. https://krewetulane.com/2023/05/02/the-resilience-of-treme-the-fight-to-reclaim-claiborne-avenue.

Bohn, Michael K. *Nerve Center: Inside the White House Situation Room.* Washington, DC: Potomac Books, 2003.

Brecht, Bertolt. *Brecht on Theatre: The Development of an Aesthetic.* Edited and translated by John Willett. New York: Hill and Wang, 1978.

Brown, K., N. Eernstman, A. R. Huke, and N. Reding. "The Drama of Resilience: Learning, Doing, and Sharing for Sustainability." *Ecology and Society* 22, no. (2017): 8. https://doi.org/10.5751/ES-09145-220208.

"Build a World of Play: A Playful Street." A Playful City. Dublin. Accessed 10 December 2024. https://www.aplayfulcity.com.

Bulbancha Is Still a Place, LLC. *Bulbancha Is Still a Place: Indigenous Culture from "New Orleans."* Zine. Edited by Ozone504 and Jeffery U. Darensbourg. POC Zine Project. Available from 10 September 2020, uploaded by George Scheer. https://www.flipsnack.com/cacno/bulbancha-is-still-a-place-v-2.html.

Butler, Judith. *Bodies That Matter: On the Discursive Limits of Sex.* London: Routledge, 1993.

Campanella, Richard. *Draining New Orleans: The 300-Year Quest to Dewater the Crescent City.* Baton Rouge: Louisiana State University Press, 2023.

———. "Why Idyllic Claiborne Avenue Was Undone by Expressway, but Planned French Quarter Highway Died." *NOLA.com,* 9 April 2021. https://www.nola.com/news/why-idyllic-claiborne-avenue-was-undone-by-expressway-but-planned-french-quarter-highway-died/article_522fc578-9946-11eb-bf02-9b7377a75c5b.html.

———. "Why Prytania Jogs at Joseph." *Preservation in Print,* October 2013. https://rich-campanella.com/wp-content/uploads/2020/02/article_Campanella_Preservation-in-Print_2013_Oct_Prytania_Joseph-1.pdf.

Carrico, Rachel. *Dancing the Politics of Pleasure at the New Orleans Second Line.* Urbana: University of Illinois Press, 2024.

———. "Un/Natural Disaster and Dancing: Hurricane Katrina and Second Lining in New Orleans." *Black Scholar* 46, no. 1 (2016): 27–36.

Chandler, David. "Editorial." *Resilience* 1, no. 1 (2013): 1–2.

Chandler, David, and Julian Reid. *The Neoliberal Subject: Resilience, Adaptation and Vulnerability.* London: Rowman & Littlefield, 2016.

Chase, Leah. *The Dooky Chase Cookbook.* Gretna, LA: Pelican, 2019.

Childs, Mark C. *Foresight and Design: Composing Future Places.* London: Routledge, 2022.

Clark, Maria, Todd A. Price, and Andrew Yawn. "Confederate Reckoning: How the New Orleans Tourism Industry Perpetuates Its Glaring Racial Wealth Gap." *The Tennessean,* 15 July 2021. https://eu.tennessean.com/in-depth/news/american-south/2021/07/15/how-new-orleans-tourism-industry-perpetuates-glaring-racial-wealth-gap/7779563002.

Coady, Christopher. "New Orleans Rhythm and Blues, African American Tourism, and the Selling of a Progressive South." *American Music* 37, no. 1 (2019): 95–112. DOI: https://doi.org/10.5406/americanmusic.37.1.0095.

Contemporary Arts Center, New Orleans. *The Float Lab: The Heartbeat of Invisible Rivers.* Exhibit, 2022. Accessed 21 February 2022, https://cacno.org/visual-arts/the-float-lab.

Coviello, Will. "Preview: Cry You One." *gambit,* 22 October 2013. Updated 20 Novem-

ber 2019. https://www.nola.com/gambit/events/preview-cry-you-one/article_fb3ac
dc6-07d4-5959-8d1b-e595b7e1b9f2.html.

Creative Capital. "Mondo Bizarro Presents 'Cry You One' at the 2015 Creative Capital
Retreat." YouTube, 7 October 2015. https://www.youtube.com/watch?v=8KogUH
rnJKQ.

Crutcher, Michael E., Jr. *Tremé: Race and Place in a New Orleans Neighborhood.* Athens:
University of Georgia Press, 2010.

Davis, Juliet. *The Caring City: Ethics of Urban Design.* Bristol: Bristol University Press,
2022.

De Certeau, Michel. *The Practice of Everyday Life.* Translated by Steven Rendall. Berkeley: University of California Press, 1984.

DeFrantz, Thomas F., and Anita Gonzalez. *Black Performance Theory.* Durham, NC:
Duke University Press, 2014.

Department of Parks and Parkways. "Neutral Grounds." Last updated 4 November 2024.
https://nola.gov/next/parks-parkways/topics/neutral-grounds/#:~:text=Neutral
%20ground%20refers%20to%20what,%2C%20board%20streetcars%2C%20and%20
more.

Dessens, Nathalie. "New Orleans, Where the Stage Is the Street." *South Atlantic Review*
76, no. 4 (2011): 7–21.

———. "Remembering in Black and White: Memorializing Slavery in 21st Century Louisiana." In *Traces and Memories of Slavery in the Atlantic World,* edited by Lawrence
Aje and Nicolas Gachon, 128–43. New York: Routledge, 2020.

Dikeç, Mustafa. *Space, Politics and Aesthetics.* Edinburgh: Edinburgh University Press,
2015.

Dinerstein, Joel. "Thirty-Nine Sundays: Social Aid and Pleasure Clubs Take It to the
Streets." In *Unfathomable City: A New Orleans Atlas,* edited by Rebecca Solnit and
Rebecca Snedeker, 107–13. Berkeley: University of California Press, 2013.

Dodd, Melanie. "Creative Cities: Managing Chaos Not Cleaning Up Mess." Cultures of
Resilience project. Accessed 10 December 2024. https://culturesofresilience.org/
creative-cities.

Dudley, K. D., and L. N. Duffy. "Tourism Discourse and Surveillance: Situational Analysis of Post–Katrina New Orleans." *Leisure Sciences* 45, no. 5 (2023): 475–93. DOI:
10.1080/01490400.2022.2162172.

Duggan, Patrick. "Catapult." Performing City Resilience, 8 June 2023. https://performing
cityresilience.com/2023/06/08/catapult.

———. "Rethinking Tourism: On the Politics and Practices of 'Staging' New Orleans."
Performance Research 24, no. 5 (2019): 44–56.

Duggan, Patrick, and Lisa Peschel, eds. *Performing (for) Survival: Theatre, Crisis, Ex-
tremity.* Basingstoke: Palgrave Macmillan, 2016.

Ecclesiastes, Asali DeVan. Informal conversation with authors. *Brass on the Boulevard,*
23 February 2022.

Elam, Harry Justin, Jr. *Taking It to the Streets: The Social Protest Theater of Luis Valdez and Amiri Baraka.* Ann Arbor: University of Michigan Press, 2001.

Erdely, Jennifer L. "Masking COVID, Crafting Community." *Liminalities* 17, nos. 1–2 (2021): 1–22.

Fakhruddin, B. S., K. Blanchard, and D. Ragupathy. "Are We There Yet? The Transition from Response to Recovery for the COVID-19 Pandemic." *Progress in Disaster Science* 7 (2020): 1–5.

Farrier, Andrew. *Mardi Gras (Yardi Gras) 2021 / A Year of Innovation for Carnival in New Orleans.* YouTube, uploaded by Free Tours by Foot–New Orleans, 6 February 2021. https://www.youtube.com/watch?v=xsxbNlCT8YA.

Federal Emergency Management Agency (FEMA). "Emergency Management in the United States." Teaching materials. Accessed 19 October 2023. https://training.fema .gov/emiweb/downloads/is111_unit%204.pdf.

Fields, Billy, Jacob Wagner, and Michael Frisch. "Placemaking and Disaster Recovery: Targeting Place for Recovery in Post-Katrina New Orleans." *Journal of Urbanism: International Research on Placemaking and Urban Sustainability* 8, no. 1 (2015): 38–56.

Fuel Theatre. *The Situation Room: Prejudice and Perception.* Accessed 11 September 2018. https://fueltheatre.com/projects/the-situation-room-prejudice-perception.

Gardner, Lyn. "Going Off-Script: Theatre Needs to Break Free of Its Echo Chamber." *The Guardian,* 9 December 2016. https://www.theguardian.com/stage/theatreblog /2016/dec/09/theatre-echochamber-fuel-situation-room.

"Gentilly Resilience District Launches Lantern Walk, Online Program, Public Art Project." *Gentilly Messenger,* 9 September 2020. http://gentillymessenger.com/gentilly -resilience-district-launches-lantern-walk-online-program-public-art-project.

Goat in the Road. "Goat in the Road Presents . . . A Scavenger Hunt." Promotional flyer, supplied to authors by the company in 2022.

———. "Goat in the Road's Scavenger Hunt!" Facebook Event Page. Accessed 27 November 2023. https://www.facebook.com/events/1351245581916327/?paipv=0&eav=A fZf8GkybqmombGiE91wGbpIuSxud5_1ymnDpxMr9CkJJuO_BehlMXSiLqapmv A4A7Q&_rdr.

Godschalk, David R. "Urban Hazard Mitigation: Creating Resilient Cities." *Natural Hazards Review* 4, no. 3 (August 2003): 136–43.

Gooden, Mario. *Dark Space: Architecture, Representation, Black Identity.* New York: Columbia Books on Architecture and the City, 2016.

Gotham, Kevin Fox. "Touristic Disaster: Spectacle and Recovery in Post-Katrina New Orleans." *Geoforum* 86 (2017): 127–35.

Grams, Diane M. "Freedom and Cultural Consciousness: Black Working-Class Parades in Post-Katrina New Orleans." *Journal of Urban Affairs* 35, no. 5 (2013): 501–29.

Green, Kristen M., Anne H. Beaudreau, Maija H. Lukin, and Larry B. Crowder. "Climate Change Stressors and Social-Ecological Factors Mediating Access to Subsistence Resources in Arctic Alaska." *Ecology and Society* 26, no. 4 (2012): n.p. https://doi.org/10.5751/ES-12783-260415.

Greene, Oliver N. "'Masking Indian—Practising Africa': Dialogue on Spirituality, Sound, and Resistance as Mardi Gras Indian Performativity." *Caribbean Quarterly* 65, no. 2 (2019): 265–84.

Groarke, Jenny M., et al. "Loneliness in the UK during the COVID-19 Pandemic: Cross-Sectional Results from the COVID-19 Psychological Wellbeing Study." *PLOS ONE* 15, no. 9, 24 November 2020. https://doi.org/10.1371/journal.pone.0239698.

Harvie, Jen. *Theatre and the City.* Basingstoke: Palgrave Macmillan, 2009.

Hawkins, Harriet. *For Creative Geographies: Geography, Visual Arts and the Making of Worlds.* New York: Routledge, 2014.

Hernborg, Axel. "40+ New Orleans Tourism Statistics, Numbers and Trends." Tripplo .com, 27 June 2022. https://www.tripplo.com/uk/new-orleans-tourism-statistics-and -trends.

Hetrick, Laura J. "Embracing Uncertainty through Embracing the Arts." *Visual Arts Research* 46, no. 2 (2020): v–vi.

Historic New Orleans Collection. *Art of the City: Postmodern to Post-Katrina.* Promotional flyer, 2019.

———. "COVID-19 Oral History: Dr. Jennifer Avegno." *From the Front Line: Narratives of the COVID-19 Pandemic in New Orleans,* 11 November 2020. https://www.hnoc .org/research/front-line-narratives-covid-19-pandemic-new-orleans.

Hodder, Ian. *Entangled: An Archaeology of the Relationships between Humans and Things.* Hoboken, NJ: Wiley and Sons, 2012.

hooks, bell. "Architecture and Black Life: Talking Space with Laverne Wells-Bowie." *Art on My Mind: Spatial Politics,* 152–62. New York: New Press, 1995.

Hough, Emily, Matthieu Langlois, and Patrick Lagadec. "Leadership in Terra Incognita: Vision and Action." *Crisis Response Journal* 15, no. 4 (2020): 14–17.

Hunter, Marcus Anthony, Mary Pattillo, Zandria F. Robinson, and Keeanga-Yamahtta Taylor. "Black Placemaking: Celebration, Play, and Poetry." *Theory, Culture & Society* 33, nos. 7–8 (2016): 31–56.

Imagine Water Works. "Who We Are." Accessed 30 November 2023. https://www.imagine waterworks.org/who-we-are.

Ingram, Joanne, Christopher J. Hand, and Greg Maciejewski. "Social Isolation during COVID-19 Lockdown Impairs Cognitive Function." *Applied Cognitive Psychology* (2021): 935–47.

"Inside the Situation Room." Obama White House Archives (blog), 18 December 2009. https://obamawhitehouse.archives.gov/blog/2009/12/18/inside-situation-room.

Iveson, Kurt, Craig Lyons, Stephanie Clark, and Sara Weir. "The Informal Australian City." *Australian Geographer* 50, no. 1 (2018): 11–27.

Ivry, Sara. "New Orleans Creatives Get to the Heart of the Matter." Mellon Founda-

tion, Online. 10 November 2022. https://www.mellon.org/grant-story/new-orleans
-creatives-get-to-the-heart-of-the-matter.

Jeannotte, M. Sharon. "When the Gigs Are Gone: Valuing Arts, Culture and Media in
the COVID-19 Pandemic." *Social Sciences & Humanities Open* 3, no. 1 (2021): 1–7.

Jones, Suzanne. "3 Days in New Orleans—What to See and Do in the Big Easy." *Travel
Bunny.* Last updated 14 October 2024. https://thetravelbunny.com/3-days-in-new
-orleans-travel-guide.

Julien, E. "Introduction to Arts of Survival: Exploring Arts and Lives in Urban Spaces."
Africa Today 65, no. 4 (2019): ix–xiv.

Kang, Simi. "'I Have a Right Not to Be Resilient': New Orleanians of Color Remember
Hurricane Katrina." *The Migrationist* (blog), 2 March 2018. https://www.academia
.edu/36069785/_I_have_a_right_not_to_be_resilient_New_Orleanians_of_color
_respond_to_Hurricane_Katrina?uc-g-sw=22958099.

Kaplan-Levenson, Laine. "Why New Orleans Leaned into Tourism." *TriPod.* Podcast. New
Orleans at 300, 19 May 2016. https://www.wwno.org/podcast/tripod-new-orleans
-at-300/2016-05-19/why-new-orleans-leaned-into-tourism.

Keith, Naima J., et al. *Prospect.5: Yesterday We Said Tomorrow.* Triennial exhibition catalog. New York: Prospect New Orleans and Rizzoli Electa, 2021.

Kershaw, Baz. "Practice as Research through Performance." In *Practice-Led Research,
Research-Led Practice in the Creative Arts,* edited by H. Smith and R. T. Dean, 104–
25. Edinburgh: Edinburgh University Press, 2011.

Khalaj, Fahimeh, Dorina Pojani, Neil Sipe, and Jonathan Corcoran. "Why Are Cities
Removing Their Freeways? A Systematic Review of the Literature." *Transport Reviews* 40, no. 1 (2020): 1–24.

Kushma, Jane, ed. *Case Studies in Disaster Recovery.* Oxford: Butterworth-Heinemann,
2023.

Laborde, Errol. "Defining a Super Krewe." *New Orleans Magazine,* February 2020.
https://www.myneworleans.com/defining-a-super-krewe.

Landry, Charles, and Franco Bianchini. *The Creative City.* London: Demos, 1995.

Law, John. *After Method: Mess in Social Science Research.* Abingdon, UK: Routledge,
2004.

Lazar, Zachary. "Brandon 'Bmike' Odums." *BOMB* magazine (Summer 2016). https://
bombmagazine.org/articles/brandan-bmike-odums.

Leach, Kirk, and Jason D. Rivera. 2022. "Dismantling Power Asymmetries in Disaster
and Emergency Management Research: Another Argument for the Application of
Critical Theory." *Risk, Hazards & Crisis in Public Policy* 13 (2022): 337–55.

Lee, Rachel. "*Cry You One* Lets the Land Speak." *Antigravity,* October 2013. https://anti
gravitymagazine.com/feature/cry-you-one-lets-the-land-speak.

LeJeune, Dominique. "Deep Gras." Practicallytragic. Instagram. Accessed 10 December
2024. https://www.instagram.com/practicallytragic.

Levendis, John, and Mehmet F. Dicle. "The Economic Impact of Airbnb on New Orleans." *SSRN*, 20 October 2016. https://ssrn.com/abstract=2856770.

Levin, Dan. "Attempt at Mardi Gras without the Reckless Abandon Falters." *New York Times*, 15 February 2021. https://www.nytimes.com/2021/02/14/us/mardi-gras-pandemic-2021.html.

Liu, Xu, and David Burnett. "Insider-Outsider: Methodological Reflections on Collaborative Intercultural Research." *Humanities and Social Sciences Communications* 9, no. 314 (2022).

Lookatthisfuckinstreet. @lookatthisfuckinstreet. *Instagram*. Accessed 10 December 2024. https://www.instagram.com/lookatthisfuckinstreet.

MacCash, Doug. *Mardi Gras Beads*. Baton Rouge: Louisiana State University Press, 2022.

MacGill, Belinda. "Craft, Relational Aesthetics and Ethics of Care." *Art/Research International: A Transdisciplinary Journal* 4, no. 1 (2019): 406–19.

Magelssen, Scott. *Simming: Participatory Performance and the Making of Meaning*. Ann Arbor: University of Michigan Press, 2014.

Mahn, Churnjeet, Caroline Scarles, Justin Edwards, and John Tribe. "Personalising Disaster: Community Storytelling and Sharing in New Orleans Post-Katrina Tourism." *Tourist Studies* 21, no. 2 (2021): 156–77.

Manyena, Siambabala Bernard. "The Concept of Resilience Revisited." *Disasters* 30, no. 4 (2006): 433–50.

Mardi Gras New Orleans. "About the Krewe of the Rolling Elvi." Accessed 10 December 2024. https://www.mardigrasneworleans.com/parades/marching-clubs/krewe-of-the-rolling-elvi.

MAYK. "A Parallel Party." Accessed 19 June 2021. https://www.mayk.org.uk/blog/this-is-not-a-mayfest-party-text.

McEntire, David A. *Disaster Response and Recovery: Strategies and Tactics for Resilience*. Hoboken, NJ: Wiley & Sons, 2022.

McKinney, Louise. *New Orleans: A Cultural History*. Oxford: Oxford University Press, 2006.

Mikkonen, Jukka. "Aesthetic Appreciation of Nature and the Global Environmental Crisis." *Environmental Values* 31, no. 1 (2022): 47–66.

Miller, DeMond Shondell. "Disaster Tourism and Disaster Landscape Attractions after Hurricane Katrina: An Auto-Ethnographic Journey." *International Journal of Culture, Tourism and Hospitality Research* 2, no. 2 (2008): 115–31.

Mingazova, Ella. "Slow Travel Writing: Anik See's Saudade: The Possibilities of Place." *Studies in Travel Writing* 23, no. 2 (2019): 175–87.

Mondo Bizarro. *Cry You One (Work Sample–St. Bernard)*. YouTube, 16 May 2020. https://www.youtube.com/watch?v=pnM7kq3z3LU&list=PLke1_9NotAlk6QC8Jn6wlP6ujELcXfIEB&index=3.

———. *Cry You One*. Mondo Bizarro and ArtSpot Productions, May 2013. http://www.mondobizarro.org/?page_id=8.

———. *Cry You One.* Mondo Bizarro and ArtSpot Productions. Accessed 3 July 2024. http://www.cryyouone.com.

Montano, Samantha. *Disasterology.* Email newsletter, 28 September 2023.

Montgomery, Alesia. *Greening the Black Urban Regime: The Culture and Commerce of Sustainability in Detroit.* Detroit: Wayne State University Press, 2020.

Mørland, Gerd Elise, and Heidi Bale Amundsen. "The Political Potential of Curatorial Practice." *On Curating,* no. 4 (2010). https://www.on-curating.org/files/oc/date iverwaltung/old%20Issues/ONCURATING_Issue4.pdf.

Morris, James R. G., and Paul I. Kadetz. "Culture and Resilience: How Music Has Fostered Resilience in Post-Katrina New Orleans." In *Creating Katrina, Rebuilding Resilience: Lessons from New Orleans,* edited by Michael J. Zakour, Nancy B. Mock, and Paul I. Kadetz, 233–56. Oxford: Butterworth-Heinemann, 2017.

Morton, Jeremy. "Slung Low Stage a Treat for Local Families." *South Leeds Life,* 29 June 2020.

Mukhija, Vinit, and Anastasia Loukaitou-Sideris. *The Informal American City: Beyond Taco Trucks and Day Labor.* Cambridge, MA: MIT Press, 2014.

Music and Culture Coalition of New Orleans. "The Good Visitor's Guide to New Orleans (or How You Can Help New Orleans Music and Culture Thrive and Survive)." Accessed 30 November 2023. https://maccno.com/good-visitor-guide-to-new-orleans.

———. "Reallocation of Tourism Revenue." Accessed 30 November 2023. https://maccno .com/reallocation-of-tourism-revenue.

Mwase, Rebecca. "A Culture of Belonging." AlternateROOTS, September 2014. https:// alternateroots.org/a-culture-of-belonging.

NBC News. "New Orleans Now Nation's Murder Capital." Online. 25 January 2023. https://www.nbcnews.com/now/video/new-orleans-now-nation-s-murder-capital -161815621643.

Newcomb Art Museum. "Monique Verdin: Return to Yakni Chitto." Accessed 30 November 2023. https://newcombartmuseum.tulane.edu/portfolio-item/return-to-yakni -chitto.

New Orleans Airlift. "Music Box Village." Accessed 17 September 2018. https://musicbox village.com.

New Orleans, City of. *Gentilly Resilience District Creative Engagement and Communications Plan.* Resilience + Sustainability, September 2017. https://nola.gov/archived /resilience-sustainability/resources/community-outreach/gentilly-comm-strategy.

NewOrleans.com. "Costume & Masking Culture: The History of Masking and Costuming in New Orleans." Accessed 27 October 2023. https://www.neworleans.com/events /holidays-seasonal/mardi-gras/costume-and-masking-culture-in-new-orleans.

———. "New Orleans Second Line History." Accessed 30 November 2023. https://www .neworleans.com/things-to-do/music/history-and-traditions/second-lines.

———. "New Orleans Signature Drink Recipe: Hurricane." Accessed 30 November 2023. https://www.neworleans.com/drink/cocktails/hurricane.

New Orleans Sustainable Tourism Task Force. "Abstract: A Pivotal Moment for New Orleans Tourism." Online, 2019. http://neworleans.sustainableuplift.org.

——. "A Culture Misunderstood." Accessed 22 March 2023. http://neworleans.sus tainableuplift.org/resources/New-Orleans-Sustainable-Tourism-Task-Force-A -Culture-Misunderstood.pdf.

Nield, Sophie. "Tahrir Square EC4M: The Occupy Movement and the Dramaturgy of Public Order." In *The Grammar of Politics and Performance,* edited by S. M. Rai and J. Reinelt, 121–33. London: Routledge, 2015.

——. "There Is Another World: Space, Theatre and Global Anti-Capitalism." *Contemporary Theatre Review* 16, no. 1 (2006): 51–61.

Nilsson, Jan Henrik. "Conceptualizing and Contextualizing Overtourism: The Dynamics of Accelerating Urban Tourism." *International Journal of Tourism Cities* 6, no. 4 (2020): 657–71. DOI: https://doi.org/10.1108/IJTC-08-2019-0117.

No Dream Deferred. "Home," "Our Mission," and "We Will Dream: New Works Festival." Accessed 23 November 2023. https://www.nodreamdeferrednola.com, https://www.nodreamdeferrednola.com/about/nddmission, and https://www.nodreamde ferrednola.com/wwd-festival-home.

NOLA Ready. The City of New Orleans Disaster Preparedness Campaign. Managed by the Office of Homeland Security & Emergency Preparedness. Accessed 12 May 2023. https://ready.nola.gov/home.

Odem, Jennifer. *Rising Tables.* New Orleans: Jennifer Odem Studio, 2019.

100 Resilient Cities. "Frequently Asked Questions (FAQ) about 100 Resilient Cities." Accessed 21 September 2018. http://www.100resilientcities.org/faq.

Oswell, Paul. "Kermit's Treme Mother in Law Lounge." Review. *Condé Nast Traveler.* Accessed 17 May 2023. https://www.cntraveler.com/bars/new-orleans/new-orleans /kermits-treme-mother-in-law-lounge.

Pakan, Sarani Pitor, and Intan Purwandani. "Itinerary, Information, Denial: Local Travel Agents and Tourist Flows Governance in Yogyakarta, Indonesia." *Tourism Planning & Development* 20, no. 5 (2022): 885–900.

Performing City Resilience. "Resisting Catastrophe: Performances of the Crescent City." Accessed 30 November 2023. Panel at the American Society for Theatre Research conference, 2022. https://performingcityresilience.com/resisting-catastrophe-perform ances-of-the-crescent-city.

Playable City. "About" and "Playable City Sandbox: How (Not) to Get Hit by a Self-Driving Car." PlayableCity.com. Accessed 20 November 2023. https://www.playable city.com/about and https://www.playablecity.com/projects/playable-city-sandbox -how-not-to.

Playing Out. "An International Movement." Bristol, UK. Accessed 20 November 2023. https://playingout.net/nearby-you/an-international-movement.

Quinn, Patrick. "Los Angeles Has Its Own Situation Room." *Art and Cake: A Contem-*

porary Art Magazine with a Focus on the Los Angeles Art Scene, 21 February 2017. https://artandcakela.com/2017/02/21/los-angeles-has-its-own-situation-room.

Radice, Martha. "Creativity, Sociability, Solidarity: New-Wave Carnival Krewes' Responses to COVID-19 in New Orleans." *Anthropologica* 63, no. 1 (2021): 1–27. DOI: https://doi.org/10.18357/anthropologica6312021230.

Ramkissoon, Haywantee. "Place Affect Interventions during and after the COVID-19 Pandemic." *Frontiers in Psychology* 12 (2021): 1–7.

Reckdahl, Katy. "A Divided Neighborhood Comes Together under an Elevated Expressway." *Next City,* 20 August 2018. https://nextcity.org/features/a-divided-neighbor hood-comes-together-under-an-elevated-expressway#:~:text=Fifty%20years%20 ago%2C%20New%20orleans,of%20culture%2C%20commerce%20and%20play.

Restore the Mississippi River Delta. *Eternal Flow: Mississippi River Views from Louisiana.* YouTube, 20 October 2021. https://www.youtube.com/watch?v=ZJiGPc84 dgY. Also available at https://mississippiriverdelta.org/eternal-flow-mississippi-river -views-from-louisiana.

Riggs, William. *End of the Road: Reimagining the Street as the Heart of the City.* Bristol: Bristol University Press, 2022.

Rimini Protokoll. *Situation Rooms.* Radioplay. 2013–19. https://www.rimini-protokoll. de/website/en/project/situation-rooms.

Roach, Joseph. *Cities of the Dead: Circum-Atlantic Performance.* New York: Columbia University Press, 1996.

———. "Dreaming New Orleans: Desire, Cemeteries, and Elysian Fields." *TDR: The Drama Review* 65, no. 1 (2021): 15–39.

Rodin, Judith. *The Resilience Dividend: Managing Disruption, Avoiding Disaster, and Growing Stronger in an Unpredictable World.* London: Profile Books, 2015.

Rogers, Amanda. "Geographies of the Performing Arts: Landscapes, Places and Cities." *Geography Compass* 6, no. 2 (2012): 60–75.

Romero, Leah. "'Spread Art Not Rona': Local Artists behind Community Scavenger Hunt." *Las Cruces Sun-News,* 9 July 2020. https://eu.lcsun-news.com/story/news /2020/07/09/coronavirus-new-mexico-covid-19-las-cruces-events-instagram-art /5390790002.

Rosefeldt, P. "Alternative Mardi Gras 2021: How the City Celebrated in Spite of Covid." *Arthur Hardy's Mardi Gras Guide.* 46th annual ed. New Orleans: Arthur Hardy, 2022.

Rough Guides. "New Orleans Travel Guide." Accessed 30 November 2023. https://www .roughguides.com/usa/new-orleans.

Sadik-Khan, Janette, and Seth Solomonow. *Streetfight: Handbook for an Urban Revolution.* New York: Viking Press, 2016.

Sakakeeny, Matt. *Roll with It: Brass Bands in the Streets of New Orleans.* Durham, NC: Duke University Press, 2013.

Sapat, Alka. "Transboundary Disasters and Nongovernmental Organizations." Natural Hazard Science. *Oxford Research Encyclopaedia,* December 2018.

Schechner, Richard. *Between Theater and Anthropology.* Philadelphia: University of Pennsylvania Press, 1985.

———. *Performance Theory.* 1988. Reprint, New York: Routledge. 2003.

Schneider, Benjamin. "Why Is It So Hard to Kill This Freeway?" *Bloomberg CityLab* (Transportation), 12 April 2023. https://www.bloomberg.com/news/features/2023 -04-12/fate-of-a-controversial-highway-still-divides-new-orleans.

Scott-Bottoms, Steve. "The Rise and Fall of Modern Water: From Staging Abstraction to Performing Place." *Theatre Journal* 71, no. 4 (December 2019): 415–35.

Scott-Bottoms, Stephen, and Maggie Roe. "Who Is a Hydrocitizen? The Use of Dialogic Arts Methods as a Research Tool with Water Professionals in West Yorkshire, UK." *Local Environment* 25, no. 4 (2020):273–89.

Setyawan, Kezia. "What Goes into a Handmade Mardi Gras Throw? Glue, Glitter and (of Course) Throwing a Party." WWNO, February 3, 2023. https://www.wwno.org/news /2023-02-03/what-goes-into-a-handmade-mardi-gras-throw-glue-glitter-and-of -course-throwing-a-party.

Shand, Rory. *The Creative Arts of Governance of Urban Renewal and Development.* London: Routledge, 2020.

Sheehan, Rebecca. "(Re)working Subjectivities and Social-Spatial Interactions in the Urban Landscape: The Camel Toe Lady Steppers Parade in New Orleans Mardi Gras." *GeoJournal* 88, no. 2 (2022): 2215–31. https://doi.org/10.1007/s10708-022-10743-z.

Shepherd, Simon, and Mick Wallis. *Drama/Theatre/Performance.* London: Taylor & Francis, 2004.

Shklovsky, Viktor. "Art as Device." *Theory of Prose.* Translated by Benjamin Sher. Elmwood Park, IL: Dalkey Archive Press, 1990.

Shukla, Pravina. *Costume: Performing Identities through Dress.* Bloomington: Indiana University Press, 2015.

Shusterman, Richard. "Bodies in the Streets and the Somaesthetics of City Life." In *Bodies in the Streets and the Somaesthetics of City Life,* edited by Richard Shusterman, 1–10. Leiden: Brill, 2019.

Sloane-Boekbinder, Karel. "African Symbolism." Ashé Cultural Center online. Accessed 24 February 2022. https://maphub.net/AsheCulturalArtsCenter/Ashe.

Sofaer, Joshua. *Scavengers.* Accessed 26 October 2023. https://joshuasofaer.com/2011/06 /scavengers.

Source10. *The Ideal City: Exploring Urban Futures.* Berlin: Gestalten, 2021.

Souther, J. Mark. *New Orleans on Parade: Tourism and the Transformation of the Crescent City.* Baton Rouge: Louisiana State University Press, 2006.

Southern Rep Theatre. "New Home for Southern Rep" and "Southern Rep Theatre." Accessed 21 September 2018. http://www.southernrep.com/plays/newhome and http://www.southernrep.com.

———. Statement. Facebook, 1 June 2020. https://www.facebook.com/SouthernRep/posts
/southern-rep-theatre-stands-against-racist-violence-and-white-supremacy-in-all
-i/10157749451803649.

Split Britches. *Situation Room.* Accessed 17 September 2018. https://www.split-britches.com
/situation-room.

Swain, Jon, and Brendan King. "Using Informal Conversations in Qualitative Research."
International Journal of Qualitative Methods 21 (2022).https://doi.org/10.1177/160940
69221085056.

Thomas, Lynnell L. *Desire and Disaster in New Orleans: Tourism, Race, and Historical
Memory.* Durham, NC: Duke University Press, 2014.

Thorpe, Amelia. *Owning the Street: The Everyday Life of Property.* Cambridge, MA:
MIT Press, 2020.

Thoumi, Andrea, et al. *Hyperlocal Covid-19 Testing and Vaccination Strategies to Reach Communities with Low Vaccine Uptake: Considerations for States and Localities.* Report.
Washington, DC: Duke-Margolis Center for Health Policy, 23 September 2021. https://
healthpolicy.duke.edu/sites/default/files/2021-09/Hyperlocal%20COVID%20Test
ing%20Vaccination_1.pdf.

"300 Unique New Orleans Moments: Construction of the Interstate Highway System
in Louisiana Began in 1957." *The Advocate,* 25 December 2017. https://www.theadvo
cate.com/300-unique-new-orleans-moments-construction-of-the-interstate-high
way-system-in-louisiana-began-in/article_a246ba14-e9f2-11e7-8caf-071f49fba794
.html.

Tierney, Kathleen. "Resilience and the Neoliberal Project: Discourses, Critiques,
Practices—and Katrina." *American Behavioral Scientist* 59, no. 10 (2015): 1327–42.

Twardowski, Weston. "'They're Tryin' to Wash Us Away': Performance, Urban Adaptation, and the New New Orleans." PhD diss., Northwestern University, 2022.
https://www.proquest.com/docview/2675659147?pq-origsite=gscholar&fromopen
view=true.

United Nations. "On the Frontlines of Climate Change." Sustainable Development
Goals, 24 July 2019. https://www.un.org/sustainabledevelopment/blog/2019/07/on
-the-frontlines-of-climate-change.

United Nations Office for Disaster Risk Reduction (UNDRR). "Response." Sendai
Framework Terminology on Disaster Risk Reduction. Online. Accessed 28 February 2023. https://www.undrr.org/terminology/response.

United Nations World Tourism Organization (UNWTO); Centre of Expertise Leisure,
Tourism & Hospitality; NHTV Breda University of Applied Sciences; and NHL
Stenden University of Applied Sciences. *"Overtourism"?—Understanding and Man-
aging Urban Tourism Growth beyond Perceptions.* Executive summary. UNWTO,
Madrid, 2018. DOI: https://doi.org/10.18111/9789284420070.

U.S. Department of Arts and Culture. "Mondo Bizarro and the Land Memory Bank,
Invisible Rivers, New Orleans, LA." USDAC Network, 26 October 2020. https://

usdac.us/pwpa-cohort/2020/10/26/nick-slie-and-monique-verdin-invisible-rivers
-new-orleans-la.

Van der Westhuizen, Helene-Mari, et al. "Face Coverings for COVID-19: From Medical
Intervention to Social Practice." *BMJ: British Medical Journal* 370 (2020). Accessed
27 November 2023. https://www.proquest.com/docview/2435390244.

Verdin, Monique. "Ebb and Flow: Migrations of the Houma, Erosions of the Coast
Southward into Vanishing Lands." In *Unfathomable City: A New Orleans Atlas,*
edited by Rebecca Solnit and Rebecca Snedeker. Berkeley: University of California
Press, 2013.

———. *Return to Yakni Chitto: Houma Migrations.* Edited by Rachel Breunlin. New
Orleans: Neighborhood Story Project. 2019.

Wade, Leslie A., Robin Roberts, and Frank de Caro. *Downtown Mardi Gras: New Carnival Practices in Post-Katrina New Orleans.* Jackson: University Press of Mississippi, 2019.

Walker, Brian, and David Salt. *Resilience Thinking: Sustaining Ecosystems and People in
a Changing World.* Washington, DC: Island Press, 2006.

Water Leaders Institute. *Building a Home in the Delta.* Uploaded 3 February 2022.
https://www.youtube.com/watch?v=2Pkz15pUdUc.

Werry, Margaret. *Theatre and Tourism.* London: Bloomsbury Methuen Drama, 2023.

"Where to Build the Walls That Protect Us." *Kaleider,* November 2013–September 2014.
http://www.stephenhodge.org/portfolio/project/where-to-build-the-walls-that
-protect-us-1.

White House. "Fact Sheet: Historic Bipartisan Infrastructure Deal." Statements and Releases, 28 July 2021. https://www.whitehouse.gov/briefing-room/statements-releases
/2021/07/28/fact-sheet-historic-bipartisan-infrastructure-deal.

Whybrow, Nicolas. "Introduction." In *Performance and the Contemporary City,* edited
by Nicolas Whybrow. Basingstoke: Palgrave Macmillan, 2010.

Winterson, Jeanette. "With His Manchester Poem, Tony Walsh Found Words Where
There Are No Words." *The Guardian,* 20 May 2017. https://www.theguardian.com
/books/2017/may/25/tony-walsh-poem-vigil-manchester-bombing.

Woynarski, Lisa. *Ecodramaturgies: Theatre, Performance and Climate Change.* Basingstoke: Palgrave Macmillan, 2020.

WWNO. "'The Monster': Claiborne Avenue before and after the Interstate." *TriPod: New
Orleans at 300,* 5 May 2016. https://www.wwno.org/podcast/tripod-new-orleans
-at-300/2016-05-05/the-monster-claiborne-avenue-before-and-after-the-interstate.

WWOZ New Orleans, "Festing in Place 2020." Flickr album. Accessed 1 March 2023.
https://www.flickr.com/photos/wwoz/albums/72157713877114722/page7.

———. "WWOZ Presents Jazz Festing in Place: An On-Air Festival," 23 April 2020.
https://www.wwoz.org/events/639916.

Wynne, Laura, and Chris Riedy. "Precinct-Scale Innovation and the Sharing Paradigm."

In *Building Urban Resilience through Change of Use,* edited by S. Wilkinson and H. Remøy, 21–37. Hoboken, NJ: Wiley & Sons, 2018.

Young, Harvey. *Theatre and Race.* Basingstoke: Palgrave Macmillan 2013.

Young, Martin, and Francis Markham. "Tourism, Capital, and the Commodification of Place." *Progress in Human Geography* 44, no. 2 (2020): 280–81.

INDEX